JOURNAL OF

THE COLLOQUIUM
FOR INFORMATION SYSTEMS SECURITY EDUCATION

Volume 8, No. 1

FALL 2020

The Colloquium for Information Systems Security Education (CISSE),
a USA Non-profit Corporation, all rights reserved.

WWW.CISSE.INFO

Copyright © 2020

Cover image © chakisatelier / Adobe Stock.

TABLE OF CONTENTS

Organization iii

Editor's Preface iv

Experiential Activities for Risk Management Education 1

Judging Competencies in Recent Cybersecurity Graduates 9

Follow the Money Through Apple Pay 19

Building Capacity for Systems Thinking in Higher Education Cybersecurity Programs 30

Do Users Correctly Identify Password Strength? 38

An Experimental setup for Detecting SQLi Attacks using Machine Learning Algorithms 44

Weak Password Policies: A Lack of Corporate Social Responsibility 49

Higher Education Social Engineering Attack Scenario, Awareness & Training Model 57

Applied Cyber Security for Applied Software Engineering Undergraduate Program 65

Quantum Cryptography Exercise Schedules with Concept Dependencies 72

Evaluating the Effectiveness of Gamification on Students' Performance in a Cybersecurity Course 80

Enhancing Cyber Defense Preparation Through Interdisciplinary Collaboration, Training, and Incident Response 86

Tempting High School Students into Cybersecurity with a Slice of Raspberry Pi 92

Integration of Blockchain Concepts into Computer Science Curriculum 96

Author Index 101

Organization

Board of Directors and Officers

William "Vic" Maconachy, Ph.D.
Chairman & Co-founder

William "Art" Conklin, Ph.D.
Director

Denise Kinsey, Ph.D.
Vice Chairman

Barbara Endicott-Popovsky, Ph.D.
Director

William Hugh Murray, CISSP
Secretary & Co-founder

Erik Fretheim
Director

Bill Butler, Ph.D.
Assistant Secretary

Stephen Miller
Director

Daniel Likarish
Treasurer

Daniel Stein
Governmental Liaison

Corey Schou, Ph.D.
Director & Co-founder

Deanne Wesley, Ph.D.
Director

Editorial Board

Erik Moore, Editor-in-Chief

Dan Likarish, Associate Editor

Denise Kinsey, Associate Editor

Andrew Belón, Design and Production Editor

Editor's Preface

In this Journal of the 24th Colloquium for Information Systems Security Education (CISSE), contributing authors address key and emerging issues in cybersecurity, cybersecurity education, and related fields. The commitment of The Colloquium to forwarding the field of cybersecurity education has been consistent since 1996, working to bring together government, industry, and academic sectors. The goal of these efforts is to ensure the resilience of our society as we increasingly rely on digital technologies that enable, automate, and enhance so many essential services that we have come to rely on for our way of life. The significance of this work is perhaps becoming clearer to citizens as popular media increases awareness of cyber threats in a time when many have moved to digitally enabled remote work and learning environments to reduce the impact of the COVID-19 Pandemic. This situation has also caused The Colloquium to adapt to a virtual format this year, ensuring an uninterrupted contribution to the cyber resilience of society.

The CISSE community at its core is composed of many leaders of the National Centers for Academic Excellence in Cybersecurity. The community meets annually to discuss developments in cybersecurity education and share ways to advance the body of knowledge in this field. The goal of the community is to further research and collaboration that forwards the discipline and yields graduates that are well prepared to assure resilience, stability, and the advancement of our cyber dependant society.

Papers for this Journal were peer reviewed with 24 submissions from across the United States. Each paper was reviewed by at least two Program Committee members and the Editorial Board. The Journal accepted 14 papers, with an acceptance rate of 58%.

The papers presented herein, contribute to knowledge at the forefront of a range of research areas in cybersecurity and cybersecurity education. These include authentication and passwords, interdisciplinary and systems thinking, advances in cybersecurity education as influenced by innovations in physics and mathematics, assessment and process improvement of cybersecurity education programs, new methods for engaging students in risk management and social engineering, and new paradigms for understanding cybersecurity.

This Journal was created with support and guidance from many individuals. We would like to thank the Program Committee members for taking significant time to complete the peer review process. Thank you Erik Fretheim for organizing the conference this year. And thanks to the Board of Directors and Officers of the Colloquium, who provided essential leadership and guidance under Chairman & Co-founder William "Vic" Maconachy.

The Editorial Board:

Erik Moore, Editor-in-Chief

Dan Likarish, Associate Editor

Denise Kinsey, Associate Editor

Andrew Belón, Design & Production Editor

Experiential Activities for Risk Management Education

Michael E. Whitman, Ph.D.,
CISM, CISSP
Kennesaw State University
Kennesaw, GA, USA
mwhitman@kennesaw.edu

Robert L. Chaput, MA, CISSP,
HCISSP, CRISC, C|EH, CIPP/US
Clearwater Compliance, LLC
Nashville, TN, USA
bob.chaput@clearwatercompliance.com

Abstract—A core premise in the instruction of Information Security/Cybersecurity is that risk management is a cornerstone of security management, as evidenced in the promotion of GRC (Governance, Risk Management and Compliance) as the strategic triad in the trade press. While a theoretical exploration of risk management is important, the provision of an experiential activity to support the theory is valuable in cementing the knowledge in students. This paper will discuss popular risk management methodologies and examine a number of tools to support the instruction of the more common methodologies by instructors without substantial cost or learning curve.

Keywords—Risk Management, Risk Assessment, Information Security Education, Cybersecurity Education, Experiential Education Background

I. Introduction

With the well-documented increase in demand for Information Security / Cybersecurity Professionals, there is a corresponding increase in academic program offering degrees in security related fields, as evidenced in the increase in Center of Academic Excellence Designated Schools [1]. Risk Management (RM) is commonly taught as part of security curriculum. RM is the identification, assessment and remediation of risk to an organization's information assets and systems [2] and is recognized as critical to the organization's security program [3, 4, 5]. While professional certifications like the CISSP, CRISC and CISM have theoretical RM content, and while current standards such as NIST and ISO promote the need for RM, there is little available to assist the instructor in developing RM curriculum, especially if the instructor seeks to provide hands-on experiential activities.

This paper examines common RM methodologies promoted by key standards organizations and offers alternatives the instructor can use to implement an experiential component with their RM theoretical instruction.

II. Popular Risk Management Approaches

There are a few RM methodologies and standards an instructor can select when developing curriculum. While there are some academic frameworks for teaching RM [e.g. 5], they lack widespread adoption and the formal support of standards-based approaches. The challenge is to select a methodology that is widely accepted enough to provide a foundation for students in their career, yet suitable for use as an instructional tool.

A. Qualitative versus Quantitative Risk Assessment

Before examining the current available RM methodologies suitable for use in information security instruction, the first fundamental question is whether to use qualitative or quantitative valuations. RM begins with an expectation that, unless mandated, one should never spend more to protect an information asset than it is worth. Risk assessment (RA) is the first major component of RM – first you find the risk and then you address it. Some RA calculations used in the popular Cost-Benefit Analysis (CBA) expect the user to value of an asset. The challenge becomes how do you *accurately* calculate the value of an information asset. Using a purely quantitative approach means the organization must assign an accurate dollar value for each of its information assets. Yet there is little in the literature that shows any real success in doing just that [6]. As a result, many organizations chose a simplistic qualitative assessment – such as a scale of "very valuable" to "not valuable at all", also implemented in some RA tools. This approach can result in an oversimplification of information asset values, which introduces problems in prioritizing RM efforts. If the organization has multiple assets with the same value, and limited funds, which assets should be protected first?

The natural evolution is to use a hybrid method of valuing information assets (or threats) using tools like weighted tables. In a weighted table approach, the organization develops categories to compare assets, such as:

- Which information asset is the most critical to the success of the organization?
- Which information asset generates the most revenue?
- Which information asset generates the highest profitability?
- Which information asset is the most expensive to replace?
- Which information asset is the most expensive to protect?

- Which information asset's loss or compromise would be the most embarrassing or cause the greatest liability? [2]

These categories are then weighted, with each asset assigned a value per category, with values calculated as the sum of category weights times values. The result is not purely quantitative nor purely qualitative, simplifying assessment, but resulting in a more granular comparison.

B. Generally Accepted Risk Management Methods

RM principles date back to the 1983 publication "Risk Assessment in the Federal Government: Managing the Process" known as the "Red Book" [7]. NIST SP 800-30 "Risk Management Guide for Information Technology Systems" provided the foundation for most U.S. government RM efforts [8]. The now retired SP 800-30 version of RM the following steps:

1. System Characterization – identification of information assets and understand of systems to identify vulnerabilities.
2. Threat Identification – examination of the threat environment for threats with the potential to impact systems and assets.
3. Vulnerability Identification – comparison of threats to assets, and identification of vulnerabilities.
4. Control Analysis – identification and examination of current controls for each Threat/Vulnerability/Asset (TVA) triple.
5. Likelihood Determination – calculation of the probability that a particular threat could exploit a particular vulnerability in an information asset, using a simple qualitative scale.
6. Impact Analysis – determination of the outcome or impact of a successful attack within a given TVA triple.
7. Risk Determination – calculation of risk of each TVA triple by combining likelihood and impact.
8. Control Recommendations – based on the residual risk, the recommendation of additional controls.
9. Results Documentation – documentation and review of the results of the RM process [8].

The "likelihood/probability" and "impact/consequences" approach is common in RM methodologies, as illustrated above and in the CISSP common body of knowledge [2, 9, 14, 16, 19, 23].

C. The NIST Risk Management Framework

With the publication of SP 800-30, Revision 1 in 2011, NIST began promoting its Risk Management Framework (RMF) as the preferred methodology for performing RM. According to SP - NIST Special Publication 800-37 Revision 2 Risk Management Framework for Information Systems and Organizations [11], there are seven steps in the RMF; a preparatory step to ensure that organizations are ready to execute the process and six main steps, as shown in Figure 1.

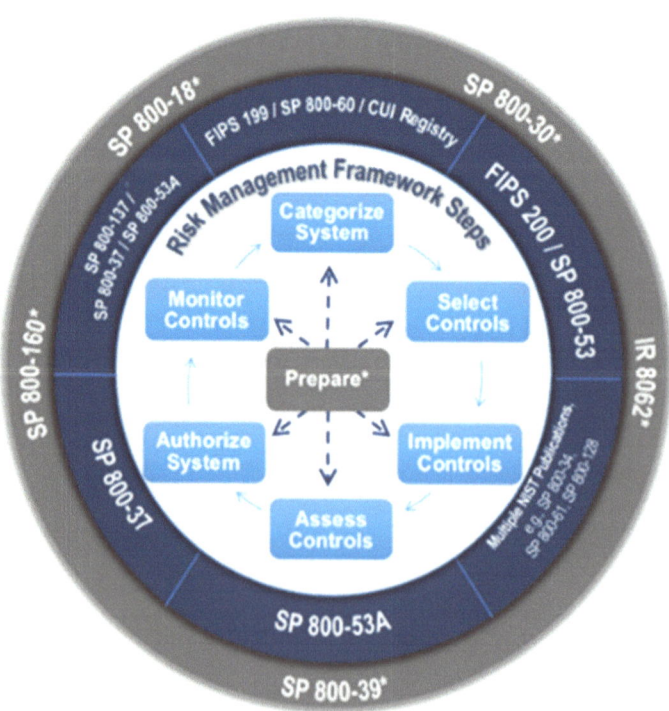

Fig. 1. NIST Risk Management Framework [12].

There are several NIST publications that address aspects of the RMF applicable to both government and non-government organizations, useful in formulating coursework [See 10, 11, 12 & 13]. One of the benefits of using NIST documents as an instructional foundation is the availability of the NIST library (http://csrc.nist.gov) to faculty and students alike.

D. The ISO Approach to Risk Management

The International Organization for Standardization (ISO; www.iso.org) has two closely related standards for RM. ISO 31000 focuses on general business risk, while ISO 27005 focuses on information security RM. The RM methodology is virtually identical in these standards.

1) ISO 31000: 2018

The ISO RM approach involves two major phases as shown in Figure 2. The RM Framework involves the development and design of the overall RM effort - the *planning* phase. The RM Process is the conduct of an iteration of risk assessment and treatment - the *doing* phase.

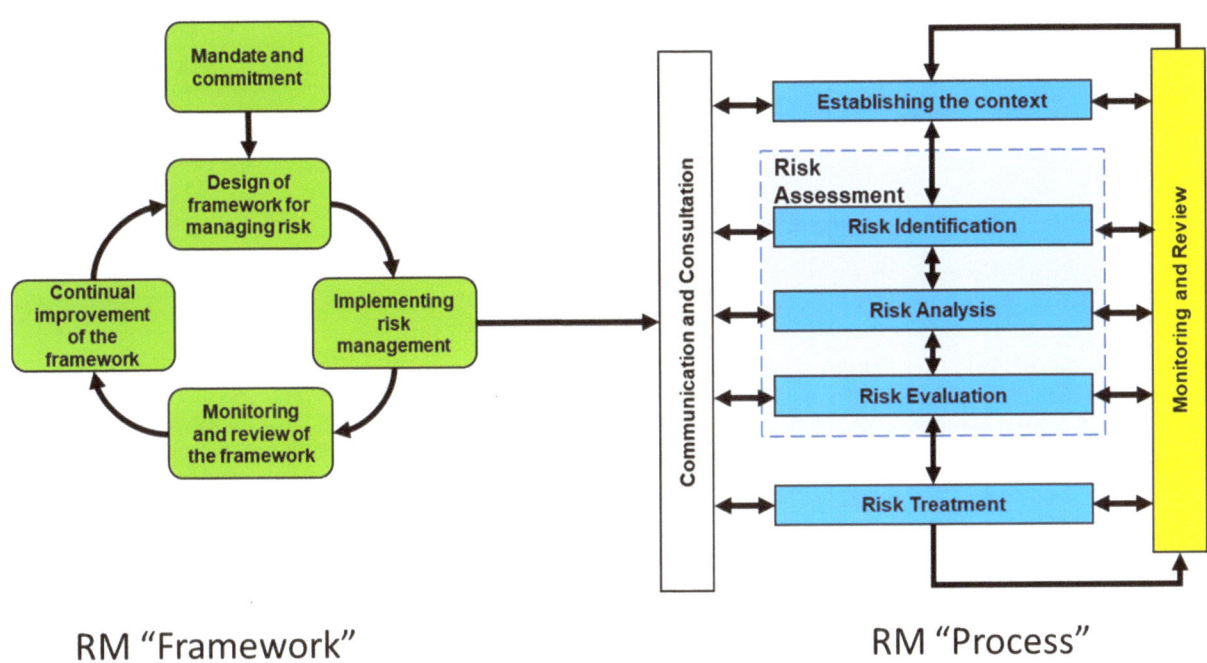

Fig. 2. ISO 31000: 2018 Approach to Risk Management [14].

The ISO RM Framework includes "integrating, designing, implementing, evaluating and improving risk management across the organization" [14], guided by leadership and commitment of the organization.

The RM Process begins with defining the RM project, its scope, personnel, resources and determine who will conduct and manage the RM project. From there the RM methodology involves two main phases. The first is Risk Assessment, which includes Risk Identification to determine the location of information assets at risk; Risk Analysis to determine the level of risk present in those information assets; and Risk Evaluation to assess whether the level of risk present exceeds the organization's risk threshold or whether additional treatment is needed. This step is followed by the second phase - Risk Treatment which is the application of additional controls to reduce risk to an acceptable level, or the decision to remove the asset from the threat environment [14].

Throughout the RM Process there is constant monitoring and review of the process and communication with organizational decision makers concerning progress, as well as formal documentation of each step in the process [14].

2) ISO 27005: 2018-07

ISO 27005:2018-07 focuses specifically on information security RM. Currently, the 27005 approach is an adaptation of the 31000 approach, focusing more extensively on the RM Process. The standard does provide a more granular look at RM, calling out risk acceptance as a separate step, as shown in Figure 3. This approach provides an easier means to educate students with, as it clarifies risk decision points that support the determination of whether the risk efforts are acceptance, or whether another iteration is needed [15].

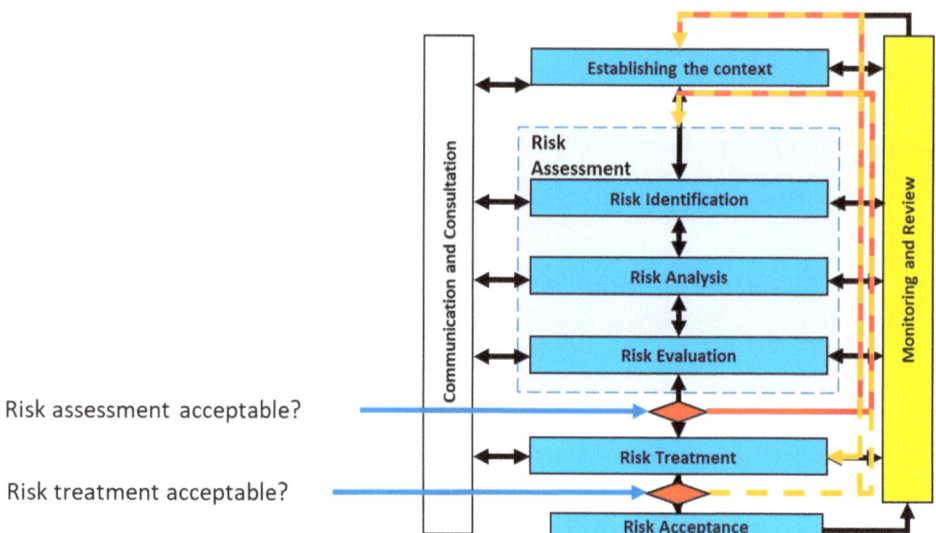

Fig. 3. ISO 27005 Approach to Risk Management [15].

E. Factor Analysis of Information Risk (FAIR)

FAIR was developed by Jack A. Jones to help organizations understand, analyze, and measure information risk. Projected outcomes are more cost-effective information RM, greater credibility for the InfoSec profession, and a foundation from which to develop a scientific approach to RM [16].

FAIR's framework comprises four stages: 1) Identify scenario components; 2) Evaluate Loss Event Frequency (LEF); 3) Evaluate Probable Loss Magnitude (PLM); and 4) Derive and articulate Risk. FAIR's likelihood is "Loss Event Frequency" and impact is "Loss Magnitude", determining and using these values to define an asset's level of risk, as shown in Figure 4.

In its early days, FAIR was a pen-and-paper exercise involving a series of qualitative values to indicate key inputs. These values were put into tables, which provided subsequent values used to determine risk levels on scales of "Severe" to "Low", also shown in Figure 4. In 2014, FAIR became an Open Group international RM standard and rebranded as Open FAIR™. In 2015, CXOWARE became RiskLens and the FAIR Institute was created [17].

F. Operationally Critical Threat, Asset, and Vulnerability Evaluation (OCTAVE)

There are other RM models available, many of which have been abandoned or discarded, including the Carnegie Mellon University Software Engineering Institute's OCTAVE methods. OCTAVE was promoted in three variants – OCTAVE for large organizations, OCTAVE-S for small organizations, and OCTAVE Allegro for concentrated RA.

OCTAVE involved a three-phase approach of 1) build asset-based threat profiles; 2) identify infrastructure vulnerabilities, and 3) develop security strategy and plans [20]. OCTAVE Allegro streamlined the risk assessment portion of OCTAVE and provided easy to use forms to use in the assessment [19]. As such OCTAVE Allegro can still serve as an effective paper-based exercise for the instruction of risk assessment

(See https://resources.sei.cmu.edu/library/asset-view.cfm?assetID=309051).

III. EXPERIMENTAL SUPPORT FOR RM INSTRUCTION

While it is generally accepted that the use of hands-on components in the instruction of security is a positive approach [20, 21], literature that describe this approach in RA/RM instruction is virtually non-existent.

A. Paper-Based Exercises

As mentioned earlier, OCTAVE Allegro is one method of using a pen-and-paper exercise to support the risk assessment process. While more complicated than other approaches, it is a realistic and usable exercise in risk assessment. OCTAVE Allegro includes worksheets and questionnaires to perform risk assessment against an academic case organization, or real-world organization in the event of service-learning assignments [19].

In addition, the original FAIR Basic Risk Assessment Guide provides an excellent tutorial for students to use to calculate risk qualitatively. While no longer supported by the FAIR Institute, this approach allows the instructor to present the fundamentals of identifying and evaluating risk for an asset [16].

Step 10 – Derive and Articulate Risk

The probable frequency and probable magnitude of future loss

Well-articulated risk analyses provide decision-makers with at least two key pieces of information:

- The estimated loss event frequency (LEF), and
- The estimated probable loss magnitude (PLM)

This information can be conveyed through text, charts, or both. In most circumstances, it's advisable to also provide the estimated high-end loss potential so that the decision-maker is aware of what the worst-case scenario might look like. Depending upon the scenario, additional specific information may be warranted if, for example:

- Significant due diligence exposure exists
- Significant reputation, legal, or regulatory considerations exist

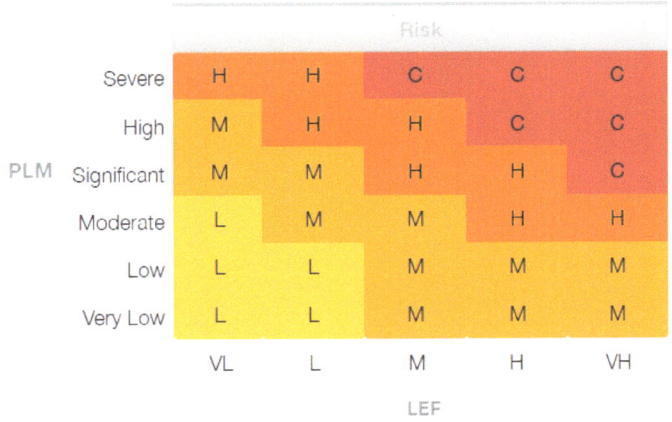

Fig. 4. FAIR Calculation of Risk [16].

B. Software-Based Exercises

For a more advanced and real-world approach to teaching risk assessment, two organizations have offered academic partnerships allowing the use of their Web-based products in the classroom.

1) RiskLens & FAIR

Risk Lens, with the FAIR Institute offer FAIR-U - a training tool based on the commercial version of the RiskLens Platform (https://www.fairinstitute.org/fair-university-curriculum). FAIR-U provides several risk assessment scenarios and is focused on training and education of the FAIR approach. The application is provided free of charge with a self-registration function. In addition, Risk Lens offers a video-based training course for the use of FAIR [See 22].

As shown in Figure 5, the application is very visual with representations of the values of the FAIR methodology presented for each scenario (such as a phishing attack resulting in a database breach). For a given scenario, the student enters several of the initial values, resulting in an annual loss exposure. Comparison of this exposure between threat/asset pairs would allow prioritization of remediation effort. For the most part, once a student has been taught this methodology, completing the tables is effectively straightforward estimation. What is not included in the software is assistance in the identification of information assets, and the understanding of the actual vulnerabilities associated with them. It does make a very effective tutorial on likelihood and impact once the terms are translated into the FAIR terminology.

2) Clearwater & IRM|Pro®

For those instructors looking for a more robust and more formal approach to performing risk assessment, Clearwater's Information Risk Management | Professional (IRM|Pro®) is a leading RM platform. While not widely advertised, Clearwater provides full complimentary access to IRM|Pro® to academic institutions to support the instruction of RM. Currently Kennesaw State University uses this application in two undergraduate and three graduate security management courses.

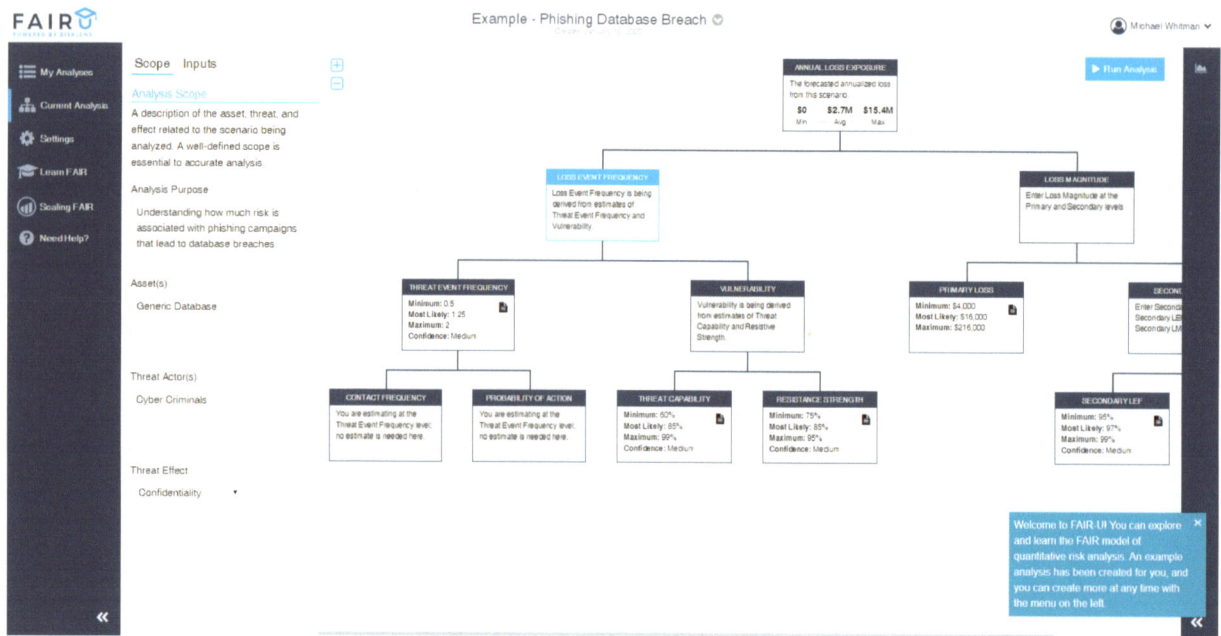

Fig. 5. FAIR-U Risk Analysis Training Application [23].

Perhaps the strongest endorsement of the product is its foundation in the NIST RM methodology, having been developed based on NIST SP 800-30 [9, 11]. While the application has improved on some of the qualitative categories used in the assessment of likelihood and impact, many definitions and examples from the SP are available in help screens.

In teaching risk assessment using this application, the instructor could provide a case organization, complete with information on information assets and supporting systems. As shown in Figure 6, users identify, then enter and describe their information assets.

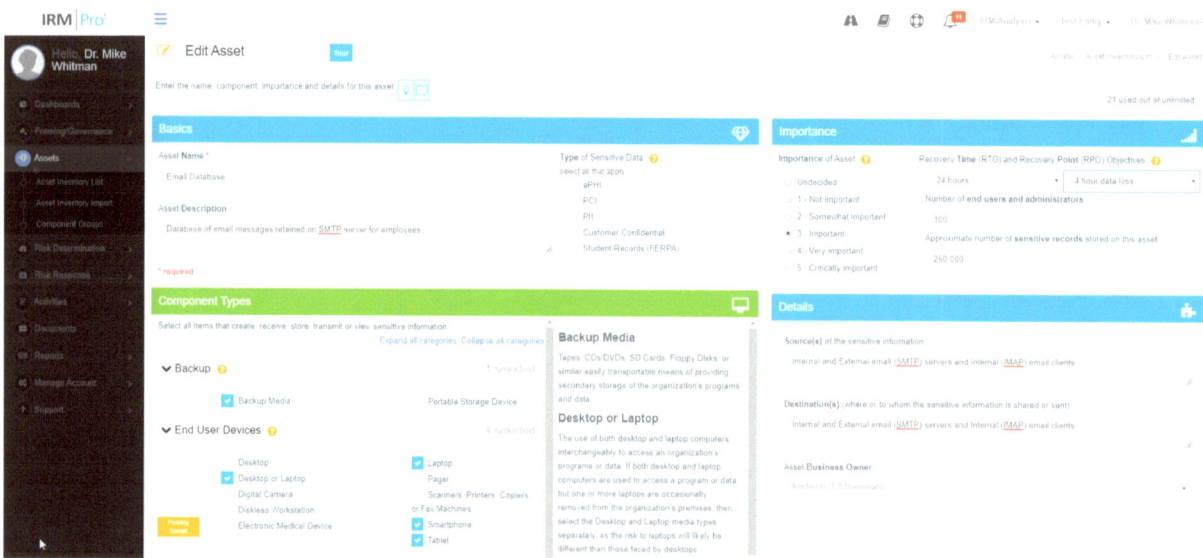

Fig. 6. Clearwater IRM|Pro® Asset Entry [24].

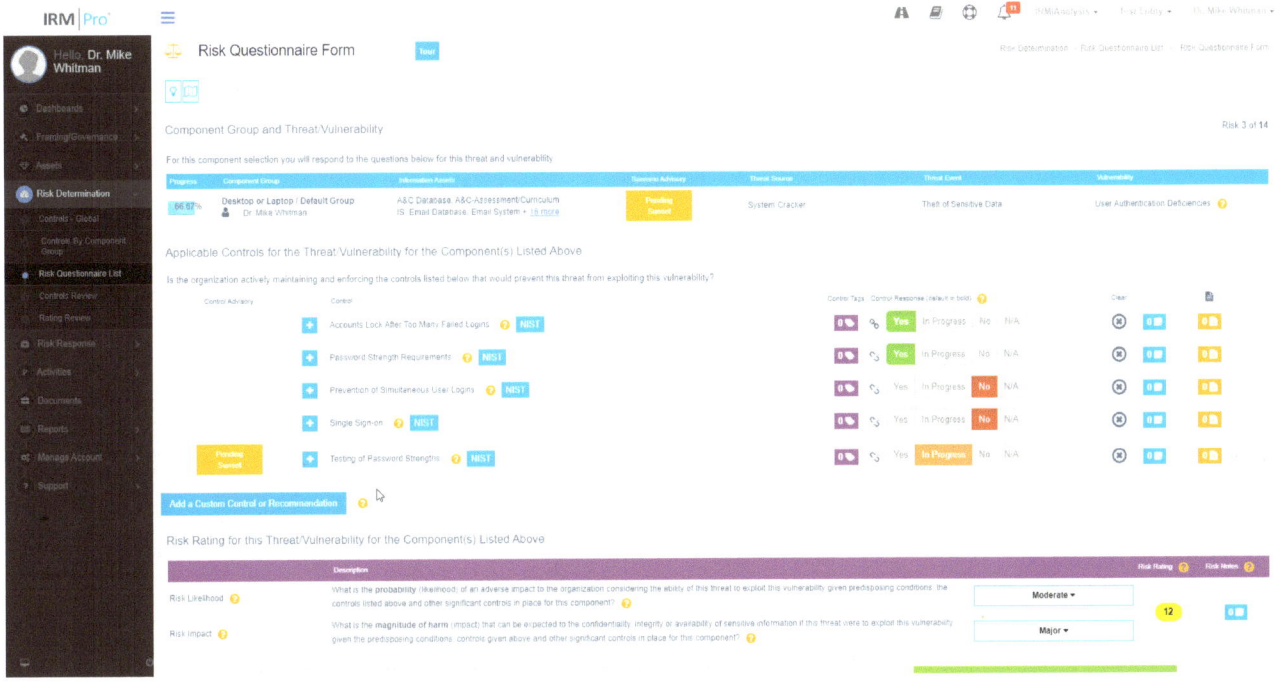

Fig. 7. Clearwater IRM|Pro® Risk Questionnaire [24].

The application separates information assets from the systems that store, process and access them. In order to manage the scope and scale of an academic project, it is recommended to limit projects to a few information assets. The application ties into the NIST SP 800-53 control structures [25], building the threat/vulnerability/asset triples commonly taught, as shown in Figure 7. In this application, users specify the current controls and safeguard implemented by selecting from available options in a Risk Questionnaire. Once all control statuses are indicated, users can specify the likelihood and impact using the scales provided.

The next step of the project involves the assignment of additional controls for TVA triples that have a current risk level exceeding the organization's risk threshold. The application allows the user to perform a risk response – projecting additional controls the organization would deploy and then estimating the residual risk if those controls were implemented. While the application can track the implementation of the controls and revision of the level of risk, a student's project typically ends with the estimation of risk response. Students can export reports for submission with their assignments.

The advantages of IRM|Pro®, beyond its foundation in NIST methodology, are in the easily understood implementation of RA assessment. Users are not expected to brainstorm the threat/asset scenarios, but simply identify the assets, define how the assets are accessed, and then answer questions as to the organization's current protection of those assets. The bulk of the work is performed by the software. The application takes the assets entered, creates TVA triples for each asset and then asks for input from the user. Once the user enters the current protection strategies, they are prompted as to whether additional security controls could be implemented based on NIST recommendations. After determining likely additional controls, the user then estimates the level of organizational risk that would exist after the additional controls are implemented, resulting in a risk reduction. The software is robust enough to allow the organization to track the implementation of these additional controls and has a sophisticated dashboard interface to oversee the current risk profile and improvement plans for the entire enterprise.

Since IRM|Pro® is designed as an enterprise solution, administration for an academic environment is trivial. At the beginning of the term, the instructor submits an Excel file with the student roster and institutional email and a support technician loads the course, clearing the work of previous classes. Each student is assigned to their own "entity", which the instructor can easily view, and thus grade, though a single drop-down menu option from their account.

Because IRM|Pro® is a commercial application, the largest drawback for classroom use is the need to provide detailed instructions for students. Clearwater does not provide training tutorials. Clearwater also updates its software regularly and without warning, which is both an advantage and a disadvantage for its use in academic instruction.

IV. SUMMARY

Teaching RM can be challenging, especially without an experiential exercise to enforce the theoretical concepts. With the use of experiential exercises, students can gain a deeper understanding and appreciation for the complexity and importance of a RM project, especially in the assessment of risk. Students can gain even more from applying these academic exercises to the real-world using approaches like service-learning to conduct risk assessments on actual organizations [26].

Whichever approach an instructor selects, it is important to ensure they follow an established methodology that the student can take with them into the workplace, as a student completing a course that includes RM may find themselves applying lessons learned in the classroom on the job.

REFERENCES

[1] NIETP. NSA/DHS National CAE in Cyber Defense Designated Institutions, Accessed 1/05/2020 from https://www.iad.gov/NIETP/reports/cae_designated_institutions.cfm (n.d.).

[2] Whitman, M.E. and Mattord, H.J. Management of Information Security, 6th ed. Cengage Learning, Inc., Boston, MA, 02210 (2019).

[3] Baskerville, R. Risk analysis: an interpretive feasibility tool in justifying information systems security, European Journal of Information Systems, Vol. 1 No. 2, pp. 121-130 (1991).

[4] Shedden, P., Ruighaver, A.B. and Ahmad, A. Risk management standards – the perception of ease of use, Journal of Information Systems Security, Vol. 6 No. 3 (2010).

[5] Spears, J.L. and Barki, H. User participation in information systems security risk management, MIS Quarterly, Vol. 34 No. 3, p. 503 (2010).

[6] Wangen, G., Snekkenes, E., and Hallstensen, C. A framework for estimating information security risk assessment method completeness. International Journal of Information Security, Vol. 17, No. 6, pp. 681-699 (2018).

[7] Greenberg, M., Goldstein, B.D., Anderson, E., Dourson, M., Landis, W, and North, D.W. Whither Risk Assessment: New Challenges and Opportunities a Third of a Century After the Red Book, Risk Analysis, Vol. 35, No. 11, pp. 1959-1968 (2015).

[8] Stoneburner, G., Goguen, A. and Feringa, A. NIST SP 800-30, Guide for Conducting Risk Assessments, Accessed 1/16/2020 from https://doi.org/10.6028/NIST.SP.800-30 (2002).

[9] Hernandez, S (Ed.) Official ISC2 Guide to the CISSP CBK, 3rd ed., CRC Press, Boca Raton, FL, 33487 (2013).

[10] NIST JTF. NIST SP 800-30, Rev. 1, Guide for Conducting Risk Assessments, Accessed 1/16/2020 from https://doi.org/10.6028/NIST.SP.800-30r1 (2012).

[11] NIST JTF. NIST SP 800-37, Rev. 2, Risk Management Framework for Information Systems and Organizations: A System Life Cycle Approach for Security and Privacy, Accessed 1/16/2020 from https://doi.org/10.6028/NIST.SP.800-37r2 (2018).

[12] NIST JTFTI. NIST SP 800-39 Managing Information Security Risk: Organization, Mission, and Information System View. Accessed 1/16/2020 from https://csrc.nist.gov/publications/detail/sp/800-39/final (2011).

[13] NIST. Risk Management Framework, Accessed 1/16/2020 from https://csrc.nist.gov/projects/risk-management/risk-management-framework-(RMF)-Overview (n.d.).

[14] ISO 31000 Risk Management – Guidelines, 2nd ed. Vernier, Geneva (2018).

[15] ISO/IEC 27005 Information technology — Security techniques — Information security risk management, 3rd ed. Vernier, Geneva (2018).

[16] FAIR Basic Risk Assessment Guide, Accessed 7/1/2013 from www.risk managementinsight.com/media/documents (2010).

[17] RiskLens. CXOWARE Becomes RiskLens, Accessed 1/15/2020 from https://www.prnewswire.com/news-releases/cxoware-becomes-risklens-aligning-with-mission-to-empower-organizations-to-manage-cyber-risk-from-the-business-perspective-300109155.html (2015).

[18] Alberts, C., Dorofee, A., Stevens, J. and Woody, C. Introduction to the OCTAVE Approach Carnegie Mellon University, Software Engineering Institute, Accessed 1/15/2020 from https://http://resources.sei.cmu.edu/library/asset-view.cfm?assetID=8419 (2003).

[19] Caralli, R.A., Stevens, J.F., Young, L.R. and Wilson, W.R. Introducing OCTAVE Allegro: Improving the Information Security Risk Assessment Process, TECHNICAL REPORT CMU/SEI-2007-TR-012, Carnegie Mellon University, Software Engineering Institute, Accessed 1/15/2020 from https://http://resources.sei.cmu.edu/library/asset-view.cfm?assetID=8419 (2007).

[20] Sharma, S.K. and Sefchek, J. Teaching information systems security courses: A hands-on approach. Computers and Security, Vol. 26, No. 4, pp. 290-299 (2007).

[21] Murthy, N. Teaching Computer Security with a Hands-On Component, R.C. Dodge Jr. and L. Futcher (Eds.): WISE 6, 7, and 8, IFIP AICT 406, pp. 204–210 (2013).

[22] FAIR. Announcing the First Video-Based Training Course for FAIR. Downloaded from https://www.risklens.com/blog/announcing-the-first-video-based-training-course-for-fair/ on 05/29/2020 (2017).

[23] FAIR. FAIR-U The Risk Analysis Training Application based on FAIR. Downloaded from https://www.fairinstitute.org/fair-u on 1/16/2020 (n.d.).

[24] Clearwater Information Risk Management, Accessed 01/16/20 from https://software.clearwatercompliance.com/ (n.d.).

[25] NIST JTF. NIST SP 800-53, Rev. 5, Security and Privacy Controls for Information Systems and Organizations, Accessed 1/16/2020 from https://doi.org/10.6028/NIST.SP.800-53r4 (2017).

[26] Spears, J.L. Gaining Real-World Experience in Information Security: A Roadmap for a Service-Learning Course, Journal of Information Systems Education, Vol. 29, No. 4, pp. 183-201 (2018).

Judging Competencies in Recent Cybersecurity Graduates

Nelbert St. Clair
School of Business and Public Management
College of Coastal Georgia
Brunswick, GA, USA
nstclair@ccga.edu

John Girard
School of Computing
Middle Georgia State University
Macon, GA, USA
john.girard@mga.edu

Abstract—This innovative research project chronicles how cybersecurity professionals and professors rate recent cybersecurity graduates in the components of Cybersecurity Competency Model. Noteworthy findings included that information technology graduates exhibit poor reading, writing, and some communication skills; there was a statistically significant difference between the two groups in their thoughts on the importance of mathematics; and there was a significant difference between the two groups pertaining to (a) planning and organization and (b) working with tools of technology.

Keywords—cybersecurity, graduates, competencies, expectations

I. Introduction

The National Cybersecurity Workforce Framework proposed to connect colleges, training vendors, students, employers, employees, and policymakers to align degrees, job training, and certifications for cybersecurity. It also developed a "comprehensive competency model for cybersecurity" [1, p. 1] by using subject matter expert from the workforce and academic. The Cybersecurity Competency Model defines "the latest skills and knowledge requirements needed by individuals whose activities impact the security of their organization's cyberspace" [1, p. 1].

The Cybersecurity Industry Model (CIM) was designed to provide a framework to help employers decide on which competencies are needed by a cybersecurity professional from an entry-level employee to management. The person designated as a cybersecurity professional will help to secure a company's network from both internal and external threats [1]. CIM defines cybersecurity or cyberspace, for the purpose of the model, as the following: "The strategy, policy, and standards regarding the security of and operations in cyberspace, whereby information and communications systems and the information contained therein are protected from and/or defended against damage, unauthorized use or modification, or exploitation" [1, p. 3].

The Cybersecurity Competency Model (CSCM) was released by The Employment and Training Administration (ETA). The overall aim of this study was to identify competencies employers expect from cybersecurity graduates and to determine if there is an expectation gap between the current cyber curriculum and employer expectations when they hire cybersecurity graduates. A prior report considered Tier 1 [2] while another report focused specifically on whether cybersecurity professionals satisfied with recent cybersecurity graduates [3]. This part of the project considered how cybersecurity professionals and cybersecurity profession rate the importance of CSCM tiers 2 through 5.

Tier 2 contains the academic skills level. This is where an employer rates a potential employee's ability to learn common core education. The employer can use this level to rule out any person without a certain Grade Point Average (GPA) or lack in a common core area. Employers may like to see if this potential employee had a previous internship. An internship would greatly enhance a person's abilities in the next three levels of Tiers. The competencies at this level are the following: reading, writing, mathematics, science, communication, critical and analytic thinking, and fundamental IT skills. For Tier 2, "Academic Competencies are primarily learned in a school setting. They include cognitive functions and thinking styles. Academic competencies are likely to apply to all industries and occupations" [3, p. 10].

Tier 3 is the working environment skills level. This is where an employer can separate a recent college graduate from someone who has been in the profession for a number of years. Most of these skills can be learned in different ways. For a recent college graduate, several of the skills can be learned through academic coursework, college-sponsored clubs, organizations, and at home. There are numerous different ways someone could learn all the different skills, but ultimately the potential employee would need to show competency in the work environment for which they are applying. The competencies for this level are the following: teamwork, planning and organizing, critical thinking, problem-solving and decision making, working with tools and technology, and business fundamentals. For Tier 3, "Workplace Competencies represent motives and traits, as well as interpersonal and self-management styles. These are generally applicable to a large number of occupations and industries" [3, p. 17].

Tier 4 is the industry standard skills level, and again at this level, the employer can separate a recent graduate from a professional. Basic skills can be taught in the classroom but, to be proficient at this level, one must have on the job experience for a certain amount of time. This experience gives employees time to learn the business and how to react in real-world situations. Employers expect potential employees to understand and execute five main functions as it relates to the company's mission. The competencies at this level are the following: cybersecurity technology, information assurance, risk management, incident detection, and incident response and remediation [3].

Tier 5 is industry sector skills level. At this level, employers can create and define an employee's role within the company. Because these skills are specialized functions, a potential employee could have one or two areas in this skill set, as their main responsibilities for day-to-day operations. This could depend on the size of the company or special needs of each company. Some of these skills can be learned within the classroom, but to understand the job or task, a particular employer needs an employee to work in the position and perform the duties. The competencies at this level include security provision systems, operate and maintain IT security, protect and defend from threats, investigate threats, collect information and operate cybersecurity process, analyze information, and oversee and govern cybersecurity work.

II. METHODOLOGY

Two surveys were used to collect the necessary data. The first survey was administered to 104 cybersecurity professionals and second survey was administered to 44 cybersecurity professors. Both surveys were designed to take no more than 10–15 minutes of the participants' time, with no more than 15 questions, depending on the participants' answers. The small number of survey questions helped to ensure that participants did not reach survey fatigue.

The criteria for group one (Professional) included (a) cybersecurity professional and (b) currently or previously employed or supervised someone in the cybersecurity industry. The rationale for this criteria selection was to gather input from employers because the best results required engaging cybersecurity professionals or supervisors already in the field. The criteria for group two (Professor) included (a) a faculty member and (b) having taught cybersecurity courses at the university level. The rationale for this criteria selection was to involve educators since it was a logical choice to engage educators on how they lecture students and how they develop curriculum.

The first part of both surveys included questions demographic and professional attributes and characteristics. The main part of the survey was divided into five questions; with each question having subtopics in which the participant was asked to rate the sub-competency areas. These five questions consisted of a 5-point Likert scale, in which participants were asked to rate competencies as very important, important, neutral, less important, or not important. The two surveys provided different questions depending on who, Professional (Pro) or Professor (Prof), took the survey. An example, (shown in Figure 1 focused on the Personal Effectiveness Competencies. The question pertained to "personal attributes essential for all life roles. Often referred to as soft skills, personal effectiveness competencies were generally learned in the home or community and honed at school and in the workplace" [3, p. 6].

Personal Effectiveness Competencies are personal attributes essential for all life roles. Often referred to as "soft skills," personal effectiveness competencies are generally learned in the home or community and honed at school and in the workplace.

Professional: How important are Personal Effectiveness Competencies when hiring or working with recent cyber security graduates?

Professor: How important do you think it is to incorporate the following Personal Effectiveness Competencies into the curriculum when teaching cyber security courses?

	Very Important	Important	Neutral	Less Important	Not Important
Interpersonal Skills	❏	❏	❏	❏	❏
Integrity	❏	❏	❏	❏	❏
Professionalism	❏	❏	❏	❏	❏
Initiative	❏	❏	❏	❏	❏
Adaptability and Flexibility	❏	❏	❏	❏	❏
Dependability and Reliability	❏	❏	❏	❏	❏
Lifelong Learning	❏	❏	❏	❏	❏

Fig. 1. Personal effectiveness competencies.

Academic Competencies are primarily learned in a school setting. They include cognitive functions and thinking styles. Academic competencies are likely to apply to all industries and occupations.

<u>Professional</u>: How important are Academic Competencies when hiring or working with recent cyber security graduates?

<u>Professor</u>: How important do you think it is to incorporate the following Academic Competencies into the curriculum when teaching cyber security courses?

	Very Important	Important	Neutral	Less Important	Not Important
Reading	❏	❏	❏	❏	❏
Writing	❏	❏	❏	❏	❏
Mathematics	❏	❏	❏	❏	❏
Science and Technology	❏	❏	❏	❏	❏
Communication	❏	❏	❏	❏	❏
Critical and Analytic Thinking	❏	❏	❏	❏	❏
Fundamental IT User Skills	❏	❏	❏	❏	❏

Fig. 2. Academic competencies

The next question (shown in Figure 2) focused on the Academic Competencies, "which were characteristics primarily learned in a school setting" (DOL, 2014, p. 10). These competencies included cognitive functions and thinking styles. Academic Competencies "were likely to apply to all industries and occupations" [3, p. 10].

One question (shown in Figure 3) focused on the Workplace Competencies, which were "represented by motives and traits, as well as interpersonal and self-management styles" (DOL, 2014, p. 17). DOL found these characteristics "generally applicable to a large number of occupations and industries" [3, p. 17].

Workplace Competencies represent motives and traits, as well as interpersonal and self-management styles. They are generally applicable to a large number of occupations and industries.

<u>Professional</u>: How important are Workplace Competencies when hiring or working with recent cyber security graduates?

<u>Professor</u>: How important do you think it is to incorporate the following Workplace Competencies into the curriculum when teaching cyber security courses?

	Very Important	Important	Neutral	Less Important	Not Important
Teamwork	❏	❏	❏	❏	❏
Planning and Organizing	❏	❏	❏	❏	❏
Creative Thinking	❏	❏	❏	❏	❏
Problem Solving and Decision-Making	❏	❏	❏	❏	❏
Working with Tools and Technology	❏	❏	❏	❏	❏
Business Fundamentals	❏	❏	❏	❏	❏

Fig. 3. Workplace competencies.

Industry-Wide Technical Competencies cover the knowledge, skills, and abilities from which workers across the industry can benefit, regardless of the sector in which they operate. These competencies are considered cross-cutting, as they allow a worker to move easily across industry subsectors. Because of this, many of the critical work functions on this tier deal with awareness or understanding, rather than performing specific job tasks.

Professional: How important are Industry-Wide Technical Competencies when hiring or working with recent cyber security graduates?

Professor: How important do you think it is to incorporate the following Industry-Wide Technical Competencies into the curriculum when teaching cyber security courses?

	Very Important	Important	Neutral	Less Important	Not Important
Cyber-security Technology	❏	❏	❏	❏	❏
Information Assurance	❏	❏	❏	❏	❏
Risk Management	❏	❏	❏	❏	❏
Incident Detection	❏	❏	❏	❏	❏
Incident Response and Remediation	❏	❏	❏	❏	❏

Fig. 4. Industry-wide technical competencies

The next question (shown in Figure 4) focused on Industry-Wide Technical Competencies. This question covered the following:

Knowledge, skills, and abilities from which workers across the industry benefited, regardless of the sector in which they operated. These competencies were considered crosscutting, as they allowed a worker to move easily across industry subsectors. Because of this, most of the critical work functions on this tier dealt with awareness or understanding, rather than performing specific job tasks. [3, p. 22

The penultimate question (shown in Figure 5) focused on Industry-Sector Functional Areas. This "established the common taxonomy and lexicon that was to be used to describe all cybersecurity work and workers irrespective of where or for whom the work was performed" [3, p. 40]. The last question of this survey was open-ended, see Figure 6. The purpose of this question was to capture any ideas, thoughts, or responses that were not available to the participants in the previous questions [4].

Industry-Sector Functional Areas establish the common taxonomy and lexicon that is to be used to describe all cybersecurity work and workers irrespective of where or for whom the work is performed.

Professional: How important are Industry-Sector Functional Areas when hiring or working with recent cyber security graduates?

Professor: How important do you think it is to incorporate the following Industry-Wide Technical Competencies into the curriculum when teaching cyber security courses?

	Very Important	Important	Neutral	Less Important	Not Important
Securely Provision Systems	❏	❏	❏	❏	❏
Operate and Maintain IT Security	❏	❏	❏	❏	❏
Protect and Defend from Threats	❏	❏	❏	❏	❏
Investigate Threats	❏	❏	❏	❏	❏
Collect Information and Operate Cybersecurity Processes	❏	❏	❏	❏	❏
Analyze Information	❏	❏	❏	❏	❏
Oversee and Govern Cybersecurity Work	❏	❏	❏	❏	❏

Fig. 5. Industry-sector functional areas.

Professional: From your experience/perspective, what competencies do you expect recent cyber security graduate(s) to have on the first day of employment?

Professor: From your experience/perspective, what recommendations would you suggest to improve quality and integrity of the current cybersecurity curriculum or course(s) you teach?

Fig. 6. Open-ended question

III. RESULTS

Cybersecurity professionals and professors from across the United States completed separate, independent surveys. The results are separated into two categories: Professionals (Pro) and Professors (Prof), with a total of 105 cybersecurity professionals and 44 cybersecurity professors who participated in this research. The overall results on academic competencies are in Table I and Table II.

TABLE I. PROFESSIONAL: ACADEMIC COMPETENCIES BREAKDOWN

Pro – Academic Competencies	Very Important		Important		Neutral		Less Important		Not Important	
	%	N	%	N	%	N	%	N	%	N
Reading	50%	53	43%	45	6%	6	1%	1		
Writing	50%	53	42%	44	7%	7	1%	1		
Mathematics	20%	21	46%	48	28%	29	6%	6	1%	1
Science and Technology	43%	45	47%	49	8%	9	2%	2		
Communication	64%	67	33%	35	2%	2	1%	1		
Critical and Analytic Thinking	87%	92	10%	10	3%	3				
Fundamental IT User Skills	63%	66	31%	33	4%	4	2%	2		

TABLE II. PROFESSOR: ACADEMIC COMPETENCIES BREAKDOWN

Prof – Academic Competencies	Very Important		Important		Neutral		Less Important		Not Important	
	%	N	%	N	%	N	%	N	%	N
Reading	79%	35	16%	7	5%	2				
Writing	68%	30	27%	12	5%	2				
Mathematics	39%	17	43%	19	14%	6	2%	1	2%	1
Science and Technology	66%	29	27%	12	5%	2			2%	1
Communication	82%	36	16%	7	2%	1				
Critical and Analytic Thinking	93%	41	5%	2	2%	1				
Fundamental IT User Skills	68%	30	27%	12	2.5%	1	2.5%	1		

A two-tailed t test was used to examine the relationship between professional and professor responses. This test is used to compare if any differences exist between two different groups. A probability of less than .05 would show a statistically significant difference between the two groups. As Table III shows, the t test results for academic competencies, between the two groups, revealed statistically significant differences with regard to reading ($t = -3.14$, $df = 97.24$, $p < .002$); writing ($t = -2.01$, $df = 92.36$, $p < .047$); mathematics ($t = -2.21$ $df = 77.63$, $p < .030$); and communication ($t = -2.17$, $df = 100.84$, $p < .032$).

TABLE III. ACADEMIC COMPETENCIES FOR PROFESSIONALS AND PROFESSORS

t Test Result – Academic Competencies	p	Result
Reading	.002	The result is significant at p < .05
Writing	.047	The result is significant at p < .05
Mathematics	.030	The result is significant at p < .05
Science and Technology	.085	The result is not significant at p < .05

t Test Result – Academic Competencies	p	Result
Communication	.032	The result is significant at p < .05
Critical and Analytic Thinking	.376	The result is not significant at p < .05
Fundamental IT User Skills	.600	The result is not significant at p < .05

A frequency analysis revealed a significant difference in that 79% of the professors agreed with 50% of the professionals that reading is very important. A significant difference existed ($p < .002$), as 42% of the professionals chose reading as important, and only 16% of the professors agreed with them (see Table I and Table II). The significant difference, as related to the reading competency, is that professors may read more than an average person and they understand the value of reading while cybersecurity professionals tend to read the technical manuals relating to the field. A study conducted by Treadwell and Treadwell [5] found that employers were dissatisfied with the academic performance from recent graduates.

Another frequency analysis showed that 68% of the professors agreed with 50% of the professionals that writing is very important. A significant difference existed ($p < .047$), as 42% of the professionals chose writing as important, and only 27% of the professors agreed with them (see Table I and Table II). Professors and professionals both agree that the writing competency is very important or important in the workforce. The significant difference in the writing competency depends on a person's job duties, which varies from position to position. Treadwell and Treadwell's found employers were not impressed when they received cover letters and resumes that had basic grammar errors and they were neutral about "Dear first name" in a cover letter when there is a relationship between the parties. [5, p. 91]

A frequency analysis showed that 64% of the professors agreed with 82% of the professionals that communication is very important. A significant difference existed ($p < .032$) between professionals (33%), who chose communication as important and only 16% of the professors (see Table I and Table II). These findings are consistent with Treadwell and Treadwell's [5] conclusion that recent graduates are not completely ready for the workforce.

The overall results for workplace competencies are in Table IV and Table V.

TABLE IV. PROFESSIONAL: WORKPLACE COMPETENCIES BREAKDOWN

Pro – Workplace Competencies	Very Important		Important		Neutral		Less Important		Not Important	
	%	N	%	N	%	N	%	N	%	N
Teamwork	51%	54	45%	47	3%	3	1%	1		
Planning and Organizing	39%	41	50%	53	8%	8	3%	3		
Creative Thinking	50%	53	42%	44	4%	4	4%	4		
Problem Solving and Decision-Making	73%	77	27%	28						
Working with Tools and Technology	50%	53	40%	42	8%	8	1%	1	1%	1
Business Fundamentals	26%	27	39%	41	29%	30	5%	6	1%	1

TABLE V. PROFESSOR: WORKPLACE COMPETENCIES BREAKDOWN

Prof – Workplace Competencies	Very Important		Important		Neutral		Less Important		Not Important	
	%	N	%	N	%	N	%	N	%	N
Teamwork	61%	27	27%	12	8%	3	2%	1	2%	1
Planning and Organizing	59%	26	36%	16	5%	2				
Creative Thinking	61%	27	34%	15	5%	2				
Problem Solving and Decision-Making	84%	37	14%	6	2%	1				
Working with Tools and Technology	70%	31	23%	10	7%	3				
Business Fundamentals	27%	12	53%	23	11%	5	9%	4		

To determine the relationship between professionals and professors, a two-tailed t test was used to determine if a difference existed. Table VI shows the t test results for workplace competencies. There were statistically significant differences between the two groups regarding planning and organizing ($t = -2.55$, $df = 98$, $p < .012$) and working with tools and technology ($t = -2.164$, $df = 98.08$, $p < .033$).

TABLE VI. WORKPLACE COMPETENCIES FOR PROFESSIONALS AND PROFESSORS

t Test Result – Workplace Competencies	p	Result
Teamwork	.815	The result is not significant at p < .05
Planning and Organizing	.012	The result is significant at p < .05
Creative Thinking	.123	The result is not significant at p < .05
Problem Solving and Decision-Making	.292	The result is not significant at p < .05
Working with Tools and Technology	.033	The result is significant at p < .05
Business Fundamentals	.353	The result is not significant at p < .05

A frequency analysis showed that 59% of the professors agreed with 39% of the professionals that planning and organizing is very important. A further significant difference existed, as 50% of the professionals chose planning and organizing as important, and only 36% of the professors agreed with them (See Table IV and Table V). A possible difference between the two groups is that professors can teach planning and organizing in a clean, static environment while professionals plan and organize in chaotic, dynamic environments. Ivancevich et al. [6] echoed this and added the importance of teamwork, time management, and understanding the needs of the clients to accomplish a given task.

A frequency analysis, of "very important" responses to the tools and technical competency, showed 70% of professors agreed while 50% of professionals agreed. Of the "important" responses, a difference, ($p < .033$) between 40% of the professionals chose to work with tools and technology as important, and only 23% of the professors agreed with them (See Table IV and Table V). There is a significant amount of software/hardware tools and technology available for any company to use to defend their network and protect their data. Higher education institutions cannot anticipate which tools and technology will be used in the workforce to help prepare cybersecurity students. These findings agree with Treadwell and Treadwell's [5] and Ivancevich et al. [6] conclusions that recent graduates are not fully ready for the workforce, which also assisted with answer research questions one and two.

The overall results on industry-wide technical competencies are in Table VII and Table VIII.

TABLE VII. PROFESSIONAL: INDUSTRY-WIDE TECHNICAL COMPETENCIES BREAKDOWN

Pro – Professional Industry-Wide Technical Competencies	Very Important		Important		Neutral		Less Important		Not Important	
	%	N	%	N	%	N	%	N	%	N
Cybersecurity Technology	62%	66	30%	31	7%	7	1%	1		
Information Assurance	54%	57	36%	38	10%	10				
Risk Management	50%	53	42%	44	8%	8				
Incident Detection	54%	57	37%	39	8%	8	1%	1		
Incident Response and Remediation	56%	59	36%	38	6%	6	1%	1	1%	1

TABLE VIII. PROFESSOR: INDUSTRY-WIDE TECHNICAL COMPETENCIES BREAKDOWN

Prof – Professional Industry-Wide Technical Competencies	Very Important		Important		Neutral		Less Important		Not Important	
	%	N	%	N	%	N	%	N	%	N
Cybersecurity Technology	75%	33	20%	9	5%	2				
Information Assurance	75%	33	23%	10	2%	1				
Risk Management	68%	30	30%	13	2%	1				
Incident Detection	59%	26	34%	15	7%	3				
Incident Response and Remediation	64%	28	32%	14	4%	2				

Table IX shows the t test results for industry-wide technical competencies. There were statistically significant differences between the two groups regarding information assurance ($t = -2.814$, $df = 106.32$, $p < .006$) and risk management ($t = -2.293$, $df = 96.45$, $p < .024$).

TABLE IX. INDUSTRY-WIDE TECHNICAL COMPETENCIES

t Test Result – Industry-Wide Technical Competencies	p	Result
Cybersecurity Technology	.129	The result is not significant at p < .05
Information Assurance	.006	The result is significant at p < .05
Risk Management	.024	The result is significant at p < .05
Incident Detection	.518	The result is not significant at p < .05
Incident Response and Remediation	.241	The result is not significant at p < .05

A frequency analysis showed that 54% of the professors agreed with 75% of the professionals that information assurance is very important. A significant difference exists, as 36% of the professionals chose information assurance as important and only 22% of the professors agreed with them (See Table VII and Table VIII). This competency is important to the business, depending on the type of business and how they view information assurance. Overall, information assurance is a critical area to both groups but distinguishing between those who chose "very important" versus "important" depended upon the respondent's business and the level of management.

Another frequency analysis showed that 50% of the professors agreed with 68% of the professionals that risk management is very important. A statistically significant difference existed ($p < .006$), as 42% of the professionals chose risk management as important and only 30% of the professors agreed with them (see Table VII and Table VIII). Overall, professors and professionals view risk management as an important competency for a cybersecurity graduate. These findings agree with the researchers who developed the CSCM [7].

The responses to industry-sector functional competencies are in Table X and Table XI, with the results in Table XII. The t test showed that there were no statistically significant differences between the groups. The Industry-Sector Functional Areas breakdown show that both groups agree on the Industry-Sector Functional Areas Breakdown levels. These competencies are a combination of various skills and attributes to the workforce, which are spread across the first five levels of the model.

TABLE X. PROFESSIONAL: INDUSTRY-SECTOR FUNCTIONAL AREAS BREAKDOWN

Pro – Industry-Sector Functional Areas	Very Important		Important		Neutral		Less Important		Not Important
		N		N		N		N	
Securely Provision Systems	46%	48	41%	43	10%	11	3%	3	
Operate and Maintain IT Security	52%	55	42%	44	3%	3	3%	3	
Protect and Defend from Threats	66%	69	30%	32	3%	3	1%	1	
Investigate Threats	54%	57	31%	33	13%	13	2%	2	
Collect Information and Operate Cybersecurity Processes	43%	45	44%	46	10%	11	3%	3	
Analyze Information	56%	59	40%	42	2%	2	2%	2	
Oversee and Govern Cybersecurity Work	24%	25	50%	53	17%	18	9%	9	

TABLE XI. PROFESSOR: INDUSTRY-SECTOR FUNCTIONAL AREAS BREAKDOWN

Prof – Industry-Sector Functional Areas	Very Important		Important		Neutral		Less Important		Not Important
		N		N		N		N	
Securely Provision Systems	48%	21	41%	18	11%	5			
Operate and Maintain IT Security	61%	27	39%	17					
Protect and Defend from Threats	70%	31	23%	10	5%	2			2%	1
Investigate Threats	64%	28	27%	12	7%	3	2%	1	
Collect Information and Operate Cybersecurity Processes	52%	23	34%	15	14%	6			
Analyze Information	61%	27	34%	15	5%	2			
Oversee and Govern Cybersecurity Work	37%	16	41%	18	20%	9	2%	1	

TABLE XII. INDUSTRY-SECTOR FUNCTIONAL AREAS FOR PROFESSIONALS AND PROFESSORS

t Test Result – Industry-Sector Functional Areas	*p*	Result
Securely Provision Systems	.594	The result is not significant at p < .05
Operate and Maintain IT Security	.083	The result is not significant at p < .05
Protect and Defend from Threats	.888	The result is not significant at p < .05
Investigate Threats	.292	The result is not significant at p < .05
Collect Information and Operate Cybersecurity Processes	.367	The result is not significant at p < .05
Analyze Information	.559	The result is not significant at p < .05
Oversee and Govern Cybersecurity Work	.146	The result is not significant at p < .05

IV. SUMMARY

This study showed that some graduates exhibit poor reading, writing, and some communication skills. Other studies, on the academic disparities between employers and recent graduates, support this conclusion. In these studies, other disciplines face some of the same issues as information technology. For example, students tend to write and speak English that is heavily influenced by slang. Some students thought that was appropriate to write and speak using slang and cryptic acronyms when they communicate with their professors. This aligns with the study of Treadwell and Treadwell [5], who showed that recent graduates lack the proper verbal and written communication skills.

This study highlighted the importance of workplace competencies. There was a significant difference between the two groups pertaining to (a) planning and organization and (b) working with tools of technology. Clearly, organizations differ as such, plan and organize according to their own missions, visions, and ideologies. To improve tools and technology education at academic institutions, universities need to address more than the technologies themselves and the rapid nature at which technologies are fielded. They must consider usability. The field of usability is equally a soft skill, highlighting the phenomena that all cybersecurity competencies are interrelated. There is a need to adequately address and bridge the differing points of view regarding the tools of technology in academia, a recommendation should be presented to higher education institutions to be proactive by constantly informing and advising students to understand and expect a difference between the tools and technologies in the classroom and the essential tools and technology skills employers expect. Higher education institutions should also encourage their students to work with different types of technology tools to be more competitive in the technology workforce.

There are differences in attitude, between employers and professors, concerning information assurance and risk management. There are a number of reasons for this. All organizations differ on how they prioritize and manage risk. For example, a company that does not collect personal identifier information (PII) may not have a robust, restrictive policy on their e-mail or telephone conversations. Conversely, a hospital, which handles highly-sensitive personal health and financial information, is required to safeguard and protect that information by law. These institutions must make risk management a high priority to address and mitigate all vulnerabilities. To address these deficiencies, companies must make a significant investment to train new cybersecurity personnel about IT policies and procedures.

Considering the limited reach and scope of this study, it would be important in the future to increase the size and scope of the dynamic data collection in universities and professionalism. Because of the short time duration of this study, its limited scope, and assessable survey participants, there is a need for greater knowledge before more dynamic generalizations can be considered. The preliminary findings of this study provide useful information for making recommendations to institutions, colleges, and universities of similar size. To generalize these findings, future studies should compare the results of this study with larger universities with greater dynamic influence in career centers, grants, and external funding. This will help develop an understanding of whether there are significant differences because of monetary constraints in budgeting, state funding, or grants.

REFERENCES

[1] "Cybersecurity Competency Model," 4 January 2015. [Online]. Available: http://www.careeronestop.org/competencymodel/competency-models/cybersecurity.aspx.

[2] N. St. Clair and J. Girard, "Personal Effectiveness Competencies of Recent Cybersecurity Graduates," *Issues in Information Systems*, to be published.

[3] N. St. Clair and J. Girard, "Employer Perceptions of Recent Cybersecurity Graduates," *The Journal of CISSE, vol. 7, no. 1*, to be published.

[4] DOL, "Cybersecurity Competency Model," 2014. [Online]. Available: http://www.careeronestop.org/CompetencyModel/competency-models/cybersecurity.aspx.

[5] P. M. Nardi, Doing Survey Research: A guide to quantitative Methods, Boulder: Paradigm, 2014.

[6] D. F. Treadwell and J. B. Treadwell, "Employer Expectations of Newly-Hired Communication Graduates," *Journal Of The Association For Communication Administration 28, no. 2*, pp. 87-99, 1999.

[7] S. Ivancevich, D. Ivancevich and R. Roscher, "The First Two Years of Employment," *CPA Journal, 79(7)*, pp. 69-72, 2009.

[8] "Bureau of Labor Statistics, U.S. Department of Labor," 25 January 2015. [Online]. Available: http://www.bls.gov/ooh/computer-and-information-technology/information-security-analysts.htm#tab-6.

[9] "Curricula Recommendations," 1 Nov 2015. [Online]. Available: http://www.acm.org/education/curricula-recommendations.

[10] M. H. Kavanagh and L. Drennan, "What skills and attributes does an accounting graduate need? Evidence from student perceptions and employer expectations," *Accounting & Finance, 48(2)*, pp. 279-300, 2007.

Follow the Money Through Apple Pay

Dominicia Williams
Department of Computer Science
Norfolk State University
Norfolk, VA, USA
d.a.williams75096@spartans.nsu.edu

Yen-Hung (Frank) Hu
Department of Computer Science
Norfolk State University
Norfolk, VA, USA
yhu@nsu.edu

Mary Ann Hoppa
Department of Computer Science
Norfolk State University
Norfolk, VA, USA
mahoppa@nsu.edu

Abstract—Rapid growth in the number of mobile phones and their users has brought ecommerce applications and mobile payments to the forefront along with raising significant new cybersecurity concerns. Consumer enthusiasm for "tap-and-go" purchases must be tempered with knowledge about new risks and responsibilities that come along with these payment technologies. This paper highlights and analyzes key risks within end-to-end mobile-payment transactions through the lens of one of the most popular services: Apple Pay. Hackers are relentlessly adapting their ploys to breach these payment systems. Proactive approaches are identified to better secure vulnerabilities in smartphones, networks, communication, consumers, merchants and banks, along with practical, proactive countermeasure and action plans.

Keywords—Apple Pay, Mobile Commerce (mCommerce), Near Field Communication (NFC)

I. INTRODUCTION

The wide penetration and personal nature of mobile phones, the overall stability of mobile communication, technology, and positive experiences with mobile commerce (mCommerce) payments have favored the adoption of mobile solutions for financial services [1].

In 2014, Apple Pay launched and has been built into every iPhone since 6/6 Plus, including the newly released iPhone X. The iPhone solution also includes a Near Field Communication (NFC) antenna (the standard for all contactless payments); the convenience and security of Touch ID and a Secure Element chip (SE). These features work together toward one goal: the ability to encrypt and securely store all payment information. All credit cards a consumer adds into their Apple Pay can be safely stored through Passbook. There are hundreds and millions of credit cards and debit cards from customers in their iTunes Store accounts. When a customer purchases an iPhone 6 or newer, they can place the card on file by inputting the card information, manually, or simply taking a picture of the card. With just a "touch", you can easily make payments through your mobile device [2].

Apple Pay originated in the United States with credit cards and debit cards from three major networks: American Express, MasterCard, and Visa. Moreover, Apple Pay is connected to the largest issuing banks in the United States including Citi Bank, Bank of America, Capital One, Wells Fargo, and Chase Bank, comprising 83 percent of all credit card volume across the nation. Apple Pay can be used in over 220,000 U.S. merchant locations that accept contactless payments and, since 2014, has been networking with some of the largest retailers to enable Apple Pay in all locations, nationally and internationally. Macy's, Bloomingdale, Walgreens, Staples, Subway, McDonalds, Whole Foods Market, Apple retail stores, and Disney are some of the businesses that welcome Apple Pay for their fast and reliable services [3].

Apple Pay security is realized through both hardware and software [4]. When a new card is added, a device-only account number is created for it and stored safely in the secure element; the card number is never stored or share with the merchant. For each consumer transaction, a one-time payment number is generated along with a dynamic security code.

Security and privacy are at the core of Apple Pay. Apple does not track what purchases the consumer makes, where the consumer makes them, nor the cost of the purchases. The transaction is among the consumer, the merchant, and the consumer's bank. According to Apple's encryption guidelines, even the cashier does not see the name of the consumer, credit card information, nor the security code [4].

The goals of this project were to develop proactive mitigation and objective strategies to:

- Develop an understanding of the many risks of mobile-payment technology methods and any associated lack of confidentiality.
- Identify damages caused by Apple Pay when affected by cybercrimes.
- Study detailed transaction mechanism of the Apple Pay system and identify security vulnerabilities of each.
- Identify if there are some solutions or a proactive approach to securing vulnerabilities and networks for Apple Pay.
- Summarize and seek optimized solutions for each vulnerability.
- Recommend policies for early detections of fraudulent activities.

The remainder of this paper is organized as follows: Section II summarizes related work and recent efforts to provide perspective on the scope and importance of Apple Mobile Payments to the mCommerce ecosystem. Section III discusses known examples of Apple Pay attacks and threats. Section IV discusses relevant updates to Apple iOS. Section V introduces actions planning to address risks. Section VI proposes recommendations. Section VII concludes the paper with some reflections on findings and suggestions for future work to build upon them.

II. Concept of Apple Mobile Payments

The popularity of mobile payments is growing at an amazing rate. There are five million ecommerce transactions within the United States alone each day, representing over $1 billion of online purchases. On Black Friday 2016, online sales from mobile devices totaled $1.2 billion, or 36 percent of the day's total sales. This was an increase of 33 percent over 2015. By 2019, worldwide mobile payments are predicted to surpass $1 trillion [3].

With Apple Pay there is "one-touch" check out, no card number entry, no disclosure of addresses when shopping online, and no sharing of card information with the merchant. Online payments and physical Point of Sale (POS) are the two methods of mobile payments. Physical POS refers to methods such as Apple and Android Pay that are processed at checkout terminals in stores. Companies such as MasterPass (MasterCard), Samsung Pay and Chase Pay use these services, but most physical POS payments use NFC technology that is built into many smartphones. This is the same technology that is used for mobile payments at brick-and-mortar retailers. Card information is not stored on the smartphone but creates a token that replaces card details to realize a confidential transaction. For example, Apple Pay requires strict security measures whereby all transactions must be verified with biometric authentication or a passcode. However, mobile payment fraud still can occur.

Mobile payments are becoming more popular, but they still face some high barriers, such as consumers' continued loyalty to traditional payment methods and fragmented acceptance among merchants [5]. New data from the PULSE 2016 Debit Issuer study shows that despite increased availability, debit users are mostly uninterested in mobile wallets [6]. In 2016, a survey was taken where 67 percent of respondents expressed concerned about the security of mobile payments. Fiserv [7] found that another 47 percent of consumers avoid mobile payments because they do not trust the advancement of technology with their confidential information. A study from Auriemma Counseling Group found that 74 percent of consumers want to avoid the use of mobile payment, collectively, due to the risks they believe their devices will be exposed to [6]. Moreover, many consumers have decided to remain loyal and dependent on traditional payment methods.

A. Definitions and Characteristics of Apple Mobile Payment

Table I shows the types of mobile payments that currently are available and have reached their peak within the U.S. Mobile payments are centralized among consumers and merchants and involve direct purchases of goods and services that can be account-based and POS. Apple Pay is considered a proximity-technology involved mobile payment in which payment credentials are stored in the mobile device and exchanged over the air, based on NFC technology, with a dedicated and compatible payment terminal [8]. Additionally, this acts as a contactless reader or Personal Identification Number (PIN), for authentication purposes, in which the consumer purchases goods and services. Apple Pay can send and receive data in which it is highly aligned with the use of trusted computing media such as Subscriber Identity Module (SIM) cards and Trusted Platform Modules (TPM).

TABLE I. Types of Mobile Payments

Type	Technology Involved
Proximity Payment • Refers to contactless payment • Payment credential stored in mobile device and exchanged over air • Mobile device acts as a contactless payment card *Remote Payment* • Covers payments that take place via mobile browser or smartphone application • Mobile device is used to authenticate personal information stored remotely • Payment transactions: face-to-face and vending machine transactions	• Mobile phone is used by the consumer to pay for goods via contactless reader, text-based, or personal identification number using NFC • NFC: communication between consumer device, payment scheme operator, and retail merchant • NFC Compatible devices can send/receive data

B. Ecosystem of Apple Mobile Payments

Figure 1 presents the cycle of the functioning of Apple Pay's NFC transaction through mobile payments. This chart depicts the ecosystem of mobile payment functions. First, authorization of the NFC proximity mobile payment via an existing Payment Service Provider (PSP) network is needed. The financial institution prepares the account data and then transfers the payment information to Trusted Service Manager (TSM) [8]. Secondly, TSM manages the deployment of mobile applications and delivers consumers' payment information over-the-air (OTA) through the mobile network to the secure element in the mobile phone. Once the payment is in phone, the consumer can utilize the mobile device as a contactless payment with merchants who accept this specific payment method.

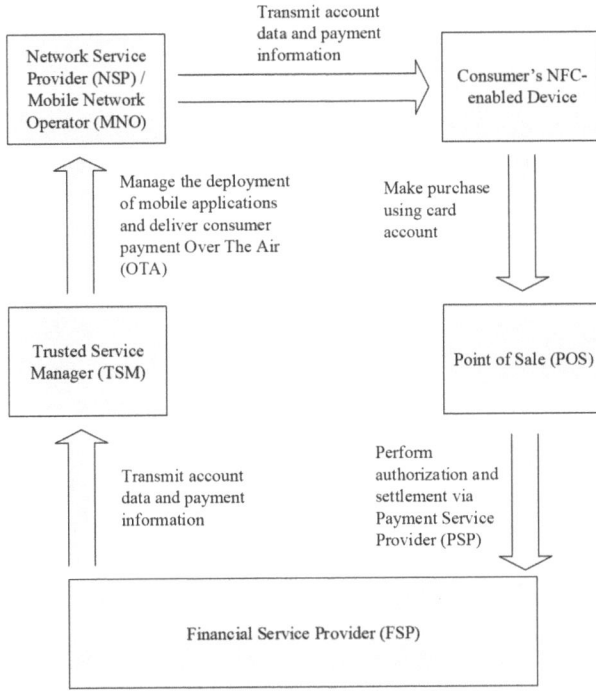

Fig. 1. Lifecycle of a Bank-Centric NFC Mobile Payment [8]

Table II presents various types of mobile payment services. They comprise independent communication service providers that own the complete telecom infrastructure for hosting and managing mobile communications among subscribed mobile users with users in the same and external wireless and wired telecom networks [9]. This creates a network of high-end telecommunication devices, specialized software, and client-end subscriber modules to issue end-to-end communication between wired and wireless telecom end-user devices. Mobile Network Operators (MNOs) install base stations, while the mobile subscribers use a circuit-like chip in iPhones to access network services.

TABLE II. MOBILE PAYMENT SERVICES

Service Provider Type	Services
Hybrid-Collaborative	Short Message Service (SMS) based payment service targeting the unbanked, prepaid mobile subscribers Google Checkout
Mobile Network Operator	SMS based system that has NFC system for mobile ticketing for mobile transport Mobile wallet services
Independent Payment Services	Peer to Peer (P2P) mobile payment company that enables mobile phone users to send/receive money through devices P2P money transfers from the sender's bank account to the recipients' bank account

C. Security and Privacy Policy of Apple Mobile Payment

Privacy is important when confidential information is being distributed across networks. Apple holds confidential information per device, encrypted, in which it is safely, individually available to the consumer [10]. Apple ensures privacy is effective through two policies:

1. No backdoors: There can be no backdoors (which may allow malicious activity in) in any software.

2. Encryption: According to the Legal Privacy Policy [4], Apple's websites, interactive application such as Apple Pay, online services, etc. use encryption such as Transport Layer Security (TLS). Encryption is a "must" in today's world.

According to Yunusov [11] Apple Pay's security measures also include using a separate microprocessor for payments, known as Secure Enclave, so that credit card data is not stored on the device or transmitted in plaintext during payments.

D. Concerns of Apple Mobile Payment

Apple Pay has received a fair amount of praise since the launch of mobile payment in September 2014. Headlines raved about this innovative category of service that has transformed mobile payments with an easy, secure, and private way to pay. Reports suggest that a lapse in verification between banks and Apple OTA transactions due to vulnerabilities within the NFC and many other payment mechanisms allows thieves to compromise information involved in mobile payments. This brings payments under the manifold protection of iOS, whether Apple's much-debated encryption or largely successful repellence of malware. Although Apple's mobile payment service can provide consumers with various benefits, it also introduces security concerns and vulnerabilities [12].

While mobile presents enticing business opportunities; it also stretches the boundaries of the threat landscape, expanding the attack surface to an increasing number of threats against the mobile banking revolution [3]. Many security researchers have confirmed that mobile provides criminals an "entrance" to stealing credit card details and hijacking transaction information. As an example, criminals who may acquire pilfered credit card data can add this information to their own Apple Pay account. Furthermore, mobile network operators are losing control of the mobile payment ecosystem [13]. Not only is the consumer and their lack of knowledge of security standards at fault, but also banks lack sufficient verification of information.

Financial institutions and MNOs compete to be the entity that will hold the customer account and receive payments. There are two models: bank-centric and nonbank-centric. The bank-centric model involves a customer account held by the bank that handles issues involving liability, transaction monitoring for fraud detection, and anti-money laundering. Apple Pay is bank centric. In the nonbank-centric model, the customer account is held at a nonfinancial organization such as an MNO or a third-party payment service [8]. When a payment is initiated, it is imperative for the consumer's bank to authorize all transactions. However, important regulations, security, and profit-sharing question have been raised. With mobile payments on the rise, cyber criminals have begun to target their efforts against mobile opportunities. Which entity will be responsible for the regulation of these services if breaches take place? National telecommunication networks? Or national banking?

Apple Pay has changed business in the field of communication and now has a method of generating financial transactions on and off the web. This in turn has helped consumers increasingly familiarize themselves with mobile payments and become accustomed to its conveniences.

III. APPLE MOBILE PAYMENT ATTACKS AND THREATS

Apple Pay may have numerous benefits when it comes to ease of use and security. However, according to researchers from the anti-fraud firm Pindrop, Apple Pay and banking partners still are not doing enough to preventing stolen credit cards, citing vulnerabilities such as SSL interception, security gaps in the secure element, and ongoing use of jailbroken iPhones [14]. When a customer adds a card, Apple connects with the bank sending them encrypted credit card data. The bank, then, imposes its own authentication checks which may require a phone call where the consumer may have to provide additional information for authentication purposes.

Pindrop researcher, David Dewey, tested out his theories regarding the safety of Apple Pay by experimenting with bank cards donated by various banks. While not revealing all the results, Dewey did disclose that he remains skeptical that banks are investing sufficient effort to prevent stolen credit cards. According to Dewey [14], Apple Pay provides the easiest work around for fraudsters to evade the protections offered by Europay, MasterCard and Visa (EMV) chips.

Apple does not implement the "rate limiting" service that rejects hackers from making too many guesses as they attempt to gain access. In other words, Apple Pay does not prevent brute force attempts. Researcher Dewey constructed a tool that would guess the correct Card Verification Values (CVV) number of a credit card, at a rapid pace. There are only 1000 different combinations of three digits, something a computer can run through in seconds [14]. Dewey stated that communication going through Apple Pay is blinded, leaving providers with no protection against brute force attacks by hackers who may try to guess the CVV code [14] [15].

Through research it has been discovered that the following are different types of attacks and threats that allow Apple Pay users to fall victim to hackers.

A. Attack I: Apple Server

iOS is designed to be reliable and secure from the moment the device is in use, with built-in security features to help protect access to personal information and data. However, experts state that around 2 percent of iPhone users make unauthorized modifications to iOS – so-called "jailbreaking" – to allow customizations and to add applications that have not been approved by Apple [16]. Jailbreaking undermines the original security features implemented by Apple [17], making them susceptible to attacks including hijackings and malware installations.

Hackers initially infect a jailbroken device with malware, then eventually acquire root privileges to gain full access to the user's device. An attacker can run tools like Cycript, GDB and Snoop-it to perform runtime analysis and steal sensitive data, including intercepting traffic like payment data en route to an Apple Server [16], damage the device, attack the network through FaceTime, and many other nefarious deeds.

B. Attack II: SSL Transaction Traffic

The Secure Socket Layer (SSL) is the standard technology for keeping an internet connection secure and safeguarding any sensitive data exchanged among systems. This prevents criminals from reading and modifying *any* information transferred, not just personal details [18]. SSL creates a secure connection through public, private, and session keys. Encrypting and decrypting with private and public keys can take a lot of processing power but is used only during the SSL Handshake to create a symmetric session key [19]. After the secure connection is established, the session key is used to encrypt all transmitted data. The browser from the devices connects to a sever to begin the transaction, secured with the SSL. The server sends a copy of its SSL certificate along with the server's public key [20].

However, hackers have mastered the art of hijacking the transaction and manipulating the traffic before the server has the opportunity to decrypt the symmetric session key. However, in the most recent years, SSL has fallen vulnerable to hackers. An attack can be performed against Apple devices by exploiting and taking advantage of jailbroken devices to inject malware and then intercept and manipulate SSL transaction traffic that users perform using Apple Pay. Hackings can intercept SSL transaction traffic, tamper with transaction data and change the amount or currency being paid using Apple Pay [21].

The first step in this attack, where hackers can compromise data, is stealing the payment token from a victim's phone. Some consumers are not aware of the risks that results from using public Wi-Fi. As remarked earlier, hackers can offer their own "fake" Wi-Fi hotspot and ask users to create a profile. This, give hackers the opportunity to steal the Apple Pay cryptogram, the key to encrypting the data. Since the delivery information is sent in clear text, hackers can use an intercepted cryptogram to make payments on the same website where the victim charged transactions [11]. These vulnerabilities can lead to additional damages such as malware dispersed throughout the network where it will spread rapidly.

To patch these vulnerabilities, consumers must disable outdated SSL servers and continuously upgrade their devices to remain in compliance with the most up-to-date security measures.

The followings are some incidents caused by SSL vulnerabilities.

1) POODLE (CVE-2014-3566)

According to the National Vulnerability Database (NVD) [22], Padding Oracle On Downgraded Legacy Encryption (POODLE) was published in October 2014 and takes advantage of two vulnerabilities. First, some Apple users still support SSL 3.0 for interoperability and compatibility with legacy systems. In this case, victims voluntarily interact with attack mechanisms resulting in unauthorized disclosure of information. The second vulnerability relates to Block Padding in SSL v3.0. POODLE uses nondeterministic Cipher Block Chaining (CBC) padding; this makes it easier for a Man-in-The-Middle (MitM) attacker to obtain clear-text data via a padding-oracle attack such as POODLE [23].

When the Apple Pay user initiates the Handshake, and sends the list of supported SSL versions, the attacker can intercept the traffic and then perform the MitM attack. This impersonates the Server until the Client agrees to downgrade the connection to the vulnerable state [24]. Once the connection between the Apple User and Server is established on the vulnerable SSL, the attacker can then perform the POODLE attack. Moreover, the vulnerability exists in CBC mode. Since Block Ciphers have fixed length, padding is added to fill the extra space. The issue here is the padding value is ignored by the Server which merely checks if padding length is accurate along with Message Authentication Code (MAC) of the plaintext [25]. In other words, the receiver will not be able to verify if the padding value has been manipulated in transit. The attacker thus will have the opportunity to decipher the plaintext value of the encryption block by modifying the padding bytes, and then seeing the corresponding response from the server.

Until systems are patched, mitigation steps need to be taken to initiate an action plan. To patch against POODLE and keep it from affecting Apple Pay, users and merchants need to implement Intrusion Prevention Systems (IPS) to secure network traffic through network scanning [25].

2) BEAST (CVE-2011-3389)

The Browser Exploit Against SSL/TLS (BEAST) attack affects SLL 3.0 and TLS 1.0. An attacker can decrypt data exchanged between two parties by taking advantage of a vulnerability in the implementation of the CBC mode in TLS 1.0. This is the tool that allows hackers to perform an attack. According to the NVD, the SSL protocol encrypts data that allows MitM attackers to obtain plaintext Hypertext Transfer Protocol (HTTP) headers via a Block-wise Chosen Boundary Attack (BCBA) on an HTTP Secure (HTTPS) session [26]. Using MitM, the attacker can inject packets into the SSL stream; the attacker guesses the initialization vector used in XORing with the message and compare the results to the ones of the block the attackers want to "decrypt" [23].

Despite the client-to-server relationship between Apple Pay users and merchants, these attacks can take place by simply browsing the web on public Wi-Fi. For this to be a successful attack, hackers must have control of the Apple Pay user's browser. Hardening TLS 1.1 and banning the Java Plug-in from the browser will prevent this attack from occurring [27].

3) CRIME (CVE-2012-4929)

Compression Ratio Info-lead Made Easy (CRIME) is a vulnerability found in TLS compression; meaning the connection can be established without any compression [23]. This feature is known to reduce bandwidth usage while preserving integrity and security when exchanging large amounts of information.

An attacker targets a victim's network to hijack. The Apple Pay user may have signed into the browser through a public Wi-Fi that contains malicious JavaScript and is controlled by the attacker. Then, the script will initiate a connection to a third party so the attacker can inject plaintext into the victim's cookies and then monitor the size of the response [28]. If the size of the response is lower than the initial response, it means the character the attacker injected is contained in the cookie value. Using this method, an attacker can brute force the cookie's value based on the feedback from the merchant.

4) BREACH (CVE-2013-3587)

Browser Reconnaissance and Exfiltration via Adaptive Compression of Hypertext (BREACH) is similar to CRIME, but targets HTTP compression where TLS compression is not required for this attack to be execute [23]. An attacker forces the victim's browser to connect to the TLS enabled third party network as they are monitoring the traffic between the Apple Pay consumer and merchant (server) by performing a MitM attack. Taken together, these factors constitute a vulnerable web application [29]:

- Being server from a server that utilizes HTTP-level compression
- Reflect user-input in HTTP response bodies
- Reflect a secret in HTTP response bodies

To prevent this attack from happening consumers must disable HTTP compression, mask secrets, protect vulnerable pages with Cross-Site Request Forgery (CSRF), and rate limit requests.

5) Heartbleed (CVE-2014-0160)

This attack compromises the TLS heartbeat extension [30] [23]. Heartbeat is found in the heartbeat extension of the cryptography library OpenSSL. The TLS heartbeat extension is used as a method between two parties to ensure the connection is not closed. The Apple Pay user sends a request to the retailer with a payload that contains the data-size of the data. The retailer must respond with the exact same request containing the data and size to reciprocate what the Apple Pay user requested. However, if the Apple Pay user sends a falsified data length, the retailer would respond with the data received by the client – including random data from its memory to meet the length requirements contingent of the Apple Pay user's request [31]. There are known cases where the retailer's private key leaked through the Heartbeat vulnerability, which means the attacker would be able to decrypt all the traffic of the server. The flaw allows a remote attack to retrieve private memory of an application that uses the vulnerable OpenSSL library [32].

Maintaining updated iOS and SSL is imperative to preventing security breaches. It also is important that retailers implement TLS to keep data secure over a network. There are some instances where badly configured servers place Apple Pay users at risk and expose confidential information. As a solution, OpenSSL 1.0.1 has been released to patch the damages, vulnerabilities, and leaks.

C. Attack III: Masque Attack

The 2015 release of iOS 8.4 fixed various vulnerabilities that allowed attackers to deploy two Masque Attacks: CVE-2015-3722/3725 and CVE-2015-3725. These exploits are known as Manifest Masque and Extension and can be used to demolish apps and other resources Apple has to offer, such as Apple Pay, Apple Watch, Apple Heath, etc. These exploits also have the ability to destroy and corrupt the app data container. Plugin Masque bypasses iOS security measures and hijacks Virtual Private Network (VPN) traffic.

A year after the launch of Apple Pay, one-third of iOS devices had not been updated to version 8.1.3 or above. Consequently, five months after the release of 8.1.3, these devices remained vulnerable to all Masque Attacks [31]. The Table below show three different types of Masque Attack that are threats to Apple Pay.

TABLE III. MASQUE ATTACKS [33] [31]

Name	Consequences Disclosed	Mitigation Status
Manifest Masque	• Demolish apps (such as Apple Pay, Apple Watch, etc.) during OTA installations	Partially fixed in iOS 8.4
Extension Masque	• Access to other application data • Prevent Apple Pay transactions and access to consumer's own data	Partially fixed in iOS 8.4
Plugin Masque	• Bypass prompt of trust • Bypass VPN plugin entitlement • Replace an existing VPN plugin • Hijack device traffic • Prevent device from rebooting • Exploit more kernel vulnerabilities	Fixed in iOS 8.1.3

1) Manifest Masque Attack

In 2014, Apple was notified of this vulnerability. Manifest Masque Attack leverages the CVE-2015-3722/3725 vulnerability to demolish an existing app on iOS when a victim installs an in-house iOS app. The demolish app (the attacker target) can either be a regular downloaded from official App Store or even an important system app, such as Apple Watch, Apple Pay, App Store, Safari, Settings, and so on during OTA installations [34]. Additionally, this vulnerability affects all version iOS 7.x and iOS 8.x devices which are Apple Pay compatible yet still vulnerable to being attacked due to being just "partially patched."

2) Extension Masque Attack

This attack takes advantage of the introduction of app extensions in iOS 8. While an app extension can execute code and is restricted to access data within its data container, a malicious extension using the same bundle identifier as the target app could give the attacker full access to the data container of the target app [35]. In this attack, an attacker can lure the victim to install an in-house app by using enterprise provisioning from a website to enable the malicious extension of the in-house app on the victim's device, thus leading to the end game of stealing data [34] [36]. On June 14, 2015, security researchers validated various severe issues on OS X which can, in fact, be leveraged by an attacker to steal all data in a target app's data container. Apple was notified and fixed this issue as part of CVE-2015-3725.

3) Plugin Masque

The final attack is the Plugin Masque. The vulnerability of Plug-in was disclosed to Apple in November 2014 and as a result it was patched on iOS 8.1.3 when Apple patched App Masque [34]. This attack is known to be more troubling than Manifest Masque and Extension Masque, because it allows for the replacement of the VPN plugin. In turn, this gives an attacker the ability to monitor all the network traffic on the device, not just Apple Pay, during transactions. It can perform authorized operations, including VPN traffic, without the user's knowledge. Although patched since iOS 8.1.3, it is still causing problems.

D. Attack Via Distributed Denial of Service Attack (DDoS)

The DDoS attack affects the availability of network resources of services by preventing Apple Pay users from accessing network assets; denying the use of services from authorized users [37]. In addition to denial, this attack delays time critical operation by preventing the Apple Pay customer, or merchant, from responding to a user's request. Hackers create these delays through resource exhaustion, where they exhaust all available bandwidth, disk space, or memory capacity.

There are three types of threats that can flood this service: consuming system resources; wasting the communication link by repeatedly downloading a large file from the server; and using the Structured Query Language (SQL) injections [38]. These flood attacks can be launched from botnet, viruses, or open Denial of Service (DoS) tools to disrupt the network service. Malicious users launch such attacks by sending a huge number of bogus requests to the servers to consume the processing power from the Apple Pay user to the merchant and flood the network bandwidth.

Apple Pay users are vulnerable to the Connectionless Volumetric Attack, where the attack does not require a session to be established before sending data packets to the Apple Pay user [39]. Volumetric Attacks are known as floods where it congests a system sending an abundant amount of traffic, on a network, that it overwhelms the bandwidth. This attack has become a frequent menace as it is commonly used to exact revenge, conduct extortion, and even to wage cyber war [40].

Causing a system malfunction during the transaction between the Apple Pay consumer and merchant creates damages to bandwidth affecting the connectivity of the Apple Pay user through flooding [41]. Moreover, hardware becomes corrupted through amplification-based flood attacks where the adversary sends requests with spoofed IP addresses in a reflection manner to a large number of reflectors exploiting the IP packet broadcast feature.

Many merchants are investing in an open source memcached project to eliminate this attack vector. The memcached 1.5.6 update disables the User Datagram Protocol (UDP) protocol, which is what DDoS attacker are using to amplify attacks. This "kill switch" flushes all commands to merchant networks and decreases the vulnerability of network traffic [42].

E. Additional Vulnerabilities, Risks, Threats, and Countermeasures

There is a synergy of both business risks and technical risks encountered as Apple Pay continues to become adopted into modern industrial society. There are some challenges and cost-value considerations for businesses preventing them from investing into Apple Pay services. Fraudsters are targeting Apple Pay; so upfront analysis and countermeasures are imperative to mitigate the risk to these devices. Traditional risks involve denial or theft of services leading to the loss of revenue, negative reputation, and lack of confidentiality. Emerging risks involve the use of mobile payment leading to the loss of revenue, exposure of confidentiality, and theft of transfers through transactions.

Risks for Apple Pay depend on the role of the entity user, network, or communication provider, or payment service providers [8]. Listed below in Tables IV and V are the various types of threats, risks, and vulnerabilities that are likely to play a role in potential malicious attacks on Apple Pay. These data further confirm that users and service providers have weaknesses that make them vulnerable to malicious attacks. A user is likely to be vulnerable to an attack through OTA transmission between an iPhone and POS due to the interception of traffic [43]. Apple Pay is susceptible to identity theft, information disclosure, and a potential re-launch of this attack will likely take place if countermeasures are not in place. A TPM, secured protocols, and data encryption need to be consistently enforced on the network.

Service providers are known to be the "backdoor" to mobile payment compromises. POS accepting OTA transmissions fall victim to malicious party flooding on POS systems with meaningless requests [8]. Consequently, this leads to the risk of DoS attack. Another vulnerability occurs when POS devices are installed at merchant premises; then masquerade attacks become a threat leading to POS tampering. Services and message modifications become a risk to consumers in which data traffic may be rerouted to complete a hacker's end game.

TABLE IV. APPLE MOBILE PAYMENT RISKS TO USERS [43] [8]

Vulnerability	Threat	Risk	Counter measures
OTA transmission between phone and POS	Interception of traffic	Identity theft, Information disclosure, Relay attacks	TPM, secure protocols, encryption
Inadvertent installation of malicious software on mobile phone	Interception of authentication data	Theft of authentication parameters, Information disclosure, Transaction repudiation	Authentication of both user and application, TPM
Absence of two-factor authentication	User masquerading	Fraudulent transactions	Two-factor authentication

TABLE V. APPLE MOBILE PAYMENT RISKS UPON SERVICE PROVIDER [43] [8]

Vulnerability	Threat	Risk	Counter measures
POS system accepts OTA transmissions	Malicious party floods POS system with meaningles requests	DoS	Request filtering at reader based on mobile device reader relative geometry
POS devices are installed at merchant premises	Masqueradea ttacks, Tampering with POS	Theft of service, Relay attack, Message modification	POS vendor vetting, Message authentications
Lack of digital rights management on mobile device	Mobile device user illegally distributes content	Theft of content and digital piracy, Risk to provider for digital rights infringement	Digital rights management (DRM) incorporated in smartphone TPM design, Cryptographica

Vulnerability	Threat	Risk	Counter measures
			lly supported DRM
Global System for Mobile (GSM) communication encryption for On The Scene (OTS) transmission	Message modification, Relay of transactions, Evasion of fraud control	Theft of service of content	Strong cryptographic protocols, SMS messaging authentications, Encryption

IV. APPLE MOBILE PAYMENT UPDATES

In January 2015, iOS 8.1.3 was released. App Masque, Uniform Resource Locator (URL) Masque, and Plugin Masque issues were patched or partially fixed [34]. Recently, researchers monitoring iOS web traffic in high-profile networks showed that one-third of all iOS traffic is still vulnerable to all the Masque Attacks [33]. Consumers should continuously update their Apple devices, when prompted, to ensure software remains up-to-date, and thereby reduce the potential for malicious attempts that can also affect Apple Pay.

A. Apple iOS Internal Feature

Apple is said to place heavy emphasis on security within Apple Pay to ensure consumers' payment information is safe and protected. When a credit or credit card is scanned into the Wallet for use with Apple Pay, it is assigned a unique device number, or a 'token' which is stored in the phone as a "code" than a card number [44] [45]. There is a special chip, secure element, containing payment information data that is said to never become exposed or uploaded to iCloud to Apple's servers.

When transactions are initiated, the Device Account Number (DAN) is sent via NFC with a dynamic security code; both which are needed for a successful transaction. The security code is a one-time use cryptogram that replaces the credit card's Credit Card Validation (CCV) functions to ensure that a transaction processes accordingly. As mentioned before, Apple Pay fosters secure enclave and secure element; both storing the payment applet certified by the payment networks and specializes in encrypted cardholder data and keys.

In addition to security, dynamic security codes and DAN, such as tokens and cryptograms are built into the NFC specification. However, recent studies have proven that Apple's "security" standards are not effective in protective Apple Pay users as they are portrayed.

B. Storing Keys in Secure Element

Apple has built in a security method designed to protect user data through Secure Enclave. This secure element ensures that a user's sensitive payment data is stored only on a user's device. To make a payment, an alias is generated that the processing backend can recognize. When a user taps their device against the POS to pay, that alias alone is transmitted along with a cryptographic code. The code is decrypted by the backend, which then compares the alias to the one it stores [46].

Maintaining a private key in a keychain is an amazing asset to ensure privacy and security. Secure Enclave is a hardware-based key manager that is isolated from the main processor to provide an extra layer of security [47]. As an example, when a consumer stores a private key in the Secure Enclave, the likelihood of the key becoming compromised is slim. Instead, the user instructs the Secure Enclave to create the key, securely store the key, and perform operations with the key. The consumer only receives the output of operation such as encrypted data or a cryptographic signature verification outcome.

Free Wi-Fi hotspot services, in public settings, could allow an attacker into the consumer's mobile devices. Security researchers have alerted Apple users about potential security flaws regarding the use of free Wi-Fi since exploiters can hack into iOS users' operating systems and/or set up a rogue Wi-Fi spot. This can lead consumers to insert their credit card information which attackers can then intercept. According to researchers, spoofers can loaf around a POS machine with an Apple Pay terminal and continuously launch such an attack.

Access to the secure element also creates a weakness the Relay Attack. This attack cannot be prevented by the application layer cryptography protocol. The timing requirements by International Organization for Standardization (ISO) 14443 are too lax to prevent relay over longer channels [48]. Possible countermeasures are shielding countless interface and distance bounding protocols; but this requires faster communication channels. Application accesses the secure element and relays Application Protocol Data Unit (APDU) commands/responses over a network interface.

Adding a secure element to a mobile phone opens a new attack vector, such as DoS and Relay Attack, which has fallen to negligence of being considered.

C. Near Field Communication

POS on the NFC Interface is potentially vulnerable to relay attacks for low- value payments. Some merchants welcome cloud-based systems where intercepted data may become spoofed, manipulating the identity of the user [49]. This factor leads to one of the vulnerabilities of NFC. When consumers send their information through the network, attackers tamper with the data with the possibility of being execute by the hacker's collection of keys. The biggest challenges are secure access and authentication of the user to the cloud.

To patch these vulnerabilities, Apple and many merchants have implemented security mechanisms such as tokenization and Point-to-Point Encryption (P2PE) [49] [50] [51]. Tokenization is known to offer a substantial measure of security for financial transactions, as opposed to host-based card emulation which is unsafe due to sensitive data being stored on mobile devices. Even without equipment or skill, attackers would be able to intercept the SSL transaction traffic and also manipulate data. Consequently, Apple Pay uses the EMV Payment Tokenization Specification to offer secure payment transactions [17].

To patch the vulnerabilities of NFC, tokenization captures card information, stores, and secures the data and keys on the mobile device [52]. It is also used during payment verification to identify the user and the keys of the payment product. Then, the user's data is tokenized to devalue the contained sensitive information, discouraging attackers from hacking. Tokenization makes use of session keys, single keys, or limited use keys that have to be validated and confirmed. However, tokenization and other payment card security technologies are only as secure as their implementation.

V. ACTION PLANNING TO ADDRESS RISKS IN APPLE MOBILE PAYMENT

Fraud is an intentional deception or misrepresentation intended to result in personal or financial gain. Security threats in mCommerce may be passive (e.g., information being monitored and released for fraudulent purposes), or active (e.g., modification of information through DoS and unauthorized access) [38]. Apple Pay brings new opportunities and new risks.

Due to the many parties that are involved in making a single transaction during a mobile payment, the network is left exposed and vulnerable to risks and threats. This can be exacerbated if important services are outsourced to potentially unregulated third parties without clear lines of accountability and oversight, or which are located overseas [8]. Multiparty transaction environments are conducive to exploitation by fraudsters using technological and sociological attack if the appropriate protection mechanisms and accountability controls are not established throughout Apple Pay's mobile payment ecosystem. With effective planning, favorable circumstances exist to make security an element of Apple Pay systems.

The fraud that can occur in the mCommerce environment are specific to e-payment systems through Apple Pay. It is imperative that Financial Service Providers (FSPs), PSPs, and Network Service Providers (NSPs) employ appropriate protections, safeguards and privacy and security governance programs. Transactions being undertaken, in an assurance manner by the authorized person, is a concern for many stakeholders. Some of the intrusions take place in mobile commerce environments; attempts from competitors, entry attempts into customer's private accounts, and attempts to spoil the reputation of the merchant vendor [38]. However, using two-factor authentication provides a substantial amount of identity protection for the consumer and high assurance of confidentiality for the merchant.

In the case of Apple Pay, through NFC transactions, protection from transactions originating from unauthorized users can be accomplished by the use of dynamic CVV [4].

The NFC chip on iPhone supports CVV as opposed to the CVV located on the magnetic strip of a credit card. If a bogus mobile device is used with Apple Pay, it will display the incorrect CVV and the transaction will be unsuccessful. In turn, this will protect the consumer, the merchant, and the service provider from foul play.

Techniques analogous to SSL should be used to ensure that only legitimate POS or service providers interact with mobile phones [20]. This represents a large pool of issues in relation to trustworthiness or identities and credentials for Apple Pay users. In a 2011 White House publication, these issues and potential strategies were discussed as part of a national strategy for trusted identities in cyberspace [8].

Data classification during transmission and storage at various nodes is another factor that needs to be addressed. It is imperative that organizations identify the data considered to be private to ensure appropriate countermeasures and mechanisms are in full effect to protect it. For example, such data could be appropriated for marketing services, and organizations could potentially be found liable for wrongful business practices for using it without consumer knowledge or consent. In terms of financial data, another important facet, aside from encryption, is the matter of data integrity. Organizations must take data integrity take into account as part of Apple Pay security.

In the case of proximity payments, risks to POS systems also must be addressed. Organizations should ensure that third parties with which they interact have robust security governance in place [8]. Immediate attention should be focused on TSM as this performs a compatibility check on the vendor supplied mobile device for Apple Pay.

VI. RECOMMENDATIONS

Many experts say mobile payment methods offered by major providers are more secure than physical cards and traditional cash due to encryption and tokenization to mask payment card account numbers. Despite protections provided by technology advancements, Apple Pay remains vulnerable to hackers and identity theft. Cyber thieves can "spoof" consumers' mobile wallet via public Wi-Fi. Major mobile wallet providers use randomly generated payment tokens for validation of privacy. However, consumers still add cards to Apple Pay using unsecured public Wi-Fi networks, inviting hackers to lurk on them to spoof registration systems.

Tim Cook, Chief Executive Officer (CEO) of Apple, has called for stronger privacy regulations for tech companies and merchants due to recent data scandals. Cook states, "I am worried about the number of people around the world who easily handed over their information without fully understanding the affects. [10]" Consumers should load credit cards onto Apple Pay using their own password-protected Wi-Fi network or simply invest in a personal VPN.

A. Using Cryptogram Only Once

Using a cryptogram introduces EMV cryptographic strength to remote payments, not only for in-app payments on the mobile device, but also for interconnected Apple devices used for Digital Secure Remote Payment (DSRP) [53]. Apple continues to recommend to consumers and merchants that the cryptogram token should be used only once; yet both parties frequently use this token multiple times. Using a cryptogram multiple times creates a vulnerability whereby hackers can manipulate delivery details to authorize fraudulent payments as the information is sent in clear text without integrity checking.

B. Precautionary Measures

Based on the findings in this study, the following measures should be undertaken to better security mobile payment services:

- Be wary about "https://" on websites. Fraudulent websites may also obtain "https://".

- Avoid Public Wi-Fi

- If public Wi-Fi use is unavoidable, then do not share any credentials (e.g., user-id, password)

- Never perform any financial transactions on public Wi-Fi

C. Be Aware of Masque Attacks

Although Apple has [partially] fixed the original Masque Attack on version 8.1.3, there still are other iOS attack surfaces and vulnerabilities to exploit during the installation process [34]. In addition, one in every three iOS devices is likely to be vulnerable to all Masque Attacks due to consumers neglecting to upgrade their devices. Users must keep their devices up-to-date with the latest software releases to ensure transactions are secured and no unforeseen interruptions take place during daily use.

VII. CONCLUSION

The iPhone has become a ubiquitous device for communication, entertainment, computation, and now contactless payment methods [5]. Apple Pay is undergoing transformations that hint at a seductive and promising future, where consumers and sellers alike will enjoy even more convenience and time savings. But areas of uncertainty remain. Key way-ahead considerations regarding the security and assurance of Apple Pay include the following:

- Key drivers from the consumer perspective

- Hardware secure element in the mobile device

- Trusted Execution Environment (Secure Enclave iOS)

- Device-specific Personal Area Network (PAN) with unique cryptogram (keys)

- NFC connectivity: EMV versions need to be consistently and continuously updated

- Taking advantage of EMV specifications

- Tokenization implementation

- Verification through biometrics (e.g., Touch ID, facial recognition)

ACKNOWLEDGEMENTS

"This work was supported [in part] by the Commonwealth Cyber Initiative, an investment in the advancement of cyber R&D, innovation and workforce development. For more information about CCI, visit cyberinitiative.org."

REFERENCES

[1] N. Mallat, M. Rossi and V. K. Tuunainen, "Mobile Banking Services," *Communications of the ACM*, vol. 47, no. 5, pp. 42-46, 2004.

[2] C. Xinru, "Information Security of Apple Pay," 2016. https://www.theseus.fi/bitstream/handle/10024/118948/Chen_Xinru.pdf?sequence=1&isAllowed=y.

[3] "Mobile Banking Security," VASCO, https://www.vasco.com/solutions/banking-cyber-security/mobile-banking-security.html.

[4] "Apple Pay Security and Privacy Overview," Apple, https://support.apple.com/en-us/HT203027.

[5] X. Lu, Y. Zhu, D. Li, B. Xu, W. Chen and Z. Ding, "Minimum cost collaborative sensing network with mobile phones," IEEE Explore, 13 June 2014. https://ieeexplore.ieee.org/document/6654784/.

[6] "This One Group is not Interested in Mobile Wallets," Business Insider, 15 August 2016. http://www.businessinsider.com/this-one-group-is-not-interested-in-mobile-wallets-2016-8.

[7] "Millennials Could Drive Mobile Wallet Adoption," Business Insider, 23 December 2016. http://www.businessinsider.com/millennials-could-drive-mobile-wallet-adoption-2016-12?r=UK&IR=T.

[8] "Mobile Payments: Risk, Security and Assurance Issues," November 2011. https://www.isaca.org/Groups/Professional- English/pci-compliance/GroupDocuments/MobilePaymentsWP.pdf.

[9] "Mobile Network Operator," Techopedia, https://www.techopedia.com/definition/27804/mobile-network-operator-mno.

[10] "Apple CEO Wants Stronger Privacy Laws," PYMNTS, 26 March 2018. https://www.pymnts.com/apple/2018/apple-ceo-privacy- laws-regulations-facebook/.

[11] J. Leyden , "Wallet-Snatch Hack: Apple Pay 'Vulnerable to Attack', Claim Researchers," The Register, 28 July 2017. https://www.theregister.co.uk/2017/07/28/applepay_vuln/.

[12] A. S. Jawale and J. S. Park, "A Security Analysis on Apple Pay," 6 March 2017. https://ieeexplore.ieee.org/document/7870214/?anchor=references.

[13] M. de Reuver and J. Ondrus, "When Techological Superiority is Not Enough: The Struggle to Impose the SIM Card as the NFC Secure Element for Mobile Payment Platforms," *Telecommunications Policy*, vol. 41, no. 4, pp. 253-262, 2017.

[14] T. Fox-Brewster, "Here's Proof Apple Pay is Useful for Stealing People's Money," Forbes, 1 March 2016. https://www.forbes.com/sites/thomasbrewster/2016/03/01/apple-pay-fraud-test/#330b50a46c6d.

[15] "Apple Pay's Low-Tech Security Problem," PYMNTS, 4 March 2016. https://www.pymnts.com/apple-pay-tracker/2016/apple-pays-low-tech-security-problem/.

[16] "Unauthorized Modification of iOS Can Cause Security Vulnerabilities, Instability, Shortened Battery Life, and other Issues," Apple, https://support.apple.com/en-us/HT201954.

[17] J. Sowells, "Apple Pay is Vulnerable to Malware," Hacker Combat, 31 July 2017. https://hackercombat.com/apple-pay-vulnerable-malware-attacks/.

[18] "What is SSL, TLS and HTTPS?," Symantec Website Security, https://www.websecurity.symantec.com/security-topics/what-is-ssl-tls-https.

[19] W. Chou, "Inside SSL: Accelerating Secure Transactions," *IT Professional*, vol. 4, no. 5, pp. 37-41, 2002.

[20] "What is an SSL Certificate and How Does it Work?," Digicert, https://www.digicert.com/ssl/.

[21] "New Malware Attack Techniques Expose Security Flaws in Apple Pay," TEISS, 27 July 2017. https://teiss.co.uk/news/apple-pay-malware-attack-techniques/.

[22] "POODLE CVE-2011-3389 Detail," National Vulnerability Database, 6 September 2011. https://nvd.nist.gov/vuln/detail/CVE-2011-3389#vulnCurrentDescriptionTitle.

[23] A. Prodromou, "TLS/SSL Explained- Examples of a TLS Vulnerability and Attack," Acunetix, 22 March 2017. https://www.acunetix.com/blog/articles/tls-vulnerabilities-attacks-final-part/.

[24] "Vulnerability and Exploit Database," Rapid7, https://www.rapid7.com/db/modules/auxiliary/scanner/http/ssl_version.

[25] "SSL V3.0 "Poodle" Vulnerability - CVE-2014-3566," Oracle https://www.oracle.com/technetwork/topics/security/poodlecve-2014-3566-2339408.html.

[26] "BEAST (CVE-2011-3389)," National Vulnerability Database, https://nvd.nist.gov/vuln/detail/CVE-2011-3389.

[27] L. Constantin, "Oracle Patches Java Flaw Exploited in SSL Beast Attack," Computer World, 19 October 2011. https://www.computerworld.com/article/2499203/enterprise-applications/oracle-patches-java-flaw-exploited-in-ssl-beast-attack.html.

[28] "CRIME CVE-2012-4929 Detail," National Vulnerability Database, https://nvd.nist.gov/vuln/detail/CVE-2012-4929.

[29] "SSL/TLS BREACH Vulnerability CVE-2013-3587," F5 Networks, https://support.f5.com/csp/article/K14634.

[30] "OpenSSL 'Heartbleed' Vulnerability (CVE-2014-0160)," United States Computer Emergency Readiness Team, https://www.us-cert.gov/ncas/alerts/TA14-098A.

[31] "Masque Attack: All Your iOS Apps Belong to Us," Fire Eye, 10 November 2014. https://www.fireeye.com/blog/threat-research/2014/11/masque-attack-all-your-ios-apps-belong-to-us.html.

[32] "The Heartbleed Bug," Heartbleed, http://heartbleed.com/.

[33] M. Gokey, "Masque Attack News: Researcher Find New Risk in iOS 'Masque Attack' Bug," Digital Trends, 6 August 2015. https://www.digitaltrends.com/mobile/ios-bug-masque-attack-news/.

[34] Z. Chen, T. Wei, H. Zue and Y. Zhang, "Three New Masque Attacks against iOS: Demolishing, Breaking and Hijacking," Fire Eye, 30 June 2015. https://www.fireeye.com/blog/threat-research/2015/06/three_new_masqueatt.html.

[35] D. Gilbert, "Masque Attacks are Back: IPhones and IPads Vulnerable to Sensitive App Data Theft," IB Times, 1 July 2015. https://www.ibtimes.co.uk/masque-attacks-are-back-iphones-ipads-vulnerable-sensitive-app-data-theft-1508816.

[36] L. Constantin, "One Third of Enterprise iOS Devices Vulnerable to App, Data Hijacking Attacks," CIO from IDG, 1 July 2015. https://www.cio.com/article/2943154/one-third-of-enterprise-ios-devices-vulnerable-to-app-data-hijacking-attacks.html.

[37] W. Alosaimi, M. Alshamrani and K. Al-Begain, "Simulation-Based Study of Distributed Denial of Service Attacks Prevention in the Cloud," 11 September 2015. https://ieeexplore.ieee.org/document/7373219/.

[38] P. Venkataram, B. S. Babu, M. K. Naveen and G. S. Gungal, "A Method of Fraud & Intrusion Detection for E-payment Systems in Mobile e-Commerce," 15 May 2017. https://ieeexplore.ieee.org/document/4197955/.

[39] "Types of DDoS Attacks," Verisign, https://www.verisign.com/en_US/security-services/ddos-protection/types-of-ddos-attacks/index.xhtml.

[40] D. Meyer, "Cloudflare and Apple Deal Fresh Blows to Neo-Nazi Sites," Fortune, 17 August 2017. http://fortune.com/2017/08/17/cloudflare-apple-neo-nazi-charlottesville/.

[41] G. V. Hulme, "DDoS Explained: How Distributed Denial of Service Attacks Are Evolving," CSO, 12 March 2018. https://www.csoonline.com/article/3222095/network-security/ddos-explained-how-denial-of-service-attacks-are-evolving.html.

[42] S. M. Kerner, "Memcached DDoS Attacks Slow Down as Patching Ramps Up," eWeek, 9 March 2018. http://www.eweek.com/security/memcached-ddos-attacks-slow-down-as-patching-ramps-up.

[43] P. L. Chatain, R. Hernandez-Coss, K. Borowik and A. Zerzan, "Integrity in Mobile Phone Financial Services- Measures for mitigating risks from money laundering and terrorist financing," May 2008. http://siteresources.worldbank.org/INTAML/Resources/WP146_Web.pdf.

[44] B. Sullivan, "How Tokenization May Change the Way You Pay," CNBC, 14 Dec 2014. https://www.cnbc.com/2014/12/12/how-tokenization-may-change-the-way-you-pay.html.

[45] E. Kovacs, "Tokenization: Benefits and Challenges for Securing Transaction Data," Security Week, 4 November 2014. https://www.securityweek.com/tokenization-benefits-and-challenges-securing-transaction-data.

[46] D. Etherington, "Tech Crunch," 16 January 2014. https://techcrunch.com/2014/01/16/apple-patents-mobile-payments-method-with-secure-element-for-protecting-account-info/.

[47] "Storing Keys in the Secure Enclave," https://developer.apple.com/documentation/security/certificate_key_and_trust_services/keys/storing_keys_in_the_secure_enclave.

[48] M. Roland, "Practical Attack Scenarios on Secure Element-Enabled Mobile Devices," Near Field Communication Research Lab Hagenberg, 13 March 2012. https://pdfs.semanticscholar.org/6826/325bb2721fafcd04fc28b1fa6220faade48c.pdf.

[49] F. D. Evans, "Digital Payments Security Discussion Secure Element (SE) vs Host Card Emulation (HCE)," Booz | Allen | Hamilton, 14 October 2014. https://www.itu.int/en/ITU- D/Regional-Presence/CIS/Documents/Events/2014/10_Baku/Session_5_Evans.pdf.

[50] "Encryption at the Point of Interaction," Velocity, https://nabvelocity.com/articles/encryption/.

[51] J. Heggestuen, "Payments Security is Undergoing a Revolution and Apple Pay is Leading the Way," Business Insider, 21 April 2015. http://www.businessinsider.com/apple-pay-leads-new-security-protocols-2015-4.

[52] "What Data Thieves Don't Want you to Know: The Facts About Encryption and Tokenization," https://www.firstdata.com/downloads/thought-leadership/TokenizationEncryptionWP.pdf.

[53] "Digital Secure Remote Payment: How Apple Pay Can Change the Future of Remote Payments," Computer Weekly, 27 March 2018. https://www.computerweekly.com/ehandbook/Digital-Secure-Remote-Payment-How-Apple-Pay-can-change-the-future-of-remote-payments.

Building Capacity for Systems Thinking in Higher Education Cybersecurity Programs

Esther A. Enright
Boise State University
Boise, ID, USA
estherenright@boisestate.edu

Connie Justice
Purdue School of Engineering and Technology, IUPUI
Indianapolis, IN, USA
cjustice@iupui.edu

Sin Ming Loo
Boise State University
Boise, ID, USA
smloo@boisestate.edu

Eleanor Taylor
Idaho National Laboratory
Idaho Falls, ID, USA
Eleanor.Taylor@inl.gov

Char Sample
Idaho National Laboratory
Idaho Falls, ID, USA
Charmaine.Sample@inl.gov

D. Cragin Shelton
Capitol Technology University
Laurel, MD, USA
dcshelton@captechu.edu

Abstract—The decentralized nature of cybersecurity programs in higher education leads to a lack of unifying knowledge, skills, and dispositions in the cybersecurity workforce. The emphasis on teaching the latest technologies and techniques without a sufficient foundation in systems thinking could result in graduating students without the capacity to function as constructive agents operating in complex systems. Having a unifying, cohesive cybersecurity systems framework can bridge some of these gaps. In this article, we argue that cybersecurity programs and courses must contextualize their instruction on a specific topic by teaching students to situate their learning on the system level. Additionally, we suggest that active learning strategies, in particular case study analysis and concept mapping, are particularly well suited to support this type of student learning. This article presents a cohesive framework for teaching systems thinking in cybersecurity programs and courses. The framework is designed to support meaningful reform in the currently decentralized, (mostly) unregulated academic ecosystem that manages the preparation of our cybersecurity workforce.

Keywords—cybersecurity, systems thinking, active learning, higher education

I. Introduction

The cybersecurity field has undergone significant changes since the early days of firewalls [1]. Today, the field serves the design and maintenance of intrusion detection systems (IDSs) [2], security information event management systems (SIEMs), and [3] more recently, artificial intelligence (AI) and machine learning (ML) [4] solutions. Even the name of the field has changed over the past 40 years as the practice has matured, addressing increasingly wider aspects of protection. What began as computer security, addressing a computer system and the data it processed, transitioned to network security as the implications of multiple, interconnected computers became apparent. More recently, practitioners shifted to calling the field information security since past names focused on the hardware and software, instead of considering the stored and manipulated data and the meaning of the data in context (information). Further analysis of the responsibility for assuring confidentiality, integrity, and availability of information led to calling the field information assurance. While this might be a more complete, accurate name, the word assurance did not communicate well with the general public, who confused it with insurance. Now, the word cyber has captured the public's attention, so cybersecurity is currently the preferred term.

As technology developed the demands on the cybersecurity workforce have changed as well. The introduction of each new technology pushes university faculty in cybersecurity programs to adjust their curricula to reflect the ever-changing demands of employers. We argue that the dynamic nature of the field of cybersecurity is often in tension with the static nature and organization of departments, programs, and courses (and their curricula) found in most university cybersecurity programs. University structures change slowly, requiring a significant amount of time, paperwork, and administrative oversight [5]. For a rapidly changing field such as cybersecurity the slow-to-change structure of most universities can create barriers to preparing a workforce with the capacity to keep pace with changing technologies and employer needs.

An additional dimension of this tension can be seen in that cybersecurity problems are systemic in nature, while our cybersecurity courses tend to teach point solutions [6], for example pentesting, forensics, policy, reverse engineering or cryptology. Often, instructors teach specific topics without contextualizing those subjects using a systems perspective [7], [8]. Yet, a cyberthreat operates through a complex system. Thus, agents working within the system need a broader understanding of that system to combat threats. In this article, we present a generalized systems-thinking approach for use at two levels in cybersecurity education. First, our framework serves as a means of designing program curriculum flexible enough to respond to rapid changes in the cybersecurity environment within and outside of the academy. Second, our framework can be used across cybersecurity-related courses to help contextualize and ground point solutions in complex cybersecurity systems to develop students with a systems approach to the field. Our cybersecurity systems framework is intended to support faculty in adapting their instruction to meet the dynamic demands of the cybersecurity field within the constraints of institutions of higher education. We recommend approaches to teaching systems thinking in higher education programs, drawing on active learning strategies and research on conceptual learning activities in higher education.

II. Literature Review

A. Situating cybersecurity programs in higher education

Historically cybersecurity grew out of computer science (CS), mathematics (Math), and information technology management (ITM) departments. CS has yet to effectively address secure coding [9]. Math is teaching cryptography and cryptanalysis, but crypto represents a subset of security topics and implementations of cryptographic key management remain troublesome [10]. ITM has traditionally been teaching information technology management. Some programs may concentrate too much on industry certifications (e.g., Microsoft, Cisco, etc.). Cybersecurity education and training is generally found in six environments: four in the traditional degree-focused academic environment, technical training (certificate) programs at commercial training enterprises, and certification and continuing education activities of professional associations. In the academic world, the four environments are at the associate, bachelor's, master's, and doctoral degree levels. These degree levels tend to have different mixes of technical training and discipline education. While associate's curricula naturally tend heavily toward training courses, bachelor and master's programs vary widely in the balance between training and education courses. The variation across types of programs makes reforming cybersecurity education even more challenging.

Cybersecurity programs exist on most university campuses in the United States. A quick query of various cybersecurity programs reflects a threat-based paradigm provided as the basis for the course offerings. The threat-based paradigm is supported by the NICE framework [11]. While the framework is rather comprehensive in defining threats, vulnerabilities, and risk, we believe there is a lack of foundational guidance for cybersecurity educators. A lack of proper foundational courses could bias the students' understanding of the topic, and in many cases, may disrupt students' capacity to transfer knowledge across domains. Attempts have been made to create cybersecurity standards, frameworks, foundational knowledge, and workforce standards through various government and professional organizations. Several initiatives exist to provide cyber security curricular guidance: National Centers of Academic Excellence (CAE) program jointly sponsored by the Department of Homeland Security (DHS) and the National Security Agency (NSA); the Joint Task Force ACM/IEEE/AIS SIGSEC/IFIP on Cybersecurity Education (CSEC 2017) [12]; and the NIST National Initiative for Cybersecurity Education (NICE) [11]. These programs focus on curricula as a discipline crossing path of study [6]. Again, these are risk assessment and threat-based frameworks. The field of cybersecurity has yet to arrive at a common body of knowledge (CBK) that allows a cohesive foundational knowledge level for the cybersecurity discipline. A CBK represents an agreed upon nomenclature that is accepted by the profession. As an extension of the CSEC 2017, UK's National Cyber Security Centre created the Cybersecurity Body of Knowledge (CyBOK) [13]. (ISC)2 maintains the CISSP Common Body of Knowledge (CBK) [14], and the European Union Agency for Cybersecurity (ENISA) created guides and tools for member states [15]. Additionally, NIST maintains an online cybersecurity glossary [16]. With the disparate curriculum, workforce, and CBKs, it is no surprise many graduates would like simply to be pentesters!

Due to the transdisciplinary nature of the field, cybersecurity programs do not have a natural home in the traditional discipline and subdiscipline organization of the department-structure of higher education. Since cybersecurity education work may involve both transdisciplinary and interdisciplinary efforts, the descriptions below will help the reader distinguish between them:

> *Transdisciplinary Research* is defined as research efforts conducted by investigators from different disciplines working jointly to create new conceptual, theoretical, methodological, and translational innovations that integrate and move beyond discipline-specific approaches to address a common problem. *Interdisciplinary Research* is any study or group of studies undertaken by scholars from two or more distinct scientific disciplines. The research is based upon a conceptual model that links or integrates theoretical frameworks from those disciplines, uses study design and methodology that is not limited to any one field, and requires the use of perspectives and skills of the involved disciplines throughout multiple phases of the research process. [17].

Cybersecurity interacts with so many disciplines that designating a particular specific standalone STEM department exacerbates the existing academic silo problem. This may explain the gap between cybersecurity education supply (i.e., graduates) and the demand (i.e., jobs). The current university organization structure is antiquated, failing to meet the challenges the field is facing [18]. To help mitigate these structural barriers, we propose a cybersecurity transdisciplinary working group to discuss various curriculum solutions to the antiquated department structure that would fit for each institution. The solution has to be localized based on personnel expertise and available resources. Two potential solutions are described below: students take a set of common content courses before a discipline-specific curriculum (Figure 1), or students take common content courses midway or at the end of a discipline-specific curriculum [6].

A common core set of content can consist of foundational courses and primary cybersecurity courses that all students will take in the *common cybersecurity curriculum*. As an example, common courses might consist of the following:

Common cybersecurity courses	
Network O/S Administration	Offensive Cybersecurity
Advanced Network Security	Digital Forensics
Advanced Network Administration	Applied Security Protocols
Wireless Security	IT Risk Assessment

Foundation courses	
Prog Constructs Laboratory	Info Security Fundamentals
Information Tech Architecture	Web Site Design
Data Communications	Intro to Data Management
Networking Fundamentals	Programming for NetSec

Then the curriculum can split into several specific cybersecurity *disciplines* such as (i) offensive security; (ii) industrial controls cybersecurity; (ii) cybersecurity risk assessment; (iv) defensive security, and (v) digital forensics. The core curriculum can come before the discipline specific content as seen in Figure 1. Alternatively, the core curriculum can be split before and in the middle of the *discipline specific* content as shown in Figure 2.

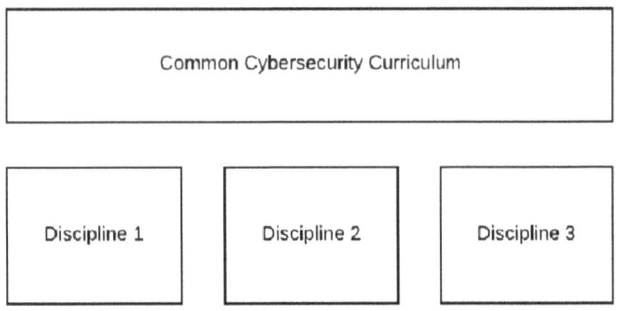

Fig. 1. Common cybersecurity curriculum preceding Disciplines

As we argued previously, cybersecurity is transdisciplinary in nature [19]. While cybersecurity touches everything, cybersecurity programs tend to exist in academic silos in higher education. There are several barriers to achieving the desired disciplinary merging. One major barrier is organizational, as attempts to introduce new courses must go through an approval process. Existing academia structure is not always set up for collaboration across departments and disciplines; the organization may even invite competition between departments, which is not conducive to transdisciplinary collaborations. For example, at a university with a strict activity-based budget model, competition over revenue could complicate collaboration efforts across departments. Another challenge within the current academic structure is communication across disciplinary divides. Even once a transdisciplinary team is formed, the team will need a common vocabulary for collaboration [16]. We believe that operating with a collaborative approach may dramatically reduce these challenges.

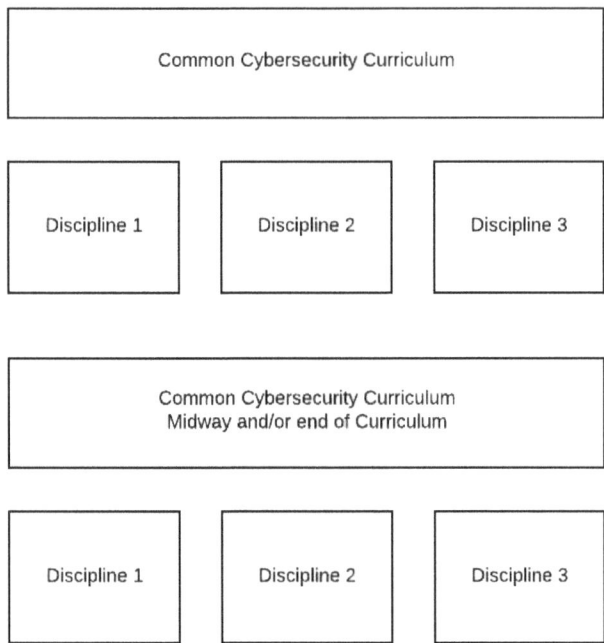

Fig. 2. Common cybersecurity curriculum interspersed with Disciplines

B. *Teaching systems-thinking across cybersecurity coursework*

In cybersecurity, we are not confronted with problems independent of each other. We manage complexity, juggle budget requirements, and plan for challenges that impact coverage, such as intended/unintended consequences, over-promising, and personnel limitations. Cybersecurity deals with people, processes, tools, technology, and metrics. Cybersecurity functions as a system of systems within an ecosystem. To understand cybersecurity well, a comprehension of system thinking is critical.

The early days of cybersecurity where signatures prevailed reflected the reductionist view since the problems were easily defined. Changes in cybersecurity have resulted in an open, dynamic environment that extends beyond hardware and software into wetware. This change requires a broader and inductive approach to student education that teaches the theoretical while reinforcing the broad concepts with applied exercises. Von Bertalanffy [7], "the father of systems theory" [8] advocated for holism. Coincidentally, cybersecurity experts have also been advocating for holism [20], and expansions into holistic thinking in cybersecurity appear with the relatively newer emphasis on situational awareness [21]. A potential benefit to cybersecurity may exist in adopting a systems approach. The systems approach to security architecture has been successfully adopted by the SABSA Institute; where security practitioners undergo additional training for various levels of SABSA certifications. This opportunity to introduce cybersecurity professionals to holistic thinking should extend to the earliest exposures so that holistic thinking becomes an automatic process.

Increasingly, aspects of complex systems such as swarming and emergent phenomenon [22] have been examined in cybersecurity research. This reflects the acknowledgment of complexity found in cybersecurity events and systems. Research efforts [23], [24], [25], [26], [27], [28], reflect the merging of complexity and cybersecurity as a means to explain cybersecurity incidents and events within a larger comprehensive framework. We argue that students benefit from understanding a systems theory framework reinforced through active learning activities. The importance of active learning in cybersecurity education is discussed in Section 3 C.

The ability to transfer cybersecurity knowledge and skills across disciplines is becoming increasingly important as illustrated by the introduction of data science into cybersecurity [29]. The increasing awareness of the interdisciplinary nature of cybersecurity requires that students and practitioners work with an overarching educational framework that can be applied to cybersecurity courses as well as other related fields. The framework would need to be foundational, so the lessons learned would be reinforced throughout the learning process. At the beginning and end of every course, students should be able to identify the part of the systems framework on which they are working. The decentralized nature of cybersecurity programs in higher education creates significant challenges to developing unifying knowledge, skills, and dispositions in the cybersecurity workforce. We argue that our cybersecurity systems framework can help bridge some of these gaps.

III. CONCEPTUAL FRAMEWORK

A. Defining system thinking

Defining systems thinking requires a contextual definition of *system*. Context is important, because related disciplines use the term *system* differently. For instance, in computer science and electrical engineering *system* refer to a *computer system*, hardware and software, neglecting the people using the computer and the procedures they follow. INCOSE provided a useful definition for systems engineering which works well in the broader systems thinking context:

> An integrated set of elements, sub-systems, or assemblies that accomplish a defined objective. These elements include products (hardware, software, firmware), processes, people, information, techniques, facilities, services, and other support elements. [30, p. 265].

Systems thinking is an approach to planning projects or solving problems that incorporates a variety of tools with the goal of using a holistic or "big picture" [30, pp. 20-21] approach. A complete explanation of systems thinking is beyond the scope of this paper; three significant sources, INCOSE [30], MITRE [31,], and SEBoK [32] each devote a major section of a chapter to the concept. That said, MITRE introduced the section on systems thinking with the following simple definition, quoting two authors:

> The ability and practice of examining the whole rather than focusing on isolated problems (P. Senge) [1]. The act of taking into account the interactions and relationships of a system with its containing environment (Y. Bar Yam, New England Complex Systems Institute) [31, p. 31].

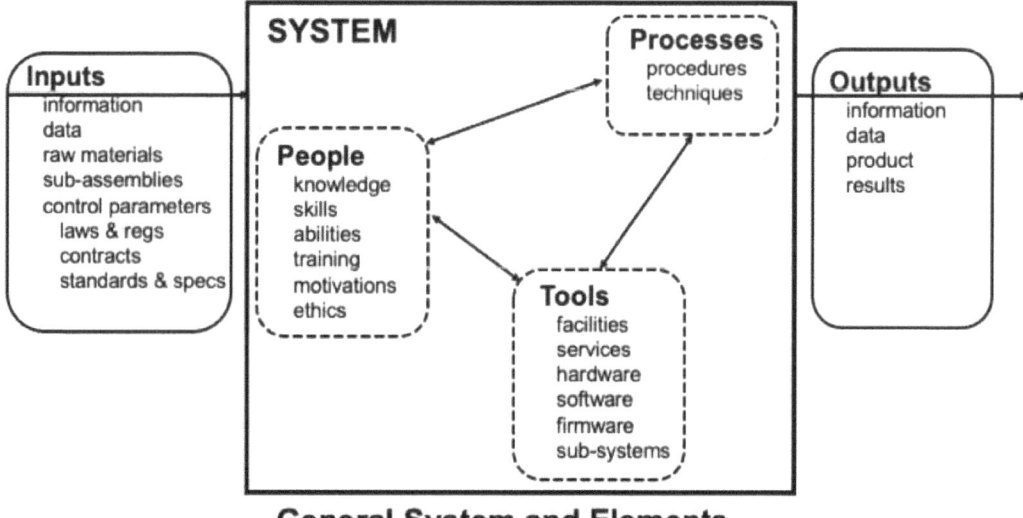

Fig. 3. General system framework

Practitioners of systems management and systems engineering often simplify the collection of system elements, grouping the elements into *people*, *processes*, and *tools*. Figure 3 illustrates this framework, useful for describing any system based on the desired output, the known inputs, and the necessary system elements. Figure 3 is a visual model of the general system framework concept, grouping system elements under the three types inside the system with a defined boundary, as well as elements of the two external groups of inputs to the system and outputs from the system. (Note that Figure 3 is not a workflow diagram, which is why no feedback loop is included.) This general framework is a useful tool for identifying the key aspects of any system, to include the known inputs, expected outputs, setting a system boundary, and identifying key elements essential to producing the output. Clear identification of the elements allows decisions on which elements to use to accomplish the goal outputs.

B. Applying systems-thinking to cybersecurity programs

Figure 4 provides an example of using the general system framework to describe an enterprise cybersecurity environment. The items listed are not exhaustive but represent what might be selected in a specific enterprise environment. Once developed to a satisfactory level of detail, the items in such a framework could be used to select topics for inclusion in courses of a structured curriculum intended to develop graduates to take part in an enterprise security practice. This example also demonstrates how a program graduate attuned to using systems thinking could approach various responsibilities while working in a security organization.

Fig. 4. A system framework for cybersecurity

C. Leveraging active learning strategies in cybersecurity instruction to foster systems-thinking

Not only are the content of and approach to teaching systems thinking in cybersecurity programs critical, the strategies used to teach systems thinking also merit attention. After reviewing the research on cybersecurity programs, we argue for the integration of active-learning strategies to improve access to meaningful learning for all postsecondary cybersecurity students. A meta-analysis of 225 studies found that students had better course outcomes in university STEM courses that utilize active learning strategies than those that utilize traditional lecturing [33]. A study on active learning in a large biology course showed that students who engaged with an active learning strategy had higher exam scores than those who did not [34]. In particular, we urge the use of conceptually oriented tasks, shown to increase students' retention, comprehension, and application [35].

One particularly promising instructional tool is case study analysis, which can be designed to be an active-learning activity as well as a conceptually oriented task. We also believe that case study analysis is particularly well suited to the integration of systems-thinking into cybersecurity coursework. Moreover, engaging students in analytical tasks as a part of case study analysis, such as concept mapping, has the potential to support students' clarification, integration, and organization of complex concepts [36]. In other terms, a key benefit of leveraging these active learning strategies -- case study analysis and concept mapping -- in cybersecurity coursework would be to help students learn to contextualize point-solutions in a complex cybersecurity system using the systems-thinking framework previously presented.

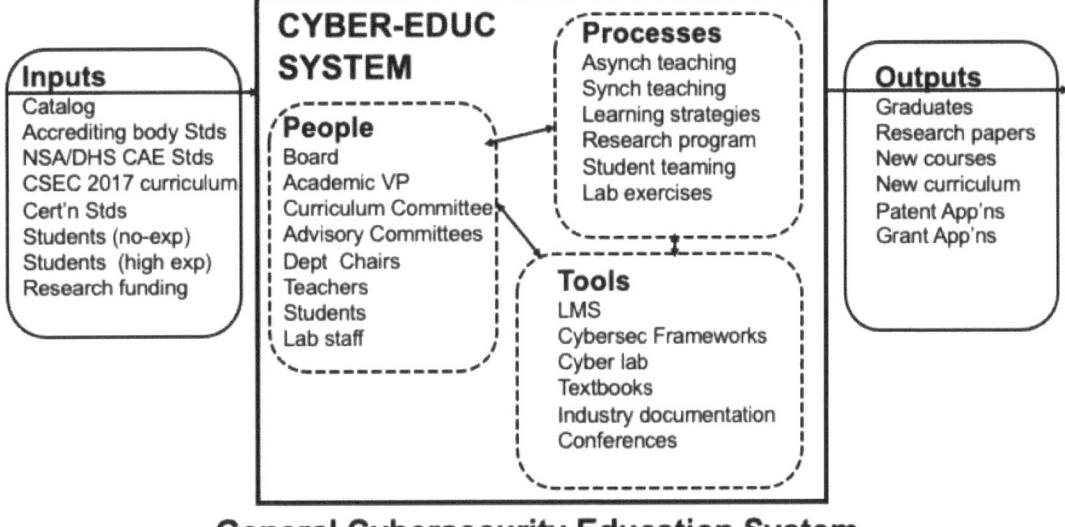

Fig. 5. A system framework for cybersecurity education

Figure 5 illustrates the use of the general system framework model to describe a cybersecurity education program as a system with identified inputs and desired outputs. As with other applications of the framework model, using this tool to explicitly identify system elements may help focus attention on selecting the optimum system elements to generate the goal outputs. For a given output (e.g. a funding grant application), this model can help determine which people can use which tools in what processes to generate the desired output. Visualizing the options in this way can assist in optimizing use of resources, and even balancing the load on high-use resources, whether people or tools.

IV. CONCLUSION AND FUTURE WORK

The challenge of achieving holistic cybersecurity depends on people – arguably even more so than on technology (tools) or policy (processes). The workforce shortage within cybersecurity is well documented - opportunities abound but hiring and staffing within the current model is not sustainable. Future careers in almost every industry and discipline will require an understanding of both technology and the underlying logic necessary to evaluate risk, mitigate threats, and adjust strategies. The need to train more cybersecurity professionals will remain but building a resilient workforce, one capable of adapting to the everchanging cyber-landscape is a promising approach to ensuring that those in the field remain engaged and are effective. This high-quality preparation requires a more active learning approach to cybersecurity education that emphasizes critical thinking, problem solving and systems thinking.

The Cyberspace Solarium Commission report [37], included several supporting recommendations to address the recruitment, development and retention of cyber talent by promoting digital literacy, civics education, and public awareness. The report also referenced the need to build societal resilience and improve cyber-oriented education. To address these needs, cybersecurity education will need to take a more holistic approach. Cybersecurity as a field is still maturing. In many ways, cybersecurity has many parallels to medicine as a field, from its organization into specialties and subspecialties to the overarching need to understand system interdependencies while working in concert to heal and do no harm. The needed skills and logic are continually developing as are the approaches to instruction and collaboration. This ecosystem is broader and more pervasive than the current domains in which it is taught, providing the opportunity to create new programs, curricula, and training, designed to reach a broader range of students. In turn, leveraging existing models to incorporate greater resilience and critical thinking, in the students and the field as a whole, may bridge gaps across our current needs, existing resources, and future demands.

Adopting systems thinking into cybersecurity education institutions may be able to improve the resiliency and robustness of the discipline while creating more resilient and adaptive students. These empowered students can utilize their problem-solving skills in the very domains that cybersecurity must interact. Furthermore, these students will possess the necessary tools to prevent obsolescence when new AI/ML based technologies replace many of the jobs for which higher education currently prepares students. Recognizing that introducing new courses is a time-consuming process, the ability to provide foundational courses in systems thinking provides a reasonable entry point.

Historically, cybersecurity has been reactive to events; this reactive focus must change to a proactive focus. For example, the patch and run model has been present since the Morris Worm. Proactive cybersecurity is the ultimate goal.

Hackers continue to test assumptions made by developers, which feeds the traditional reactive model resulting in a significant amount of certification training. Professionals attempt to remain relevant in the field through these certificates, yet those programs are limiting. As technology continues to grow, and the AI footprint in cybersecurity grows as well, professionals will need cybersecurity programs that extend beyond point solutions to help them learn to be resilient and adaptive. Integrating systems thinking into these programs could provide the needed adaptive processes.

Cybersecurity educators are facing increasing challenges to better support students through their teaching. The rise of AI along with the transdisciplinary nature of the field requires students to become conversant in other complementary subjects as well as cybersecurity. If we do not educate students in other areas we will create gaps that run the risk of inconsistent solutions. Cybersecurity as a field must both mature and broaden. These goals often exist in tension since in order to mature a field focuses inward gathering metadata for abstraction, which can make expansion a challenge. Cybersecurity must become more resilient to the changing landscape. Additionally, cybersecurity educators need to ensure broader access and participation in the field, which among other initiatives, means utilizing active learning strategies. As cybersecurity as a field becomes more mature, broader, and more resilient, cybersecurity education also needs to develop in pace with advances in higher education teaching and learning to provide cybersecurity students with rich learning opportunities that develop their systems-thinking.

REFERENCES

[1] W. R. Cheswick, S. M. Bellovin, and A. D. Rubin, *Firewalls and Internet security: repelling the wily hacker*. Addison-Wesley Longman Publishing Co., Inc. 2003.

[2] H. J. Liao, C. Lin, C. H. R., Lin, Y. C., and K. Y. Tung. "Intrusion detection system: A comprehensive review". *J. of Netw. and Comput. Appl.*, vol. 36, no. 1, pp. 16-24, 2013.

[3] H. Debar and J. Viinikka, "Intrusion detection: Introduction to intrusion detection and security information management," in *Foundations of security analysis and design III*, Springer, Berlin, Heidelberg, pp. 207-236, 2005.

[4] A. L. Buczak and E. Guven. "A survey of data mining and machine learning methods for cyber security intrusion detection," *IEEE Commun. Surveys & Tutorials*, vol. 18, no. 2, pp.1153-1176, 2015.

[5] B. Sporn, "Governance and administration: Organizational and structural trends," in *International Handbook of Higher Education*. Springer, Dordrecht, 2007.

[6] Justice, C. Sample, and E. Darraj, "Future Needs of the Cybersecurity Workforce", 2020. *19th European Conference on Cyber Warfare and Security, ECCWS 2020*, University of Chester, UK, 25 - 26 June 2020. unpublished. [Online] https://www.academic-conferences.org/conferences/eccws/

[7] L. Von Bertalanffy. "The history and status of general systems theory," *Acad. of Manage. J.*, vol. 15, no. 4, pp. 407-426, Dec. 1972 [Online] doi: 10.2307/255139. Available: https://www.jstor.org/stable/255139

[8] J.P. Van Gigch, *System Design Modeling and Metamodeling*, New York, NT, USA: Plenum Press, 1991.

[9] J. Viega and G. McGraw, *Building Secure Software: How to Avoid Security Problems the Right Way*, Addison-Wesley, Reading, MA, USA: 2011.

[10] I. Curry, *An Introduction to Cryptography and Digital Signatures*, Entrust. 2001. [Online] Available: https://www.entrust.com/wp-content/uploads/2013/05/cryptointro.pdf

[11] W. Newhouse, S. Keith, B. Scribner, and G. Witte, *National Initiative for Cybersecurity Education (NICE) Cybersecurity Workforce Framework (SP 800- 181)*. Gaithersberg, MD, USA: NIST, 2017. [Online] Available: https://doi.org/10.6028/NIST.SP.800-181

[12] Joint Task Force on Cybersecurity Education (JTF), Cybersecurity Curricula 2017, [Online] Available: https://cybered.hosting.acm.org/wp/ Download: https://cybered.hosting.acm.org/wp-content/uploads/2018/02/newcover_csec2017.pdf

[13] *The Cybersecurity Body of Knowledge*. Crown Copyright, The National Cyber Security Centre 2019. [Online] Available: https://www.cybok.org

[14] J. Warsinske, M. Graff, K. Henry, C. Hoover, B. Malisow, S. Murphy, C. P. Oakes, G.e Pajari, J. T. Parker, D. Seidl, and M. Vasquez, *The Official (ISC)2 Guide to the CISSP CBK Reference, 5th Ed.*, Hoboken, NJ, USA: Wiley, 2019.

[15] European Union Agency for Cybersecurity (EISA) [Online] https://www.enisa.europa.eu/topics/national-cyber-security-strategies

[16] *Glossary*, NIST Computer Security Resource Center [Online] Available: https://csrc.nist.gov/glossary

[17] S. W. Aboelela, E. Larson, S. Bakken, O. Carrasquillo, A. Formicola, S. A. Glied, J. Haas, K. M. and Gebbie, "Defining Interdisciplinary Research: Conclusions from a Critical Review of the Literature," *Health Services Res.*, vol. 42, 2007, pp. 329–346, 2007, doi: 10.1111/j.1475-6773.2006.00621.x as cited in *Definitions, Harvard Transdisciplinary Research in Energetics and Cancer Center* [Online] Available: https://www.hsph.harvard.edu/trec/about-us/definitions/

[18] S. A. McChrystal, T. Collins, D. Silverman, and C. Fussell. *Team of teams: new rules of engagement for a complex world*. New York, USA, Penguin Random House, 2015.

[19] D. Craigen, N. Diakun-Thibault, and R. Purse, "Defining cybersecurity" *Technology Innovation Manage. Rev.*, 4(10). 2014.

[20] K. T. Dean, *Cyber-Security Holism: A System of Solutions for a Distributed Problem*. USMC C&S Col, Quantico, VA, USA: Pennyhill Press, 2013.

[21] H. Tianfield, Cyber security situational awareness. In *2016 IEEE int. Conf. on Internet of Things (iThings) and IEEE green computing and communications (GreenCom) and IEEE cyber, physical and social computing (CPSCom) and IEEE smart data (SmartData)* (pp. 782-787). IEEE, Dec. 2016.

[22] G. A. Fink, J. N. Haack, A. D. McKinnon, and E. W. Fulp, "Defense on the move: anti-based cyber defense," *IEEE Secur. & Privacy*, vol. 12, no. 2, pp. 36- 43, 2014.

[23] S. M. Loo and L. Babinkostova, "Cyber-physical Systems Security Introductory Course For Stem Students," *2020 Annual ASEE Conf.*, June 20-24, Montreal, Canada.

[24] C. Sample, S. M. Loo, C. Justice, E. Taylor, and C. Hampton, "Cyber-Informed: Bridging Cyber Security and Other Disciplines," *19th European Conference on Cyber Warfare and Security*, June 25-26, 2020, Chester, UK.

[25] Centre for Complexity Science, U. of Warwick, [Online] Website: https://warwick.ac.uk/fac/cross_fac/complexity

[26] L. Chittka, Queen Mary U. London, [Online] Website: https://www.qmul.ac.uk/sbcs/staff/larschittka.html

[27] B. J. West, B, "Colloquium: Fractional calculus view of complexity: A tutorial." *Reviews of Modern Physics*, vol. 86 no. 4, p. 1169, Dec. 2014. [Online] Available: https://journals.aps.org/rmp/abstract/10.1103/RevModPhys.86.1169#fulltext

[28] B. P. Turnbull, Researcher, Univ New S. Wales, [Online] Website: https://research.unsw.edu.au/people/dr-benjamin-peter-turnbull

[29] D. McMorrow, ED. *Science of cyber-security* (Report No. JSR-10-102). McLean, VA, USA: JASON Program Office, MITRE Corp, 2010.

[30] D. D. Walden, G. J. Roedler, K. J. Forsberg, and T. M. Shortell, Eds. *Systems Engineering Handbook, 4th ed.* Hoboken, NJ, USA: John Wiley & Sons, 2015.

[31] G. Rebovich, Jr., Ed. *MITRE Systems Engineering Guide*, Burlington, MA, USA: MITRE Corp., 2014. [Online] Available: https://www.mitre.org/publications/technical-papers/the-mitre-systems-engineering-guide

[32] R.J. Cloutier, Ed. in C., SEBoK Editorial Board. *The Guide to the Syst. Eng. Body of Knowl. (SEBoK), v. 2.1,* . Hoboken, NJ. 2019. [Online] Available: https://www.sebokwiki.org/ Download: https://www.sebokwiki.org/w/images/sebokwiki-farm!w/8/8b/SEBoK_v2.1.pdf

[33] S. Freeman, S. L. Eddy, M. McDonough, M. K. Smith, N. Okoroafor, H. Jordt, and M. P. Wenderoth, "Active learning increases student performance in science, engineering, and mathematics," *Proc. of the Nat. Acad. of Sciences*, vol. 111, pp. 8410-8415, 2014.

[34] P.A. Ertmer, J. A. Quinn, and K. D. Glazewski, Eds., *The ID casebook: Case studies in instructional design, 5th ed.*, Evanston, IL, USA: Routledge, 2019.

[35] M. A. Ruiz-Primo, D. Briggs, H. Iverson, R. Talbot, and L. Shepard, "Impact of undergraduate science course innovations on learning," *Science*, vol. 331, pp. 1269-1270, 2011.

[36] B. J. Daley and D.M. Torre, "Concept maps in medical education: an analytical literature review." *Medical Educ.*, vol. 44 no. 5, pp. 440-8, 2010.

[37] A. King and M. Gallagher, Eds., *Cyberspace Solarium Commission [Report]*, Washington, DC, USA: Cyberspace Solarium Commission, March 2020. [Online] Available. https://www.solarium.gov/, https://drive.google.com/file/d/1ryMCIL_dZ30QyjFqFkkf10MxIXJGT4yv/view

Do Users Correctly Identify Password Strength?

Jason M. Pittman
High Point University
High Point, NC, USA
jpittman@highpoint.edu

Nikki Robinson
Capitol Technology University
Laurel, MD, USA
nrobinson@captechu.edu

Abstract—Much of the security for information systems rests upon passwords. Yet, the scale of password use is producing elevated levels of cognitive burden. Existing research has investigated the effects of this cognitive burden with a focus on weak versus strong passwords. However, the literature presupposes that users can meaningfully identify such. Further, there may be ethical implications of forcing users to identify password strength when they are unable to do so. Accordingly, the purpose of this study was to measure what socioeconomic characteristics, if any, led participants to identify weak and strong password strengths in a statistically significant manner. We gathered 436 participants using Amazon's Mechanical Turk platform and asked them to identify 50 passwords as either weak or strong. Then, we employed a Chi-square test of independence to measure the potential relationship between three socioeconomic characteristics (education, profession, technical skill) and the frequency of correct weak and strong password identification. The results show significant relationships across all variable combinations except for technical skill and strong passwords which revealed no relationship.

Keywords—passwords, password strength, authentication, ethics, socioeconomic factors

I. Introduction

Password-based authentication is a prominent feature in modern life. Unfortunately, password authentication has grown to be an overwhelming burden to users [1]. In fact, Shay et al. [2] discovered the act of changing passwords on the premise of increasing password strength bothered users. Couple such results with the fact that users keep approximately 25 password- protected accounts [3][4], entering a password, on average, up to eight times each day, and one can imagine how sizable the growing cognitive epidemic may be.

The topic of conventional text-based passwords has been well studied [4][5][6]. In fact, there has been earnest effort to combat the inherent flaws in conventional password authentication through variations in form and recall modality [7][8][9][10]. However, the existing literature presupposes that users identify password strength accurately [11][12]. Indeed, Carnavalet [12] determined that the inconsistency in the password strength may be related to a misunderstanding of the characteristics required in a stronger password. This led us to wonder if an underlying motivation for such misunderstanding might be related to the users themselves. Accordingly, the purpose of this study was to measure what socioeconomic characteristics, if any, led participants to identify weak and strong password strengths in a statistically significant manner.

Furthermore, we considered not only password comprehension but also how ethics may be related to decisions to choose weaker passwords. That is, passwords strength is an ethical imperative from the perspective of an organization as many users work from home machines or workstations [13]. Later, research [14] found individuals are increasingly using more personal devices in the workplace because of the spreading trend of Bring Your Own Device (BYOD). Employees working on sensitive information have a duty to protect such information, and to have strong passwords on personal accounts. Thus, we arrive at the question of whether it is ethical for an individual to choose a weak password, even if the individual is under the impression the selected password is strong, when safeguarding sensitive information. To thoroughly investigate such an inquiry, we must first understand if users can reliably identify password strength.

II. Method

Broadly, we conjectured that subjects would be able to identify weak passwords consistently. Password characteristics such as length, capitalization, inclusion of alphanumerical and symbol characters serve as significant context clues. Further, we imagined subjects would not be able to consistently identify strong passwords, particularly when such were intermingled with weak passwords of similar length and combination. More technically, the goal of this correlational research was to determine if socioeconomic characteristics have measurable interactions with password identification and to what extent any such correlation is positive or negative. To that end, we operationalized subject education level, profession, and self-reported technical skill as socioeconomic variables on one hand and successful identification of weak and strong passwords as password identification variables on the other. Further, we imagined a single instrument as a means of collecting data to evaluate our hypotheses.

A. Instrumentation

We designed our data collection instrument in three sections. The first section held a standard informed consent, including opt-out procedures, and required affirmation of participation before continuing to the second section. We did not collect personally identifiable information. Instead, we coded and organized data with a simple integer index ranging between one and 436.

The instrument's second section held all the demographic questions. We asked subjects to self-report on age, gender, profession, technical skill level compared to others they knew, as well as how many passwords they used daily. The first three questions in this section served to collect categorical data for our socioeconomic variables. Further, we designed the last question as a screening mechanism insofar as we wanted to include only those individuals using at least one password daily.

Then, a third section held 50 passwords with a bounded response set of weak and strong which also served to collect categorical data. These passwords were randomly generated in two phases according to standardized definitions of weak and strong [15]. The first phase generated 100 weak passwords, parameterized as length of one to seven characters, the set of characters bounded to alphanumerics only, and any numerical characters positioned at the end of string. Concurrently, the first phase generated 100 strong passwords, parameterized as greater than 8 characters, the set of characters bounded to alphanumeric, punctuation, and special symbols, and the numeric or symbolic characters randomly placed within the string. The second phase consisted of removing any obvious weak (e.g., a single character or short, blatant sequence like 123) and then random selection of 25 passwords in each category into a randomly ordered list.

B. Participants

To achieve a suitable sample, we used Amazon's Mechanical Turk [16][17][18] to recruit individuals from a general population (scoped to Mechanical Turk users, biased towards the subset willing to take part in a questionnaire-based study, and being native or near-native English speakers) as opposed to a specific profession, age, or education category. According to Amazon, Mechanical Turk has a disparate and global user population of more than 500,000 people from over 190 countries. Thus, a more diverse and representative sample could be obtained by using Mechanical Turk instead of a traditional recruitment (e.g., email). Further, participants proactively responded to the work posting as opposed to us soliciting individuals.

The final sample size was 436 after we removed 11 participants data for being incomplete. We did not provide subjects with any instructional information about password strength. While not controlled for, we did ask participants to avoid (a) searching for password strength definitions; (b) use tools such as password strength checkers; (c) or any form of outside help. That said, we recognize a limitation in our protocol exists insofar as we did not control for any of these behaviors.

The sample was demographically distributed with respect to age, gender, profession and self-reported technical skill [19]. Only two participants were under the age of 18, making them members of a vulnerable population (more on this below). However, our IRB review, which included the potential for protected category participants, categorized the risk for harm as minimal given the anonymity of both our instrumentation and Mechanical Turk.

C. Hypotheses

We broadly conjectured participant education, profession, and technical skill would show a relationship with successful identification of weak and strong passwords. Disambiguated however, this general hypothesis turns into six discretely testable statements. That is, each variable-education, profession, and technical skill- manifested one hypothesis for successful identification of *weak* passwords and one hypothesis for successful identification of *strong* passwords.

III. RESULTS

In total, our sample participants generated 21,800 discrete password identification trials. We ran a Chi-square test of independence against these data using pairs of variables in sequence with our stated hypotheses. Further, we analyzed the set of passwords in our instrumentation according to entropy measures and nominal strength compared to overall perception of each password by participants. While not associated with our primary focus, we felt at least a cursory description of these results may shed light on where participants correctly or incorrectly identified passwords as weak and strong.

A. Education

We examined education as a potentially related variable first. We compared the level of education (9 levels) and frequency of correctly and incorrectly identifying both weak and strong passwords (Table I). For weak password analysis, participants with some high school and individuals at the doctorate level identified correct passwords 56% and 57% of the time, respectively. The other education levels, High School, Some College, Trade School, Associate's Bachelor's, Master's, and a form of Professional degree, ranged from 68% to 79% able to correctly identify weak passwords. All education levels were able to correctly spot weak passwords 70% of the time. While it is interesting that the least amount of education (Some High School), and most (Doctorate), had the lowest average, the overall average displayed the ability for participants to find the weak password.

TABLE I. FREQUENCY OF IDENTIFYING WEAK AND STRONG PASSWORDS CORRECTLY AND INCORRECTLY

Education	Weak Correct	Weak Incorrect	Strong Correct	Strong Incorrect
Some High School	14	11	13	12
High School	439	186	305	320
Some College	962	338	644	656

Education	Weak Correct	Weak Incorrect	Strong Correct	Strong Incorrect
Trade School	257	68	149	176
Associate's	544	206	374	376
Bachelor's	3804	1246	2282	2768
Master's	2011	564	1268	1307
Professional	204	96	157	143
Doctorate	130	95	116	109

Note: For *Weak* - [8] = 64.89, p = 5.10E-11, α = 0.05, critical value of 15.5.

For *Strong* - [8] = 33.71, p = 4.58002E-05 0.05, critical value of 15.5. We reject the null hypothesis in both cases.

To dig into strong password analysis, all education levels were within an 8- point percentage, between 45 and 52%, able to spot a strong password. The groups with the highest scores of 52% were Some High School and Professional degrees, with a Doctorate level education missing by one point, at 51%. Average ability to spot a strong password was at 49%, showing a major decline in ability to spot a strong password. Each group of education level was able to spot a weak password than a strong password more often.

B. Professions

The second variable we evaluated for a relationship was participants' self- reported profession. As a variable, Profession showed a significant relationship with identifying weak passwords ([32] = 153.19, p value of 0.00, α of 0.05 and a critical value of 46.19). Consequently, we rejected the null hypothesis. The only professions to correctly identify a weak password less than an 80% of the time were Manufacturing - Electrical (53%) and Religious (71%). The professions which were able to identify weak passwords between an 80 and 89% were Agriculture, Education-K-12, Construction, Government, and Scientific. All other categories of professions were able to correctly find weak passwords over 90% of the time. The professions which were able to correctly identify weak passwords 100% of the time were Broadcasting, Legal, Mining, Publishing, and Retail. Of all professions, the average score for finding weak passwords was 90%.

We also evaluated participants' profession against identification of strong passwords. We rejected the null hypothesis for this variable as well based on the Chi-square test of independence results ([32] = 66.11, p value of 0.0003, α of 0.05 and a critical value of 46.19).

Strong passwords saw a much lower result from weak passwords, with an average of all professions only able to identify them 40% of the time. The professions with scores lower than 40% were Broadcasting, Education-College, Finance, Legal, Manufacturing - Other, Religious, and Transportation. This was interesting because both Broadcasting and Legal professions found the weak passwords 100% of the time.

The only group which was not able to identify any strong passwords was Manufacturing - Electrical, which showed this group had the lowest identification for both weak and strong passwords combined. The group with the highest overall identification rate of 60% was Mining.

C. Technical Skill

Overall it seemed that the participants were able to accurately depict technical skill level when it came to perceiving weak passwords (Table II). The group which self-reported as much less skilled than their counterparts averaged 72% when identifying weak passwords. The less skilled group up to the much more skilled group averaged 91% ability to identify weak passwords. Of all the groups, participants averaged an 87% ability to find weak passwords correctly. Finally, we compared technical skill to successful identification of strong passwords. Unlike with previous tests, we found no relationship between these variables (Table II).

TABLE II. OBSERVED FREQUENCIES OF PARTICIPANT TECHNICAL SKILL IDENTIFYING PASSWORDS

Technical Skill	Weak Correct	Weak Incorrect	Strong Correct	Strong Incorrect
Much less skilled	16	6	8	20
Less skilled	355	23	271	401
Same skill	2119	201	1367	1913
More skill	4097	411	2585	3607
Much more skilled	1778	155	1077	1390

Note: For *Weak* - [4] = 14.95, p value of 0.005, α = 0.05, critical value of 9.5.

For *Strong* - [4] = 5.93, p value of 0.205, α = 0.05, critical value of 9.5. We reject the null hypothesis in both cases.

D. Password Analysis

After completing the Chi-square tests for independence, we wanted to more closely examine details associated with passwords used in the instrument. The goal was to develop a richer picture of what participants perceived based on their weak or strong selections and the entropy of associated passwords. We offer only descriptive analysis here of associations between data points; there was no attempt to infer causation.

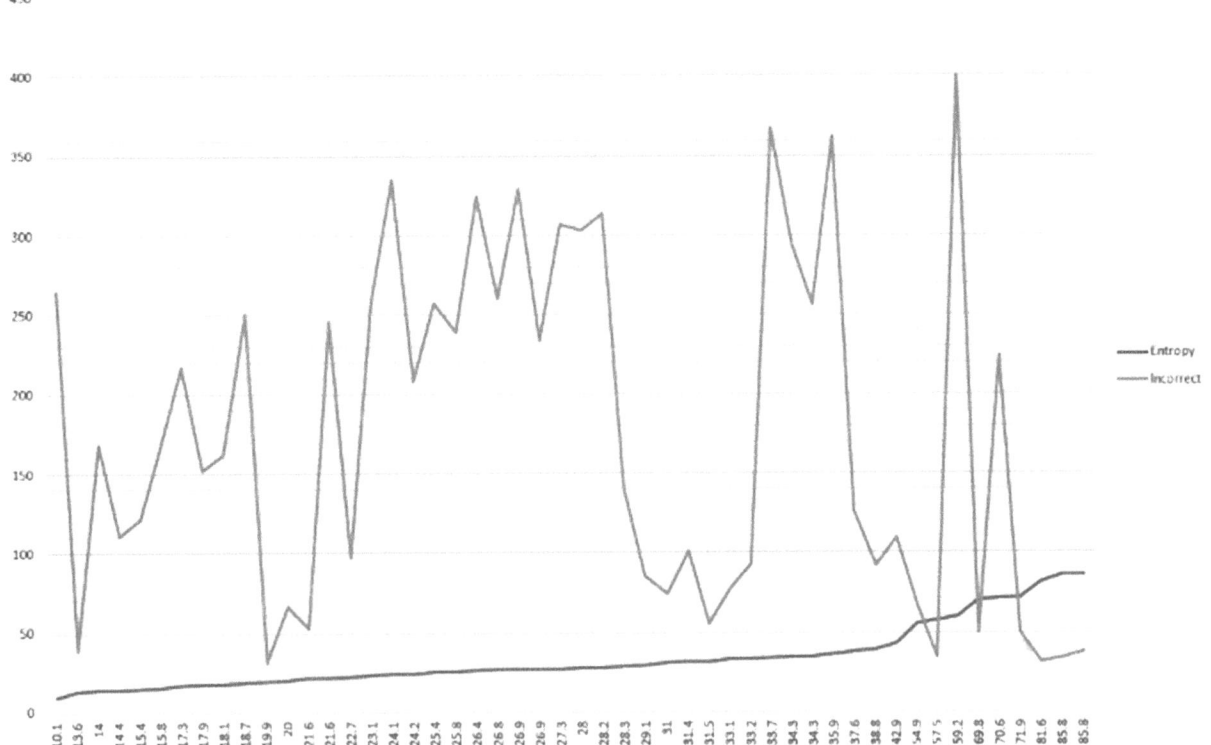

Fig. 1. Trend of incorrect perception of password strength as entropy in string rises

To begin, the most common incorrect choice was for the string G@m30f7hr0n3$. Four hundred participants incorrectly perceived this to be a weak password compared to 36 that correctly identified this as a strong password. The entropy is 59.2. Conversely, the most common correct choice was a tie between the string 1FcgiEF46Xy06jVS1 and qwerty. The former was a strong password while the latter was a weak password, and both were identified by 415 participants as such. The entropy of the two strings was 81.6 for the strong password and 19.9 for the weak. The biggest misconception for users was about strong passwords; overall, participants had a harder time identifying strong passwords. It would be interesting to find out why one password G@m30f7hr0n3$ was misidentified so often as a weak password. And if users felt this was such a weak password, why did they correctly identify 1FcgiEF46Xy06jVS1 as a strong password?

IV. CONCLUSIONS

The purpose of this work was to measure to what extent participant education, profession, or technical skill level are related to successful identification of weak and strong passwords. Towards this goal, we asked 436 human participants to judge whether 50 passwords were weak or strong. After data collection, we ran a Chi-square test for independence to measure relationships between variables and evaluate our hypotheses.

Education was significantly related to successful identification of weak and strong passwords alike. Further, each individual educational stratum showed higher frequencies of correct identification than incorrect. Based on these results, we can infer perception of what constitute a weak or strong password are not confined to any one educational stratum.

Profession was significantly related to successful identification of weak and strong passwords too. However, here we saw individual profession strata incorrectly identify password strength more often than correctly identifying password strength. While a stratum like Homemaker or Retired may not surprise anyone, the three Information Technology strata all more frequently misidentified strong passwords which is surprising.

There are a variety of follow up questions to be explored within the coupling of profession and perception of password strength. Experimental follow up may be of future interest to uncover what precisely causes specific professions to correctly identify weak passwords but incorrectly identify strong passwords. For a future study, we could focus specifically on individuals in IT fields, but target systems administrators, database administrators, and the like.

Interestingly, self-reported technical skill was significantly related to identifying weak passwords but not related to strong passwords. We wonder about the potential underlying factors contributing to this situation and emphatically suggest follow up research in this area. Because we saw some trending towards incorrect identification of strong passwords in various professions (e.g., Information Technology), we must wonder if such professions inherently harbor mentalities associated with incorrectly identifying strong passwords. Thus, we suggest any future work with technical skill not rely on self- reporting. Such study could robustly establish technical skill through empirical measurement.

Based on the inability to consistently identify weak and strong passwords, we wonder why individuals could not see clear patterns in password combinations. This could be due to the wide variety of password strength meters on websites, ranges in requirements for password strength, or even the sheer amount of different accounts users must create. Individuals will have a multitude of online accounts for business and personal reasons and would surely see conflicting information depending on the type of account. Without a dependable password format or template for all user accounts, individuals must use best guesses for creating secure passwords.

Participants without as much self-identified technical skill certainly had a more difficult time identifying weak passwords, which indicated that they are unable to create strong passwords in both business and personal accounts. Accordingly, a recommendation for these individuals is to evaluate their own passwords used on different accounts and create an exercise to change all passwords. This would allow the individual to explore current passwords versus a new set of stronger or more secure passwords. It would also provide an opportunity to use different passwords on all accounts, advancing their security awareness and education on password strength.

Based on these outcomes, we postulate that individuals with less self- identified technical skill will not have strong passwords in either business or personal user accounts. This leads to the question that if the participants do work in a professional setting, is there an absence of security training on strong passwords? Do the businesses these participants work in not have strong password requirements, or potentially unclear requirements? Superior security training and education should be made available to individuals in all industries. Tailored security guidance, specifically on password security and management, may enhance the ability to identify password strength. Along such lines, examples from this study could be used to support security training and explicitly demonstrate the differences between strong and weak passwords.

We would also strongly encourage that if users are still unable to identify weak passwords, to use multi-factor authentication (MFA) such as tokens or authentication applications to address this. MFA is a well-known tactic to protect against password attacks from malicious actors. Password attacks such as dictionary attacks, rainbow tables, and brute force attacks are common, and simple for a hacker to perform against any account. If security awareness training has not addressed password weakness issues, using MFA techniques would address security concerns and can be used in most business settings, and in personal accounts.

A few limitations were identified related to the conclusions. One limitation was the strength of the passwords; characteristics which define password strength are constantly evolving [20][21][22]. It is important to note that at the time of this study, the parameters for strong and weak passwords were based on current guidelines. And while the pool of passwords was quite large, the participants were limited to 100 passwords for the participants to evaluate. A final limitation was the self-reported information which was used to determine education, profession, and technical skill. The researchers chose these categories and options based on most relevant information in each field.

Lastly, we feel the ethical considerations of password selection ought to be investigated. While our findings demonstrate users' ability to correctly identify passwords, we are left wondering if users experience any ethical dilemma when selecting a new password. The dissonance between our results and the propensity for users to gravitate towards creating weak passwords hints at underlying factors worthy of inquiry. Similarly, we speculate there may be a discoverable balance related to how organizations force users to interact with passwords.

REFERENCES

[1] De Joode, D. (2012). Does password fatigue increase the risk on a phishing attack? (Master's Thesis). Tilburg University, Tilburg, The Netherlands.

[2] Shay, R., Komanduri, S., Kelley, P. G., Leon, P. G., Mazurek, M. L., Bauer, L., Christin, N., Cranor, L. F. (2010). Proceedings of the Sixth Symposium on Usable Privacy and Security. doi: 10.1145/1837110.1837113

[3] Dhamija, R., & Dusseault, L. (2008). The seven flaws of identity management: Usability and security challenges. IEEE Security and Privacy, 6(2), 24-29. doi: 10.1109/MSP.2008.49

[4] Florencio, D. & Herley, C. (2007). A large-scale study of web password habits. Proceedings of the 16th international conference on World Wide Web, Banff, Canada, pp. 657-666. http://franklin.captechu.edu:2123/10.1145/1242572.1242661

[5] Notoatmodjo, G., & Thomborson, C. (2009). Passwords and perceptions. 7th Australasian Conference on Information Security.

[6] Komanduri, S., Shay, R., Cranor, L. F., Herley, C., & Schechter, S. (2014). Telepathwords: Preventing weak passwords by reading users' minds. 23rd USENIX Security Symposium.

[7] Brostoff, S. & Sasse, M. A. (2000). Are passfaces more usable than passwords? A field trial investigation. In Proceedings of HCI 2000.

[8] Jansen, W. A. (2003) Authenticating users on handheld devices. National Institute of Standards and Technology.

[9] Jermyn, I., Mayer, A., Monrose, F., Reiter, M., & Rubin, A. (1999). The Design and Analysis of Graphical Passwords. 8th USENIX Security Symposium.

[10] Wiedenbeck, S., Waters, J., Birget, J. C., Brodskiy, A., & Memon, N. (2005). Authentication using graphical passwords: Effects of tolerance and image choice. Proceedings of the 2005 Symposium on Usable Privacy and Security.

[11] Ur, B., Kelley, P. G., Komanduri, S., Lee, J., Maass, M., Mazurek, M. L., Passaro, T., Shay, R.,

[12] Carnavalet, X. C. & Mannan, M. From very weak to very strong: Analyzing password-strength meters. NDSS Conference. San Diego, CA.

[13] Dearman, D., Pierce, J. S. (2008). It's on my other computer!: Computing with multiple devices. Proceedings of the SIGCHI Conference on Human Factors in Computing Systems. doi: 1148/1357054.1357177

[14] Fleck, R., Cox, A. L., Robison, R. A.V. (2015). Balancing boundaries: Using multiple devices to manage work-life balance. Proceedings of the 33rd Annual ACM Conference on Human Factors in Computing Systems. doi: 10.1145/2702123.2702386

[15] Grassi et al. (2017). NIST Special Publication 800-63B, US Department of Commerce, National Institute of Standards and Technology, Gaithersburg, MD, https://doi.org/10.6028/NIST.SP.800-63b

[16] Turk, A. M. (2012). Amazon mechanical turk. Retrieved August, 17, 2012.

[17] Paolacci, G., Chandler, J., & Ipeirotis, P. G. (2010). Running experiments on amazon mechanical turk. Judgment and Decision making, 5(5), 411-419.

[18] Kittur, A., Chi, E. H., & Suh, B. (2008). Crowdsourcing user studies with Mechanical Turk. In Proceedings of the SIGCHI conference on human factors in computing systems (pp. 453-456).

[19] Pittman, J. M., & Robinson, N. (2020). Shades of Perception-User Factors in Identifying Password Strength. arXiv preprint arXiv:2001.04930.

[20] Stavrou, E. (2017). A situation-aware user interface to assess users' ability to construct strong passwords: A conceptual architecture. International Conference on Cyber Situational Awareness, Data Analytics and Assessment. doi: 10.1109/CyberSA.2017.8073385

[21] Hart, D. (2015). Two studies on password memorability and perception, In 10th Annual Symposium on Information Assurance.

[22] Kankane, S., DiRusso, C., & Buckley, C. (2018). Can we nudge users toward better password management?: An initial study. In Extended Abstracts of the 2018 CHI Conference on Human Factors in Computing Systems (p. LBW593).

An Experimental setup for Detecting SQLi Attacks using Machine Learning Algorithms

Binh An Pham
West Texas A&M University
Canyon, USA
bpham1@buffs.wtamu.edu

Vinitha Hannah Subburaj, Ph.D.
West Texas A&M University
Canyon, USA
vsubburaj@wtamu.edu

Abstract—SQL injection attacks (SQLi attacks) have proven their danger on several website types such as social media, e-shopping, etc. In order to prevent such attacks from occurring, this research effort investigates on efficient ways of detection and prevention, so that we can preserve each cyber-user's right of privacy. This research effort is aimed at investigating and looking at different ways to protect websites from SQL injection attacks. In this research effort, machine learning algorithms were used to detect such SQLi attacks. Machine Learning (ML) algorithms are algorithms that can learn from the data provided and infer interesting results from the dataset. We used SQL code and user input as our data and ML algorithms to detect malicious code. The machine learning model developed in this research can detect such attacks from happening in future. The precision and accuracy of the machine learning algorithms in terms of predicting the SQLi attacks has been calculated and reported in this research paper.

Keywords—cybersecurity, SQL injection attacks, machine learning algorithms

I. INTRODUCTION

SQL injections (SQLi) are attacks in which an attacker sends SQL statements to an SQL database; the SQL statements allow the attacker to control what the server does. By doing so, an attacker can take full control over the server [1]. Attackers can send code by simply inputting an SQL statement in place of a username and password. The only way an attacker can use this exploit is by looking for inputs on the website in question. Assuming no security measures were taken towards the creation of the web application, this SQL statement would list all customers in the Customer database.

SQL statements can also allow attackers to gain administrator rights to the database as well, which means the attacker can add, edit, or delete data with nothing stopping them from doing it. The login boxes or inputs are the places where the SQL statements are typed, which then sends the malicious code to be run on the server hosting the database [2]. There are several types of SQL injection attacks that could be deployed [3]. Depending on what the attacker's goal is, the SQL injections are sent to the server one after another or all at the same time. Once the attacker gets to the database, they will be able to impose threats from several perspectives. The attacker may have access to very sensitive information and, therefore, can perform obliteration and alteration on that information.

Due to the increasing number of cyber-attacks and security compromises carried out in the Information Technology sector, quality research is carried out in the areas of cybersecurity to prevent such attacks from happening is becoming very crucial. This research has set up an experimental model that can not only be used for continuing research but also used inside classrooms for teaching purposes. The results obtained through this research effort has opened many doors for us to continue working on this project to obtain more accurate results. Since, there is not much research done in this area of using machine learning algorithms to predict SQLi attacks, we believe that the results disseminated in this paper may be useful to the entire computer science research community.

The rest of the paper is structured as follows. Section II discusses the state of the art. Experimental setup is described in Section III. Section IV discusses the results from the research. Section V concludes the paper with future work.

II. RELATED WORK

SQL-DOM [4] is one of those prevention methods that was developed to handle the injected HTML's commands. SQL-DOM can turn HTML into structured data thus making it hard for the hackers to enter HTML commands as input. Another preventive way is SQLrand [5], a method that transforms the application Instruction-Set Randomization to an SQL language, and the result of the transformation will be appended by a random number, with which the hacker who tries to perform any SQL injection will not be able to guess the appended number. AMNESIA [6] uses static analysis and runtime monitoring of application code to detect and prevent SQLI attacks. SQL injection, Fast Flux Monitor, Machine Learning, and Ardilla tools are methods to detect SQL injection attacks, while Noxes tool, SQLMap, and Session Shield are methods used to detect and prevent SQL injection simultaneously [7]. Joshi and Geetha in [8] have used a classifier which uses a combination of Role Based Access Control mechanism and Naïve Bayes machine learning algorithm for detecting SQL Injection attacks. Valeur et al. [9] in their paper, discussed a learning-based approach to detect SQL attacks. Ladole and Phalke [10] in their paper have used Query tree, Fisher Score, and Support Vector Machine classification to detect SQL injection attacks. What differentiates the proposed research from existing work is the experimental setup that can be used across different machine learning algorithms to detect SQL Injection attacks. Rawat and Kumar [11] in their paper have talked about detecting SQL injection attacks using SVM classification algorithm.

Chen. et. al. [12] in their paper discussed a rule matching method of SQL injection detection using machine learning. The paper discussed the use of word vector text representation method and support vector machine (SVM) classification model to detect malicious SQL queries. Gu. et. al. in their paper [13], discussed a traffic-based SQL injection detection framework named DIAVA. This framework used a regular expression model to analyze the work traffic of SQL operations. DIAVA framework used a front-end to collect network related to SQL injection attacks and a backend to evaluate the vulnerability using dictionary attack analysis. Multilevel RegExp model is used to detect the attacks and to determine the vulnerability of leaked data. DIAVA framework used Hyperscan by Intel to perform multilevel matching of RegExps. Das. et. al. [14] in their paper have described edit-distance approach to classify a dynamic SQL query as safe or malicious using a web- profile that is prepared during the training phase along with the dynamic SQL queries. The authors used well-known supervised approaches such as Naive Bayesian, SVM, and Parse-tree based approach to analyze the dataset. The paper does a comparative study of the edit-distance and binary-distance methods with the machine learning classification algorithms. The proposed method of classification had good results with dynamic SQL queries with few overheads.

III. EXPERIMENTAL SETUP

In this research effort, we used different machine learning algorithms to detect SQL Injection attacks. The dataset used for this research consisted of both vulnerable and safe SQL code. The datasets considered as input must be preprocessed and a set of features must be extracted from this dataset through a process called feature extraction. The results obtained from the classification were used to determine the vulnerable code. At the end, the classification accuracy, precision, and confusion matrix of each of the machine learning algorithms used will be determined. The model used in this research effort to predict SQLi attacks can be found in Figure. 1.

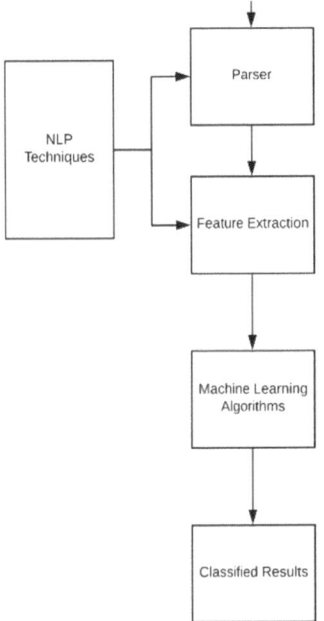

Fig. 1. Proposed model to Detect SQL Injection Attacks using Machine Learning Algorithms

A. Technologies

Python (3.7) was the language of choice because of its relatively simple syntax and the extent of supported libraries aimed at data science is second to none. The selected libraries were sklearn, which provided a wide variety of built-in machine learning algorithms and exceptionally fast setup time, xgboost, which was one of the best libraries to deploy extreme gradient boosting model, and pandas, which was a powerful library for data science. The development environment was IDLE, and the output was in the integrated shell.

B. Datasets

The process of collecting SQL injection (SQLi) malicious and safe queries was very challenging. We initially tried datasets that were manually created. After spending a significant amount of research, we ended up using two online sources primarily to gather our test and training datasets. Malicious queries, which tally up to 783 queries, were taken from [15] and benign queries, which tallies up to 700 queries, were taken from [16-19], and were put together into a text file. Then we assigned the queries with labels, label 0 for benign and label 1 for malicious.

C. Proposed Model

In this section, we proposed a unique model using machine learning to detect SLQi attacks. Instead of tackling the injection on the injection attacks on the server side by guarding the database, this model is designed to act as a filter on the client side. As a result, most of our data are text-based.

1) Data Preparation

For the purpose of reducing data noise and improving precision, unnecessary spaces and escape sequences were

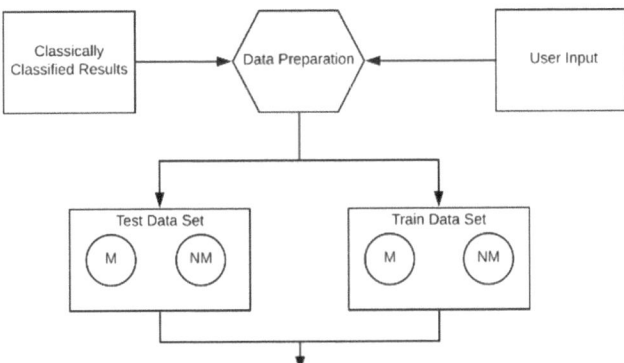

eliminated and all the queries were converted into lowercase form.

2) Training and Testing Datasets

The training and testing sets are taken randomly from the dataset with a conventional ratio of 80-20 (80% for training and 20% for testing) using train_test_split function built into sklearn library:

train_test_split(trainDF['text'], trainDF['label'], test_size = 0.2)

3) Parser

Our model came across a common adversity during the data processing phase where traditional machine learning model explicitly takes in structured tabular numeric data, but our collected data are entirely non-structured texts. This is where parser for text comes into play. Text parsing is the process of transforming given series of text into desired smaller components based on some specific rules. There are two common ways to parse texts: regular expression separation and tokenization. The former parses the targeted text using desired regular expressions such as "[a-z]", "[\t]". The latter divides the text into tokens, where each token can be a character, a word or a phrase. In the case of SQLi attacks, the regular expressions do not determine the malice of a query, the appropriate text parsing method for this model is tokenization. Queries are split into tokens of words. For example:

Parsing "or 1=1 -- 1" into "or", "1=1", "--", "1"

4) Natural Language Processing (NLP) techniques and feature extraction

For NLP, there are many featured engineering techniques, but the one that proves to be the most useful for this SQLi attacks detecting model is Word Level TF-IDF Vectors. TF-IDF stands for Term Frequency and Inverse Document Frequency, which is an important index for term searching and figuring out the relevancy of specific terms in a document. Term Frequency specifically measures how often a word occurs in a document, where Document Frequency determines how often a word occurs in an entire set of documents. The formula to calculate the relevancy of a specific word is as follows:

$$\frac{Term\ Frequency}{Document\ Frequency}$$

or

$$Term\ Frequency \times Inverse\ Document\ Frequency$$

The most significant advantage of TF-IDF is that it will assume that the documents are just bags of words, where each word does not have any correlation to another. This method is simple but powerful for our use case since in SQL, there are no tense or grammar rules like human languages.

5) Machine Learning Algorithms

The proposed model used the following machine learning algorithms:

- Naïve Bayes Classifier
- Support Vector Machine
- Decision Forest
- Logistic regression
- Extreme Gradient Boosting

To preserve the experimental aspect of our model, every parameter for the algorithms are kept to default.

D. Alignment with NICE Framework

The undergraduate research project discussed in this paper includes many of the NICE Framework Knowledge areas [20] such as K0069 - Knowledge of query languages such as SQL (structured query language), K0070 - Knowledge of system and application security threats and vulnerabilities (e.g., buffer overflow, mobile code, cross-site scripting, Procedural Language/Structured Query Language [PL/SQL] and injections, race conditions, covert channel, replay, return-oriented attacks, malicious code), K0234 - Knowledge of full spectrum cyber capabilities (e.g., defense, attack, exploitation). K0235 - Knowledge of how to leverage research and development centers, think tanks, academic research, and industry systems, K0236 - Knowledge of how to utilize Hadoop, Java, Python, SQL, Hive, and Pig to explore data, and K0238 - Knowledge of machine learning theory and principles.

IV. RESULTS & DISCUSSION

A. Evaluation Metrics

In each of the algorithms used the precision, recall, F1 score, support, macro average, weighted average, and the confusion matrix was determined.

1) *Precision*: is the ratio of tp to tp + fp where tp represents the number of true positives and fp represents the number of false positives [21].

2) *Recall*: is calculated by the ratio tp to tp + fn, where tp represents the number of true positives and fn represents the number of false negatives [21].

3) *F1-score*: is the weighted harmonic mean of the precision and recall [21].

4) *Weighted average*: is calculated by calculating the metrics of each label and then determining the average weighted by support [21].

5) *Confusion matrix*: is defined as a matrix C such that C_{ij} is equal to the observations that are known to be in group i but predicted to be group j [22].

B. Results

Figure. 2 show a sample classification report and confusion matrix of Extreme Gradient Boosting algorithm used in this research effort.

```
Classification report

              precision    recall  f1-score   support

           0       1.00      1.00      1.00        76
           1       1.00      1.00      1.00        99

    accuracy                           1.00       175
   macro avg       1.00      1.00      1.00       175
weighted avg       1.00      1.00      1.00       175

Confusion Matrix

         Predicted Class 0   Predicted Class 1
Class 0           76                   0
Class 1            0                  99
```

Fig. 2. Classification report and Confusion matrix for Extreme Gradient Boosting algorithm

Table I below summarizes the evaluation results on different metrics used by this machine learning model setup. On this test run, there are a total of 175 support data points, with 76 for class 0 (non-malicious) and 99 for class 1 (malicious). Based on the results, 3 out of 5 algorithms tested yielded 100% accuracy, except for Naïve Bayes (77%) and Support Vector Machine (57%).

TABLE I. EVALUATION RESULTS

Algorithms	Metrics (Class0/Class1)				
	Precision	Recall	F1-score	Weighted average	Accuracy
Naïve Bayes	1.00/0.71	0.46/1.00	0.63/0.83	0.74	0.77
Logistic Regression	1.00/1.00	1.00/1.00	1.00/1.00	1.00	1.00
SVM	0.00/0.57	0.00/1.00	0.00/0.72	0.41	0.57
Rando Forest	1.00/1.00	1.00/1.00	1.00/1.00	1.00	1.00
Extreme Gradient Boosting	1.00/1.00	1.00/1.00	1.00/1.00	1.00	1.00

V. CONCLUSION & FUTURE WORK

Through this research effort, 1) An experimental setup to run different machine learning algorithms to detect SQL Injection attacks was developed; 2) Research results produced can be used by the research community working on Cyberattacks; 3) Accuracy of the machine learning algorithms used in research were determined; and 4) Research has the potential to be expanded in the future by adding more machine learning algorithms.

This research effort has led to a novel approach in terms of predicting SQLi attacks using machine learning algorithm and provides an alternative approach to the traditional models like AMNESIA, SQLrand, and SQLdom. This research effort if continued in the right direction might result in a SQLi attacks detecting model that can be used across different platforms to detect and prevent SQLi attacks from happening in the future. The results obtained through this research effort are preliminary and needs to be optimized for better results. The experimental model developed must be tested out with larger and more diverse datasets to improve the reliability and accuracy. Furthermore, a more powerful and cutting-edge methodology like deep learning will be taken into consideration, which would improve the automation and longevity of the model developed.

REFERENCES

[1] Acunetix. "What Is SQL Injection (SQLi) and How to Fix It." Web.

[2] Tajpour, Atefeh, Suhaimi Ibrahim, and Mohammad Sharifi. "Web application security by sql injection detectiontools." IJCSI International Journal of Computer Science Issues 9.2 (2012): 332-339.

[3] Vinitha Subburaj, Daniel Thomas Loughran, MayarKefah Salih, "All About SQL Injection Attacks", CISSE 2018, New Orleans, LA.

[4] McClure, Russell A., and Ingolf H. Kruger. "SQL DOM: compile time checking of dynamic SQL statements." Software Engineering, 2005. ICSE 2005. Proceedings. 27th International Conference on. IEEE, 2005.

[5] Boyd, Stephen W., and Angelos D. Keromytis. "SQLrand: Preventing SQL injection attacks." International Conference on Applied Cryptography and Network Security. Springer, Berlin, Heidelberg, 2004.

[6] Halfond, William GJ, and Alessandro Orso. "AMNESIA: analysis and monitoring for NEutralizing SQL-injection attacks." Proceedings of the 20th IEEE/ACM international Conference on Automated software engineering. ACM, 2005.

[7] Alwan, Zainab S., and Manal F. Younis. "Detection and Prevention of SQL Injection Attack: A Survey." (2017).

[8] Joshi, A., & Geetha, V. (2014). SQL Injection detection using machine learning. Control, Instrumentation, Communication and Computational Technologies (ICCICCT), 2014 International Conference on, 1111-1115.

[9] Valeur, Fredrik, Darren Mutz, and Giovanni Vigna. "A learning-based approach to the detection of SQL attacks." International Conference on Detection of Intrusions and Malware, and Vulnerability Assessment. Springer, Berlin, Heidelberg, 2005.

[10] Ladole, Aniruddh, and DA, Phalke. "SQL Injection Attack and User Behavior Detection by Using Query Tree Fisher Score and SVM Classification." International Research Journal of Engineering and Technology 3.6 (2016).

[11] Rawat, R. & Kumar, S. (2012). SQL injection attack detection using SVM. International Journal of Computer Applications.

[12] Chen, Zhuang, and Min Guo. "Research on SQL injection detection technology based on SVM." MATEC Web of Conferences. Vol. 173. EDP Sciences, 2018.

[13] Gu, Haifeng, et al. "DIAVA: A Traffic-Based Framework for Detection of SQL Injection Attacks and Vulnerability Analysis of Leaked Data." IEEE Transactions on Reliability (2019).

[14] Das, Debasish, Utpal Sharma, and D. K. Bhattacharyya. "Defeating SQL injection attack in authentication security: an experimental study." International Journal of Information Security 18.1 (2019): 1-22.

[15] https://github.com/client9/libinjection.git

[16] https://archive.ics.uci.edu/ml/machine-learning-databases/00237

[17] https://www.kaggle.com/wjburns/common-password-list-rockyoutxt

[18] https://www.kaggle.com/hackerrank/developer-survey-2018

[19] https://www.kaggle.com/siddharthkumar25/malicious-and-benign-urls

[20] Newhouse, William, et al. "National initiative for cybersecurity education (NICE) cybersecurity workforce framework." NIST Special Publication 800.2017 (2017): 181.

[21] https://scikitlearn.org/stable/modules/generated/sklearn.metrics.precision_recall_fscore_support

[22] https://scikit-learn.org/stable/modules/generated/sklearn.metrics.confusion_mat

Weak Password Policies:
A Lack of Corporate Social Responsibility

Tobi A. West, CISSP, GCFE
Dakota State University
The Beacom College of Computer and
Cyber Sciences
Madison, SD, USA
Tobi.West@trojans.dsu.edu

Abstract—Data breaches continue to occur as weak password policies prevail on major websites, at costs reaching billions of dollars annually. Password attacks are a known cause of data breaches and abuse of user accounts. Enforcing strong password policies should be considered part of an organization's corporate social responsibility. Major technology companies are socially obligated to go beyond internal policies to strengthen their password policies for external-facing consumer accounts to help reduce the risk of data breaches or sensitive data exposure. Strong, enforceable password policies are beneficial to reduce the risk of successful network attacks and prevent unauthorized access to sensitive data stored in online consumer accounts. This study includes a compilation of current password policies for major social media sites, online streaming services, and online retailers to demonstrate the lack of strong password requirements across multiple industries and spanning decades of corporate establishment in the online environment. Recommendations are provided for organizations to strengthen their password policies to align with NIST Special Publication 800-63-3 as part of their corporate social responsibility to provide protection for sensitive consumer data for millions of customers and online marketplace sellers.

Keywords—cybersecurity, cyber security, passwords, password policy, password management, password guidelines, password attacks, password cracking, corporate social responsibility

I. INTRODUCTION

Social media sites and online merchants have an obligation to society, a corporate social responsibility, to help raise awareness of cybersecurity issues and protect user information stored on their networks, such as securing account credentials through strong password policies. Chen (2019) refers to corporate social responsibility (CSR) as self-regulated, that organizations can use the business model to remain socially accountable to consumers and all business stakeholders. Corporate citizenship is relevant to all aspects of society to enhance social objectives, including those that have environmental, economic, and quality of life impacts (Boulouta and Pitelis, 2014).

In February 2018, The White House's Council of Economic Advisers reported that the estimated annual cost of malicious cyber activity is between $57 billion and $109 billion (Anonymous, 2018). With data breaches having such a negative financial impact on the government and private sectors, organizations have a moral and social responsibility to develop a strong security posture and to raise consumer awareness about cybersecurity topics that impact customers, including establishing strong password requirements to curtail vulnerabilities. The most widely used mechanism for user authentication to access a website is a text-based password (Han, et al., 2018). Organizations providing online services should recognize the CSR associated with strong passwords.

Password requirements are the criteria of a password policy that determine the strength and complexity of the combination of characters input when a password is setup or reset (Afonin, 2017). According to Raponi and Di Pietro (2020), poor password policies allow users (i.e., consumers) to setup weak passwords that can be cracked nearly instantly. Sophisticated cracking dictionaries can break weak hashing algorithms and reveal collections of breached passwords, leaving organizations vulnerable to network intrusion (Krasznay, 2018; Raponi and Di Pietro, 2020). The following study provides an assessment of password policy guidelines identified by the government and industry followed by an analysis of password requirements for popular websites, including streaming media, social media, and online shopping. The findings of the analyses were used to formulate recommendations for development of password policies to strengthen cybersecurity best practices relative to enforcement of password requirements.

II. ANALYSIS OF PASSWORD REQUIREMENTS OVER THE YEARS

Decades ago, prior to the World Wide Web with online shopping, the computer password was first used in 1961 to accommodate multiple users for the same computer system, known as the Compatible Time-Sharing System (Bonneau, et al., 2015; Hiscott, 2013). Soon after in 1962, the password list for that system was hacked with a simple file printing request by one of the system users for non-nefarious reasons, his intent was simply to gain access to more time using that system by entering with other user's passwords. Since then password policies have not changed dramatically even though there is significantly more sensitive information online to be protected (Hiscott, 2013).

In addition to computer password policies set by the big name companies (e.g., Microsoft, Google, Amazon) that may be considered influential in the market, there are many factors that have shaped and guided how online merchants and service providers have developed their password policies for customer accounts over the years. It appears that user convenience dominates as one of the primary reasons that password policies continue to be weak on heavy-traffic websites (Florencio and Herley, 2010; Raponi and Di Pietro, 2020). Considering that users often access more than 25 password-protected sites per day, this takes significant attention to detail on the user's part if each password is different (Hiscott, 2013; Raponi and Di Pietro, 2020).

A. Password Policy Guidelines

On many of the early operating systems developed by Microsoft Corporation, the password length can be set to any number of characters between 0 and 14 (Microsoft, 2016). This Microsoft password configuration suggests that the system administrator can change the password length to zero characters which will then require no password at all for a computer login. While this type of policy may have been considered acceptable years ago for single-user systems such as Windows 7, it is not considered best practice for multi-user systems such as Windows Server 2008 or Windows Server 2012 R2, even according to Microsoft. The recommended password configuration on the Microsoft site now is to set the password length to 14 characters and enforce the password complexity rules.

Although the National Institute of Standards and Technology (NIST) established secure password guidelines in Special Publication 800-63 published in June 2004, new guidelines have since superseded with Special Publication 800-63-3 in June 2017 (Grassi, et al.). These guidelines include several specific characteristics, the password shall be at least 8 characters, ASCII characters and the space character should be accepted, redundant spaces may be condensed, no truncation of the password shall be performed, and the password shall be compared to known compromised, commonly used, or expected passwords.

According to NIST, expected passwords to be rejected may include passwords from previous breach lists, dictionary words, username, and repetitive or sequential characters (e.g., 'eeeeeeee' or 'abcdefgh'). If the password is rejected based on the expected password criteria, a reason for the rejection shall be provided and the user shall be required to choose a different password. Additionally, a password strength meter should be provided to offer guidance to the account creator.

Attempts at raising public awareness about password strength and complexity has resulted in World Password Day, which is calendared annually for the first Thursday of May (Avast, 2019). The Avast Security News Team (2019) reported that up to 18% of United States users have never changed their password and 83% have weak passwords. With the complexity and number of passwords to be remembered for daily use, it would be beneficial to have a secure place to keep them. The multitude of passwords can be stored using a password manager that can handle the variety and complexity, which may offer some relief for users with an abundance of passwords to be entered daily on frequently visited websites.

B. Managing Passwords

An application known as a password manager can be used by consumers and business organizations to keep track of passwords for multiple sites to reduce the confusion and prevent re-use of passwords to other sites (Han, et al., 2018; Towner, 2019). According to Forbes, 60 million users find a password manager useful to maintain their passwords in an encrypted fashion (O'Flaherty, 2019). For those that do not use a password manager, they may choose to re-use the password across multiple sites and/or they may choose to use the least number of characters to make the password easier to remember (Han, et al., 2018; SpecOps, 2019).

A lengthy password known as a passphrase can be used in place of a short password to add length and complexity to the password, making it more difficult to crack compared to the types of password complexity schemes suggested by NIST back in 2003 (Clark Estes, 2017; Krasznay 2018). Additionally, Krasznay (2018) and SpecOps (2019) recommends an easily memorable passphrase of at least 20 characters. Memorizing multiple passphrases may not be easy for users, that is where a password manager could be useful.

C. Password Attacks

Passwords allow access to protected and sensitive information, in some cases it is a personal account and in other cases it may be access to entire enterprise systems (Krasznay, 2018; Spitzner, 2018). A database full of passwords is a prime target for cyber criminals and may lead to loss of credentials for all users on the system. Whether that password data is stored in a plaintext readable format or a hashed format, it is a treasure trove for an attacker because the passwords can often still be cracked even if they are hashed (Dale, 2018). Password re-use on multiple accounts could mean that if one password is compromised then the other accounts for that user may be compromised as well (Raponi and Di Pietro, 2020).

There are various attacks that can be used to gain access to a user's password, including social engineering and more technical attacks. Different types of social engineering include phishing email in which a user may simply be tricked into providing their login credentials (i.e., username and password) to a website by spoofing to look like a familiar link and leading to a familiar looking website (e.g., financial institutions). Another social engineering attack may be more personal, attempting to convince a user to provide their login credentials simply by acting as a familiar company or government organization (e.g., Internal Revenue Service) (Bisson, 2019). Technical attacks include the use of brute force, rainbow tables, and dictionary attacks in which cyber criminals can use system tools to crack passwords quickly as the password is compared to a combination of characters or a list of known passwords.

According to Dellinger (2019), the quickly stolen Disney+ accounts were already worth $3 to $11 each on the hacking forums within a couple weeks after Disney+ began its online streaming services. Passwords are a prime target for attackers because the accounts can be sold for profit. Disney claims that this was not a widespread attack but was due to the types of passwords that users setup for their accounts (Dellinger, 2019). Included in the next section is the Disney+ password policy: a minimum of 6 characters, case sensitive with at least one number or special character. This a simple password policy and does not meet the NIST guidelines noted in the prior section. Surprisingly, Disney+ required that the credentials match the account setup for the user's Disneyland annual passport.

A brute force attempt taken out on a 6-character password may take as long as 10 hours with a powerful video card, or it could be instant if that password has already been compromised or is on the list of common passwords (Afonin, 2017). Multi-factor authentication (MFA) can help to reduce the abuse of cracked passwords, such as in the Disney+ situation mentioned previously. Some sites allow users to setup an additional method of verification that may involve human interaction, perhaps a one-time passcode sent via text message that must be entered after the login credentials, or a phone call to verify that the user interacts with the system. Some believe multi-factor authentication methods can lead to a loss of convenience and privacy because of the additional steps needed and the additional data stored for verification (Hiscott, 2013).

III. PASSWORD POLICY COMPARISONS

A comparison of password policies from popular online sellers and service providers is necessary to view the landscape of account creation and the password requirements of major online retailers with large market shares. These password policies may have broader impacts and global implications on cybersecurity, in that these policies may shape and guide how users choose to setup passwords for other sites.

In order to understand the password requirements of a variety of popular websites, 15 online organizations were selected for new account creation in December 2019, using a personal email address previously created on the Google site. New accounts were created for Streaming Media Providers: *Disney+*, *Hulu*, *YouTube*, *Twitch*, and *SmashCast*; Social Media Providers: *Facebook*, *Instagram*, *Snapchat*, *Pinterest*, and *LinkedIn*; and Online Retailers: *Target*, *Walmart*, *Etsy*, *Amazon*, and *eBay*. The accounts were created similarly to identify the type of username that was required, to check whether password requirements were initially visible on screen or required a poor password attempt for the requirements to be displayed, to identify password strength and complexity requirements, and whether a password strength indicator was available to guide users with password creation.

Customer account creation on a website may include a request for some personal information or as little as an email address and password. Typically, the login type for account creation may include either a user-generated name or an email address. If a user-generated name is allowed then it is usually compared to existing usernames for that site to reject duplicates, avoiding the possibility of a user creating the same username as one previously stored for another user.

Of the 15 accounts created for this study, 4 allowed the user to generate a login name with minimum character values ranging between 4 and 8 characters. Password requirements varied with 10 of the 15 accounts requiring 6 character minimum, and 8 of the 15 accounts accepting sequential characters such as 'abcdef' for the password. Only 2 of the 15 accounts offered a password strength meter to guide users on the strength or complexity of the password being entered for the new account.

A variety of online retailers and service providers were selected to compare password policies for websites that were created over the past 25 years and that have different target audiences. For example, LinkedIn is a social media platform for professionals while Hulu is for anyone that wants to stream movies or shows. In this study, Amazon has the longest running site, since 1994, while Disney+ is one of the newest, having launched less than one month ago in November 2019 (Sherman, 2019). All of the sites have one thing in common relative to password policies, a simple minimum of 6 characters and an email address to get an account started.

A. Password Policies on Popular Sites

Table I in Appendix provides a comparison data collected during account creation, including provider name, login type, password requirements, the inclusion of a password strength indicator on-screen, the number of users reportedly accessing the site, and the year the website was established on the World Wide Web.

Some of the websites included in this study have been in existence for decades and each one has millions or more accounts containing sensitive information. With this much time providing products and services to the community and with such heavy traffic, it would stand to reason that the organizations are aware that the password policies are weak and that there are many options available as guidelines for developing stronger password policies. These organizations have a corporate social responsibility to follow the latest password guidelines provided in NIST SP 800-63-3 and change the minimum requirements for their password policies to protect the sensitive customer information stored on their systems.

In 2018, on the Amazon Web Services (AWS) blog site, Rains included "weak, leaked, and stolen passwords" as the number three-way organizations initially get compromised. The post goes on to describe the implementation of complex password policies for AWS and the Identity and Access Management (IAM) systems, which are not currently implemented on the Amazon commercial site. The Amazon retail site still allows customer account creation with as few as six alpha characters and no complexity requirements.

According to Bocetta's Dark Reading article (2019), following are the most common passwords exposed during breaches:

```
123456 123456789 password qwerty 12345 qwerty123
1q2w3e 123123 111111 12345678 1234567 1234567890
abc123 anhyeuem iloveyou password1 123456789
123321 qwertyuiop 654321 123456 121212 asdasd
666666 zxcvbnm 987654321 112233 123456a 123123123
123qwe 11111111 aaaaaa qwe123 dragon 1234
1q2w3e4r5t reset zinch 25251325 monkey a123456
1qaz2wsx 1q2w3e4r 123654 159753 222222 asdfghjkl
147258369 999999 5201314 123abc qweqwe 456789
555555 7777777 qazwsx princess qwerty1 1111111
football j38ifUbn asdfgh 66bob 888888 163.com
147258 asd123 azerty sunshine 789456 3rJs1la7qE
159357 michael 789456123 88888888 1234qwer daniel
Password abcd1234 myspace1 computer 987654321
shadow qqqqqq 1234561 killer superman pokemon
987654 master q1w2e3r4t5y6 baseball 777777
123456789a charlie 11223344 333333 soccer
x4ivygA51F
```

The above collection of re-used, breached passwords demonstrates the simplicity of many passwords and that users are often still including many sequential characters in their passwords which allows for the password to be easily cracked or hacked. For the most part, the accounts setup in this study would all have allowed any of these passwords for account creation. Hughes (2017) notes that DashLane's examination of password policies on major websites revealed that most had failed to implement even the most rudimentary password guidelines, having given ratings of 0 to popular streaming sites such as Netflix, Pandora, and Spotify.

An online password strength indicator often reflects the characteristics of a user password in either a numeric value, a Likert-scale value, or a color-coded meter to represent the complexity of the password entered. This helps users gain visibility to whether the password they are creating could easily be compromised by an attacker. The DashLane examination reports that 76% of consumer sites failed to provide any form of on-screen password assessment (Hughes, 2017). Over 30% of consumer sites do not support two-factor authentication, according to Hughes (2017), which leaves users without the choice to take extra precautions to protect sensitive information on those accounts.

B. Limitations of the Study

This study included only the options for entry of the password on the account setup screen and did not continue with the login process, password reset process, or other factors affecting the form in which it may be stored or the way the user may interact further with the password (e.g., typing in the password, using a password manager or previously stored password, or multi-factor authentication).

IV. RECOMMENDATIONS

With Facebook boasting over 2.45 billion monthly active users worldwide, the impact of the weak password policy cannot be any more profound (Clement, 2019). Facebook has deleted billions of fake accounts in 2019 alone (Stewart, 2019). These organizations should recognize the corporate social responsibility for the weak password policies that allow the abuse of account setup because the consequences are so far reaching.

Opderbeck (2017) is of the mindset that large transnational corporations have a corporate responsibility to consider implications for cybersecurity and international security in product and service development. Due to the significant reliance on digital technology for the global economy and social processes, cybersecurity is imperative to protect sensitive data that could be used to harm others financially or physically. With that in mind, there is a high level of responsibility to protect user accounts and "to reduce the most probable cyber risks" (Christen, et al., 2017). For these reasons, organizations have a corporate social responsibility to develop strong password policies that help protect sensitive user information, maintaining user privacy and preventing fraudulent use of customer accounts.

The Microsoft Identity Protection Team reports seeing over 10 million attacks every day on username/password pairs (Hicock, 2019). Microsoft provides recommendations to IT Administrators based on this experience, including a minimum of 8 characters, a ban on common passwords, enforcement of multi-factor authentication, and risk-based multi-factor authentication challenges. Similar to recommendations from other organizations, Microsoft's policy also includes the elimination of the character-composition requirements and the elimination of the periodic password reset (Hicock, 2019).

A. Password Policy Improvements for Organizations

Following are the recommendations for organizations when developing a password policy, especially on heavy-traffic sites. These suggestions from NIST SP 800-63-3 (Grassi, et al., 2017) and Krasznay (2018) apply to both password setup and password reset.

- Always require the use of passwords for accounts and systems containing sensitive data
- Set minimum requirements to 14 characters
- Prevent use of known-compromised passwords
- Ban commonly used passwords
- Prevent use of passwords known to be in cracking dictionaries, especially top 10
- Do not allow the username or service name to be included in the password
- Do not require periodic password reset
- Allow multi-factor authentication

- Continuous password monitoring using known-compromised passwords and common passwords to maintain an updated dictionary

- Require input of the current password on password reset requests

- Do not require reuse of the same credentials across different systems without single sign-on

B. Strong Passwords for Users

Following are recommendations for users when setting up or resetting a password, especially on sites that store sensitive or personal data. Some of these suggestions are from NIST SP 800-63-3 (Grassi, et al., 2017).

- Use a passphrase of at least 16 characters that can easily be remembered but not easily guessed

- Enable multi-factor authentication whenever possible

- Do not choose commonly used passwords or sequential passwords that are easy to guess

- Avoid words that are related to the service being protected or yourself

- Avoid words or numbers related to pet names, children's names, phone numbers, addresses, birthdates, or anniversaries

- Avoid phishing scams and other social engineering attempts that may try to obtain your password

- Avoid using public Wi-Fi that is not encrypted to protect your password

- Avoid using public computers to log into secure websites where credentials may be retrieved by other users

- Do not re-use passwords on multiple sites

- Do not share your password with others

V. CONCLUSION

Many of today's major online retailers, service providers, and social media sites continue to have weak password policies despite strong password policy guidelines and recommendations from industry and government being widely available. Of those studied, most sites require only 6 characters on the password setup which can be cracked instantly by hackers to gain access to online accounts containing sensitive information, including credit card numbers. The majority of users in the United States continue to have weak passwords that go unchanged for great periods of time.

This paper included a historical look at the evolution of the password and recommendations, covered an analysis of password policies for popular heavy-traffic websites, and provided recommendations for organizations and consumer users to develop stronger password policies and passwords for use online. Of the recommendations for organizations provided, the ones to be emphasized are increased minimum character limits and multi-factor authentication to be enabled for all users. Of the user recommendations, the most emphasized are to use multi-factor authentication whenever possible, to avoid re-using the same password on multiple sites, and do not share your password with others.

Short and simple passwords can be cracked quickly by hackers with malicious intent, exposing sensitive information, leaving accounts and computer networks open to data theft. Organizations have an obligation to customers to help to protect the accounts containing sensitive information on corporate systems. Corporate social responsibility dictates that organizations help to defend customer accounts by developing appropriately strong password policies to prevent users from creating simple passwords that can potentially be easily cracked leading to account compromise.

REFERENCES

[1] Afonin, O. (7 Apr 2017). How Long Does It Take to Crack Your Password? Elcomsoft: Desktop, Mobile, and Cloud Forensics. Retrieved from https://blog.elcomsoft.com/2017/04/how-long-does-it-take-to-crack-your-password/

[2] Anonymous. (2018). HINDSIGHT. Risk Management, 65(3), 54-55.

[3] Avast Security News Team. (1 May 2019). World Password Day 2019 – Is your password strong enough? Avast Blog. Retrieved from https://blog.avast.com/strengthening-passwords-on-world-password-day

[4] Bisson, D. (5 Nov 2019). 5 Social Engineering Attacks to Watch Out For. The State of Security. Retrieved from https://www.tripwire.com/state-of-security/security-awareness/5-social-engineering-attacks-to-watch-out-for/

[5] Bocetta, S. (9 Aug 2019). It's (Still) the Password, Stupid! Dark Reading. Retrieved from https://www.darkreading.com/endpoint/its-(still)-the-password-stupid!/a/d-id/1335430?ngAction=register&ngAsset=389473

[6] Bonneau, J., Herley, C., Van Oorschot, P., & Stajano, F. (2015). Passwords and the evolution of imperfect authentication. Communications of the ACM, 58(7), 78-87.

[7] Boulouta, I., & Pitelis, C. N. (2014). Who needs CSR? the impact of corporate social responsibility on national competitiveness. Journal of Business Ethics, 119(3), 349-364. DOI:10.1007/s10551-013-1633-2

[8] Chen, J. (27 Nov 2019). Corporate Social Responsibility (CSR). Investopedia. Retrieved from https://www.investopedia.com/terms/c/corp-social-responsibility.asp

[9] Christen, M., Gordijn, B., Weber, K., et al. (2017). A Review of Value-Conflicts in Cybersecurity. The Orbit Journal, volume 1. Retrieved from https://doi.org/10.29297/orbit.v1i1.28

[10] Clark Estes, A. (8 Aug 17). The guy who invented those annoying password rules now regrets wasting your time. Gizmodo. Retrieved from https://gizmodo.com/the-guy-who-invented-those-annoying-password-rules-now-1797643987

[11] Clement, J. (19 Nov 2019). Number of monthly active Facebook users worldwide as of 3rd quarter 2019. Statista. Retrieved from https://www.statista.com/statistics/264810/number-of-monthly-active-facebook-users-worldwide/

[12] Dale, C. (27 Nov 2018). Passwords and Authentication - Get Up to Speed on Attacks and Defenses. SANS Webcasts. Retrieved from https://www.sans.org/webcasts/passwords-authentication-speed-attacks-defenses-108865

[13] Dellinger, AJ. (25 Nov 2019). Setting Up A Disney+ Account? Don't Use A Princess As Your Password. Forbes. Retrieved from

https://www.forbes.com/sites/ajdellinger/2019/11/25/setting-up-a-disney-account-dont-use-a-princess-as-your-password/#6740a4c42551

[14] Florencio, D. and Herley, C. (2010). Where Do Security Policies Come From? Microsoft Research. Retrieved from https://www.microsoft.com/en-us/research/wp-content/uploads/2016/02/WhereDoSecurityPoliciesComeFrom.pdf

[15] Grassi, P., Newton, E., et al. (Jun 2017). NIST Special Publication 800-63B. Digital Identity Guidelines. National Institute for Standards and Technology (NIST), US Department of Commerce. Retrieved from https://pages.nist.gov/800-63-3/sp800-63b.html

[16] Han, W., Li, Z., Ni, M., Gu, G., & Xu, W. (2018). Shadow Attacks Based on Password Reuses: A Quantitative Empirical Analysis. IEEE Transactions on Dependable and Secure Computing, 15(2), 309-320.

[17] Hicock, R. (17 Jul 2019). Microsoft Password Guidance. Microsoft Identity Protection Team. Retrieved from https://www.microsoft.com/en-us/research/wp-content/uploads/2016/06/Microsoft_Password_Guidance-1.pdf

[18] Hiscott, R. (30 Dec 2013). The Evolution of the Password — And Why It's Still Far From Safe. Mashable. Retrieved from https://mashable.com/2013/12/30/history-of-the-password/

[19] Hughes, M. (9 Aug 2017). Study: Most major websites have dreadful basic password security. The Next Web. Retrieved from https://thenextweb.com/insider/2017/08/09/study-most-major-websites-have-dreadful-basic-password-security/

[20] Krasznay, C. (2018). Fixing the Problems with Passwords. Risk Management, 65(6), 14-15.

[21] O'Flaherty, K. (20 Feb 2019). Password Managers Have A Security Flaw -- Here's How To Avoid It. Forbes. Retrieved from https://www.forbes.com/sites/kateoflahertyuk/2019/02/20/password-managers-have-a-security-flaw-heres-how-to-avoid-it/#246e53f84e16

[22] Opderbeck, D. (2017). Cybersecurity, Encryption, and Corporate Social Responsibility. Georgetown Journal of International Affairs, 105-111.

[23] Microsoft. (30 Aug 2016). Minimum password length. Retrieved from https://docs.microsoft.com/en-us/previous-versions/windows/it-pro/windows-server-2012-r2-and-2012/hh994560(v%3Dws.11)

[24] Rains, T. (17 Oct 2018). The Five Ways Organizations Initially Get Compromised and Tools to Protect Yourself. AWS Public Sector Blog Team. Retrieved from https://aws.amazon.com/blogs/publicsector/the-five-ways-organizations-initially-get-compromised-and-tools-to-protect-yourself/

[25] Raponi, S., & Di Pietro, R. (2020). A Longitudinal Study on Web-sites Password Management (in)Security: Evidence and Remedies. IEEE Access, 8, 1.

[26] Sherman, A. (13 Nov 2019). Disney+ already has 10 million subscribers — here's how that compares with rivals. CNBC. Retrieved from https://www.cnbc.com/2019/11/13/disney-10-million-subscribers-vs-competition.html

[27] Specops. (30 Jul 2019). 3 best passphrase practices. Retrieved from https://specopssoft.com/blog/3-passphrase-best-practices/

[28] Spitzner, L. (2019). Security Awareness Topic #6 - Passwords. SANS Security Awareness. Retrieved from https://www.sans.org/security-awareness-training/blog/security-awareness-topic-6-passwords

[29] Stewart, E. (23 May 2019). Facebook has taken down billions of fake accounts, but the problem is still getting worse. Vox. Retrieved from https://www.vox.com/recode/2019/5/23/18637596/facebook-fake-accounts-transparency-mark-zuckerberg-report

[30] Towner, N. (1 Feb 2019). CNET Asks: Do you use a password manager? CNET. Retrieved from https://www.cnet.com/news/cnet-asks-do-you-use-a-password-manager/

APPENDIX

TABLE I. PASSWORD REQUIREMENTS OF POPULAR WEBSITES

Provider Name	Login Type	Password Requirements	Password Strength Indicator	Number of Users	Year Established
STREAMING MEDIA					
Disney+	Email address	Minimum 6 characters Case sensitive At least one number or special character	Yes	10 million	2019
Hulu	Email address	Minimum 6 characters Initially no indicators displayed	No	28.5 million	2007
YouTube	Gmail address	Uses third-party Google sign-in	N/A	110 million	2005 (purchased by Google in 2006)
Twitch	Username (4 to 25 chars)	Minimum 8 characters Must qualify as at least "Weak" At least one number and one alpha character Password creation help page	Yes	148 million	2011
SmashCast	Username (6 chars minimum)	Minimum 6 characters	No	No data	2017

Provider Name	Login Type	Password Requirements	Password Strength Indicator	Number of Users	Year Established
SOCIAL MEDIA					
Facebook	Email address	Minimum 6 characters Combination of numbers, letters, and punctuation	No	2.45 *billion* (monthly active users) and 60 million business pages	2004
Instagram	Username	Minimum 6 characters	No	1 *billion* (monthly active users) and 25 million business accounts	2010

Provider Name	Login Type	Password Requirements	Password Strength Indicator	Number of Users	Year Established
SOCIAL MEDIA					
Snapchat	Username (5 chars minimum and must start with a letter)	Minimum 8 characters	No	310 million (monthly active users)	2011
Pinterest	Email address	Minimum 6 characters	No	265 million (monthly active users)	2010
LinkedIn	Email address	Minimum 6 characters	No	610 million	2003

Provider Name	Login Type	Password Requirements	Password Strength Indicator	Number of Users	Year Established
ONLINE RETAILERS					
Target	Email address	Minimum 8-20 characters. At least 2 of the following: lower case letters, uppercase letters, numbers, special characters except < >	No; but has a req. met indicator	140 million (monthly active users)	1999 (founded in 1902)
Walmart	Email address	Minimum 8-20 characters	No	132 million (monthly active users)	2000 (founded in 1962)
Etsy	Email address	Minimum 6 characters	No	54 million (2.1 million sellers)	2005
Amazon	Email address	Minimum 6 characters	No	300 million (2.5 million sellers)	1994
eBay	Email address	Minimum 6 characters. At least one number or symbol	No	182 million (6.7 million sellers)	1995

Higher Education Social Engineering Attack Scenario, Awareness & Training Model

Thai H. Nguyen
School of Computer Science and Engineering
Jack Welch College of Business & Technology
Sacred Heart University
Fairfield, CT, USA
nguyent62509@mail.sacredheart.edu

Sajal Bhatia
School of Computer Science and Engineering
Jack Welch College of Business & Technology
Sacred Heart University
Fairfield, CT, USA
bhatias@sacredheart.edu

Abstract—In today's information security ecosystem, hackers and threat actors are increasingly using social engineering tactics to circumvent advanced technical security technologies. While every year there are vast leaps in technical security systems, one critical dynamic, the human psychology still needs a dire upgrade to their operating system. The human dynamic and our innate psychological processing algorithms need a new approach to mitigate social engineering attacks. Higher education institutions are prime target for social engineering engagement missions as they house a large diverse population of faculties, students, alumni, and employees in their ecosystem. This diversity paired with increasing inclusion of international individuals only expands the existing dynamic vulnerable landscape, thereby requiring innovative methods to secure it. In this paper, the authors utilize an existing framework to develop nine specialized and publicly available social engineering attack scenarios geared toward a higher education environment. The paper also proposes preliminary models for social engineering awareness and training to combat such attacks. The effectiveness of the proposed models will be assessed by comparing pre- and post- awareness surveys as part of the future work.

Keywords—Information Security, Social Engineering, Social Engineering Attack Scenario, Social Engineering Awareness Model, Social Engineering Training Model, Social Engineering Ethics

I. INTRODUCTION

In the 21st century, information technology (IT) is ingrained into the fabric of nearly every society in the world. There isn't an industry that IT is not utilized from Financial, Government, Healthcare, Education, Industrial, Hospitality, Entertainment, Transportation, Retail, Telecommunication, and more. Technology that we all use today is also the very same technology that is used against us to cause harm to ourselves and society, either physically, mentally, and/or financially. Information security (IS) is continually becoming an essential in-demand and on-demand service for all of society's industries. It is critical that society's industries protect data at-rest, in-transit, and in-use from internal and external threats. The need for more IS has created a steadfast emergent of hardware and software technologies to combat a multitude of technical vulnerabilities and threats [17, 18, 23, 26 – 28]. It has made it harder for hackers and threat actors (the authors will refer to them as "attackers") to circumvent the technical security technologies but has not made it impossible.

Attackers are turning to social engineering (SE) tactics to circumvent the technical securities emplaced. SE is the deliberate act of manipulating an individual or group of individuals into giving access to confidential and unauthorized information voluntarily [1 – 14, 17, 21 – 23]. Research showed that an ontological definition of SE by Mouton et al. provided a more concrete definition of SE stating, "the science of using social interaction as a means to persuade an individual or an organization to comply with a specific request from an attacker where either the social interaction, the persuasion or the request involves a computer-related entity" [2]. The techniques that attackers will use in a SE attack (SEA) are identified by Mitnick as, "research, developing rapport and trust, exploiting trust, and utilize information" [4].

The authors surveyed ethical concerns pertaining to SE penetration testing and research [9, 10, 11]. SE penetration testing and research are crucial in assessing and evaluating the weaknesses in an industry such as higher education (HE). Experimentation and live executions of SEA can yield significant results, but conducting such excursions raise ethical concerns. To gather unfettered and unbiased results from the experiments, deception is a critical factor in testing and research missions [9, 10, 11]. Attackers are not restrained by the ethical constraints that penetration testers and researchers are held to. The authors propose that crafting specialized SEA scenarios based on real-world SE events can come close to those that attackers will utilize in their profession and satisfy ethical concerns.

To assess the current state of SE awareness training policies in HE institutions, the authors examined several publicly available HE institutions information via a search engine index. The findings showed that all provided information security awareness training to their students, faculty, and employees. The authors could not assess the actual content of the training material as they were only authorized to their appropriate institutions[1-6]. From the surface level information assembled, one institution provided about two 5 min general IS awareness videos[7] and another provided only a broad generalized IS awareness text-based information[8]. Although HE institutions are providing IS awareness training, the propriety nature and generalization of IS awareness is holding back the good it can provide to the educational community.

Due to these limitations, in this paper the authors proposes utilizing an open source approach in developing and providing specialized SEA scenarios based on Mouton et al. proposed, Social Engineering Attack Framework, which expands on Mitnick's "Social Engineering Cycle" [3, 4]. The proposed scenarios are based on real-world SE events, which will replicate actual prior SEAs and be able to satisfy ethical concerns. SEA scenarios will focus specifically on the threat landscape of HE institutions. By incorporating specialized SEA scenarios into SE Awareness and Training, technical and non-technical individuals will be able to spot SEAs [6, 7, 17, 19 – 25]. This will provide individuals within institutions a superior security awareness and be more vigilant against such types of SEAs [3].

The rest of the paper is organized as follows: Section II provides an overview of the impact of SE on HE institutions, and the ethical constraints of conducting SE experimentation by penetration testers and researchers. Section III provides a detailed overview of the Social Engineering Attack Framework used in the paper for developing attack scenarios. Section IV details the authors' contribution to mitigating higher education social engineering attacks with specialized crafted SEA scenarios. Section V outlines the authors' proposed SE awareness and training model to be implemented by HE institution's in their ecosystem. Finally, Section VI concludes and summarizes the research and outlines future directions for research in this area.

II. BACKGROUND AND RELATED WORK

Social engineering (SE) is on the rise and higher education (HE) institutions are faced with an increasing vulnerable landscape [27 - 32]. Every year there are massive migrations of local, national, and international high school graduates, transfer students, faculty and employees hire. All interfacing with HE institution systems, adding hundreds to thousands of dynamic vulnerabilities to their information technology and information security (IT/IS) ecosystem [19 – 26]. These individuals need to adapt to the IT/IS systems to be able to conduct their duties as students, professors, and employees.

HE institutions are a prime target for attackers because of the stockpiles of valuable information (VI) they collect and store [26]. As well as the openness and transparency of institutional public information provides enormous amounts of open source intelligence (OSINT) information. Information is a critical necessity involved in running a HE institution, which offer attackers a one-stop-shop for VI. Firstly, types of VI include the following: Personal Identifiable Information (Students, Parents, Faculty, and Employees), Protected Health Information, Free Application for Federal Student Aid, Financial Information, Employment Information, Institutional Endowment Donors, Intellectual Property, Academic Research, 3rd Party Vendor Information, and Payment Card Information. Secondly, OSINT information include the following: Full Name (First, Last, Middle), Job Title & Role, Social Media Accounts, Individual & Institutional News Feed, Old Version of Websites, Institutional Directory (Department, Phone, & Email), Google Map & Satellite Imagery, and Photo Repository (Flickr, Google Image, etc.). The multiple public-facing information that attackers can compile in their research to formulate a refined engagement mission against an individual or group of individuals at a HE institution [17, 21].

Individuals at every level in HE institutions are mandated at one point to provide multiple data points when entering the institution's ecosystem. Attackers will not need to initiate SE engagement missions into individual industries. Attackers merely need to conduct a single SE engagement mission on an unprepared HE institution and gain access to a treasure trove of VI. VI can be utilized in a follow up SEA into other industries. Armed with enough time, motivation and unchained ethical constraints, attackers will achieve their goals of infiltrating HE/IT infrastructure. HE institutions around the world have a lot to lose in the aftermath of a security breach. Types of negative impacts on HE institutions include the following: Financial Losses, Loss of Trust, Legal Action, Negative Publicity, Reputation Damage, Decline in Retention Rate, Decline in Admission Rate, and Loss of Research Grants [26, 27].

For professional penetration testers and researchers conducting live social engineering attack (SEA) experimentations for the improvement of society, to attain accurate and unfettered results from their experimentations, penetration testers and researchers must engage in a high level of deception and manipulation [9, 10, 11]. By executing tactics that malicious social engineers will utilize in their own engagement missions against real-world targets, they are able to enlighten the organization(s) of the weaknesses in their environment. The individual or group of individuals conducting SEA experimentations must also abide by ethical guidelines to satisfy their respective ethical oversight committee such as their institutional review board [11].

---

1 https://is.richmond.edu/infosec/securityawareness/training/index.html
2 https://cybersecurity.yale.edu/mss/yale-mss-12.1
3 https://www.technology.pitt.edu/security/information-security-awareness-training
4 https://it.arizona.edu/seecurity
5 https://cuit.columbia.edu/ciso/security-training
6 https://its.gse.harvard.edu/services/information-security/awareness-training
7 https://informationsecurity.princeton.edu/training
8 https://its.ucsc.edu/security/training/index.html

According to Mouton et al. penetration testers and researchers must adhere to the 3 major normative ethics principles of virtue ethics, utilitarianism, and deontology, to be viewed as ethical [9]. If there are any deviation from the 3 principles, then the individual or group of individuals are unethical in their actions. In the following, the authors emphasize the distinctions between ethical and unethical in each principle [9].

A. Virtue Ethics

The actions of an individual in the context of virtue ethics is considered to be ethical or "virtuous" if the individual is adhering to a defined moral code or code of ethics[9]. If the actions taken by the individual deviates from the moral code or code of ethics, then they are considered unethical. For penetration testers and researchers, Mouton et al. focuses on the Code of Ethics described by the IEEE & ACM as the guiding principles [9].

B. Utilitarianism

Utilitarianism, also known as consequentialism, considers an individual to be ethical if the individual's actions benefits society[10]. Otherwise, if the individual's actions do not benefit society it is considered unethical. Penetration testers and researchers conducting SEA are considered ethical if it provides beneficial outcomes to the greatest number of people. It disregards the consequences it has on the victim in which the SEA was directed toward [9].

C. Deontology

Deontological ethics defines what individual(s) should and should not do by the moral standards of society[11]. If such actions by the individual deviates into morally forbidden norms of society then it is considered unethical. According to Mouton et al., SEA needs to strictly adhere to the deontological rules of the world from the very beginning, regardless of the consequences [9].

There is no substitute to genuine live SEA, but conducting these experimentations require thorough and precise navigation to be within ethical standards. Malicious attackers are uninhibited by such ethical limitations. The authors recognize the limitations that penetration testers and researchers face in conducting meaningful SEA experimentations. To bridge the unethical advantages of malicious attackers, the authors proposes using Mouton et al. proposed social engineering attack framework (SEAF) [3]. Penetration testers and researchers can step into the mindset of a malicious social engineers and plan full spectrum SEA engagements targeted at their specific environment. SEAF will allow penetration testers and researchers to create a multitude of ethical and unethical SEA scenarios. An additional benefit for penetration testers and researchers in utilizing SEAF is the ability to provide detailed execution procedures of their experiment to their respective ethical oversight committee for review.

III. SOCIAL ENGINEERING ATTACK FRAMEWORK

Mouton et al. proposed social engineering attack framework (SEAF) expanded upon their ontological SEA model defines 7 components [2] and 6 core phases [3]. SEAF provides a comprehensive outline of the processes that attackers utilize in conducting their social engineering attack (SEA). The authors recognize the thoroughness of SEAF, and it is the basis to the authors' specialized crafted higher education (HE) social engineering (SE) scenarios. The authors outlines the 7 components then 6 core-phases of SEAF. In the following, the 7 components of SEAF:

1. **Communication**: Direct (includes Bidirectional & Unidirectional) & Indirect
2. **Social Engineer**: Individual or Group of Individuals
3. **Target**: Individual or Organization
4. **Medium**: Method of Initiating Communication (Social Engineer to Target)
5. **Goal**: Financial Gain, Unauthorized Access, or Service Disruption
6. **Compliance Principles**: Reasons why a Target complies with the Social Engineer's Request
7. **Technique**: Method(s) a Social Engineer utilizes in achieving their Goal

The authors recognized that the medium component can be broken down into 2 types of defined methods, human-based and technology-based [8, 17]. Workman and Aldawood et al. defined human-based and technology-based medium allows individuals and organizations to better recognize and categorize the medium in which social engineers are utilizing in their attack. In the following, the 6 core-phases of SEAF:

1. **Attack Formulation**: Goal Identification & Target Identification
2. **Information Gathering**: Identify Potential Sources, Gather Information from Sources & Assess Gathered Information
3. **Preparation**: Combination and Analysis of Gathered Information & Development of an Attack Vector
4. **Develop Relationship**: Establishment of Communication & Rapport Building
5. **Exploit Relationship**: Priming the Target & Elicitation

---

9 https://plato.stanford.edu/entries/ethics-virtue/
10 https://plato.stanford.edu/entries/consequentialism/
11 https://plato.stanford.edu/entries/ethics-deontological/

6. *Debrief*: Maintenance, Transition & Goal Satisfaction

Refined advancements Mouton et al. implemented to their ontological SEA model in creating their SEAF provides an important step forward for penetration testers and researchers [2]. For penetration testers, it provides the individual or team of individuals a preliminary tool to utilize in formulating their authorized SEA mission. For researchers, the comprehensiveness of every phase and associated steps of the SEAF provides accurate repeatable results which can be utilized in verifying and comparing to other models, processes and frameworks within SE [3].

IV. PROPOSED SOCIAL ENGINEERING ATTACK SCENARIOS IN HIGHER EDUCATION

Utilizing Mouton et al. proposed Social Engineering Attack Framework [3], the authors developed 9 total higher education social engineering attack scenarios. Attack scenarios are separated into 3 Bidirectional Attacks, 3 Unidirectional Attacks, and 3 Indirect Attacks. Below the authors provides an example of a Bidirectional Attack.

A. Higher Education Information Technology Technician Attack

Description of Attack Scenario: A social engineer (SE) impersonates an institution's information technology technician. The SE convinces a faculty member that he/she needs to gain access to their office data ports to conduct a network communication test. From there the SE install a man-in-the-middle device between the network port and the faculty's computerized terminal.

Components:

1. *Communication*: Bidirectional Communication
2. *Social Engineer*: Individual
3. *Target: Primary*: Higher Education Institution, Secondary: Faculty
4. *Medium*: Face-to-Face (Human-Based)
5. *Goal*: Gaining Unauthorized Access
6. *Compliance Principles*: Consistency Principle
7. *Technique*: Pretexting

Phases:

1. *Attack Formulation*

    - **Goal Identification**: The goal is to gain unauthorized access to the higher education institution's computerized terminal.

    - **Target Identification**: "Primary target" of the attack is the higher education institution. To engage their primary target, the SE will initiate attacks on any faculty member within the institution. The "secondary target" have the ability to grant the SE access to the institution's computerized terminal.

2. *Information Gathering*

    - **Identify Potential Sources**: Potential intelligence sources include but not limited to higher education's internet facing website, social media accounts, and physical reconnaissance. Social media intelligence sources can encompass any faculty member, ranging from national, international, undergraduate professor, and graduate professor, that are associated with the institution. As well as information on everyone in the institution's information technology department. Physical reconnaissance intelligence gathering include roaming reconnaissance of information technology department locations.

    - **Gather Information from Sources**: Assemble intelligence from the above sources.

    - **Assess Gathered Information**: Compiled intelligence into a cohesive insight of the attack vector. Type of faculty members that have access to computerized terminal(s). Type of IT Technicians that work for the institution's IT Department. Type(s) of clothing and uniform specific IT Technicians wear. Compile a detailed mapping of faculty members' location. Detailed mapping of the IT Department's main and sub locations. Compile a timeline of when faculty members are located that have access to computerized terminal(s). A timeline of when IT technicians are located in specific locations in the institution's footprint.

3. *Preparation*

    - **Combination and Analysis of Gathered Information**: Determine the best time slot when faculty members and IT technicians are actively located in the same location. The SE will ensure to wear the prescribed uniform of the institution's IT technician.

    - **Development of an Attack Vector**: Develop an engagement plan that detail the specific time and location of the attack. Details include the types of IT technician uniform, location of faculty member, and precise conversation script used in the attack.

4. *Develop Relationship*

    - **Establishment of Communication**: SE will engage in conversation with the faculty member. Informing the faculty member that the IT Department has to check the data communication of their data port. This is to ensure the faculty member doesn't have any unplanned network interruptions.

- **Rapport Building**: SE will engage in friendly conversation and build a relationship with the faculty member at the institution to gain their trust.

5. *Exploit Relationship*

- **Priming the Target**: SE is required to inform the faculty member that the work needs to be done so the faculty member can stay productive. This primes the target to allowing and assisting the attacker in resolving possible network issues.

- **Elicitation**: SE offers to assist the faculty member in any future IT issues that he/she might have. Provides the faculty member with a fake IT helpdesk phone number.

6. *Debrief*

- **Maintenance**: After the SE has install the MITM device and conducted the network check. The attacker informs faculty member that their network communication is OK and will not be interrupted.

- **Transition**: Attacker was able to successfully gain access to the unauthorized computerized terminal and then proceeds to the "Goal Satisfaction" step.

- **Goal Satisfaction**: SE successfully completed the initial goal of gaining unauthorized access to a computerized terminal.

All the specialized higher education social engineering attack scenarios are publicly available on open source GitLab repository [33].

V. PROPOSED SOCIAL ENGINEERING AWARENESS AND TRAINING MODELS

Current technical information security (IS) commodities have provided organizations across major industries greater capabilities in securing their information technology (IT) infrastructure. While every year there are incremental advances in IS products, they still fail to secure the human operators [26]. It is due to the expansion of technical IS solutions have pressed attackers into conducting social engineering (SE) engagements against an individual(s) of an organization [12 – 14, 20, 21, 25, 26]. The authors theorize that it is due to the lack of awareness and knowledge of SE tactics which is the main factor in increased social engineering attacks (SEA). Technical and non-technical individuals do not need to understand the weaknesses in an IT system. They need to be aware of the tactics used by attackers to circumvent the technical security systems [19 – 21, 23, 24, 26]. If a person sees something suspicious, they can report and stop the incident from escalating to compromised IT systems.

Individuals are an essential component to the IS landscape. Not only are individuals a part of the IS problem, but they are an integral part of the IS solution [12, 26]. Organizations across the industries have implemented security awareness and training solutions to enhance their organizational human security. An example is The Department of Homeland Security's (DHS): National Cybersecurity Awareness Month[12] (NCSAM). NCSAM does a great job in providing annual guidance and awareness to industries and the general public for the month of October.

The authors propose developing a High Education (HE) Awareness and Training Model similar to Mohammed et al. and Jansson et al. [13, 14] but improves upon their limitations. By incorporating specialized crafted social engineering attack (SEA) scenarios into awareness and training programs. It will greatly increase the level of preparedness in student, faculty, and employees when challenged with a SEA. In the following sections are the Higher Education Awareness and Training Models.

A. *Higher Education Awareness Lifecycle Model*

HE awareness model is tailored to 3 human domains (HD) in HE institutions. HD encompasses: (1) Students, (2) Faculty, and (3) Employees. Segmenting awareness education allows for effective absorption of the information [13]. Each HD combined together interface with varying ITs and hold varying levels of access privileges. Tailored awareness education provides each HD clarification to their defined responsibilities in their realm of influence. Method of distributing awareness materials will take the form of physical and electronic mediums. Figures 1 below detail the types of mediums:

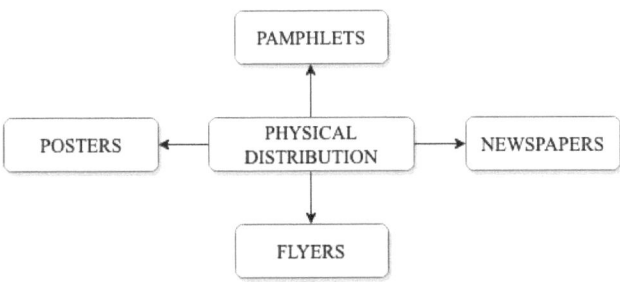

Figure 1a: Physical Distribution Medium

---

[12] https://www.cisa.gov/national-cyber-security-awareness-month

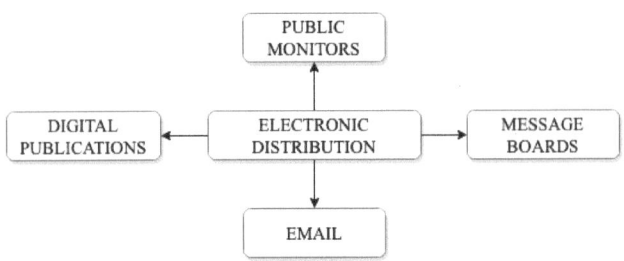

Figure 1b: Electronic Distribution Medium

Fig. 1. Awareness Training Distribution Mediums

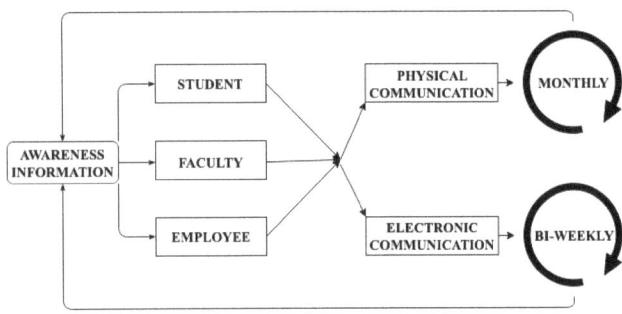

Fig. 2. Higher Education Awareness Lifecycle Model

The authors propose a continuous rotating lifecycle approach to HE awareness education. This approach can also be classified as passive learning. Awareness information is distributed but does not mandate the HD to engage with it. The proposed lifecycle tailors specialized awareness information for each HD, utilizing each communication medium, and refreshes monthly and bi-weekly. Figure 2 below details the HE Awareness Lifecycle Model:

B. Higher Education Training Lifecycle Model

Similar to the proposed HE Awareness Lifecycle Model, HE Training Lifecycle Model proposes an active learning approach. The proposed model will mandate incoming or transfer, undergraduate or graduate students, new faculty, and employees to physically participate in an IS on-boarding program with an institutional directed IS professional. The on-boarding program will provide guidance and orient individuals to the higher education's specific IT ecosystem and IS policies. Throughout the individual's duration in the institution, electronic refresher training is required. Refresher training will be conducted in a tri-annual cycle. The proposed tri-annual timeline commences January, May, and September. Training will also include review of on-boarding concepts and up-to-date SE attacks. Figure 3 details the Higher Education Training Lifecycle Model.

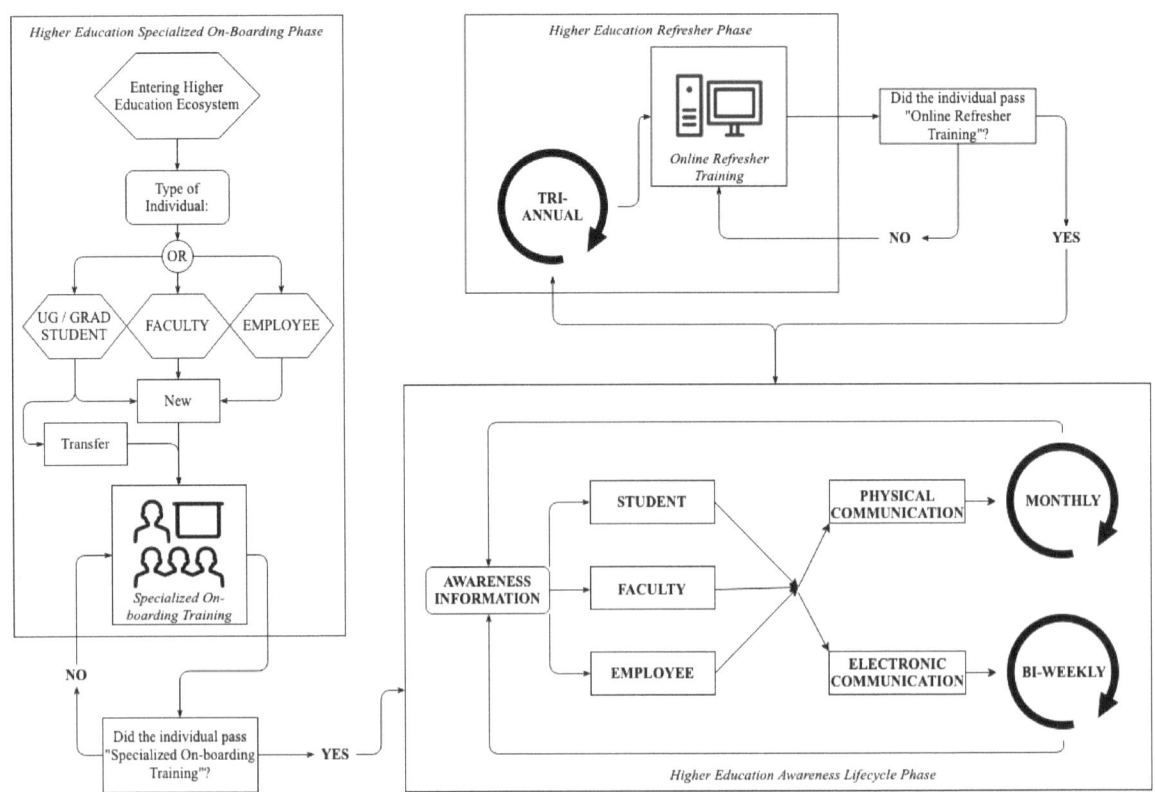

Fig. 3. Higher Education Training Lifecycle Model

VI. Discussion and Future Work

The paper proposes 9 specialized social engineering attack (SEA) scenarios focusing on the higher education (HE) landscape. These attack scenarios provide a detailed mission plan for SEAs on higher education institutions. The social engineering attack framework (SEAF) allows penetration testers and researchers to step through each phase an attacker will take in conducting a SEA. This grants penetration testers, researchers, and ethical oversight committees another tool in fulfilling their professional obligations. For penetration testers and researchers, it allows them to engage in both ethical and unethical SEA planning and research. For ethical oversight committees it allows the committee body to review the work of penetration testers and researchers so that they are within ethical standards.

The authors theorize the proposed HE social engineering awareness and training models will assist in securing the human dynamic. Through policies of continuous social engineering awareness and training, across every level of the human dynamic, HE institutions will be able to actively and passively educate an individual the moment they enter the institution's technology ecosystem until they leave. This affords HE institutions a comprehensive information security defensive formation alongside their physical security, hardware and software security technologies.

The authors realize the necessity for quantifiable data on the effectiveness of proposed HE social engineering awareness and training. With the foundation of the specialized higher education social engineering attack scenarios created, the authors propose a 3-phase methodology in gathering the data set and conduct efficiency analysis of proposed awareness/training models. In the authors' future work, the first phase is collecting a baseline awareness of social engineering concepts and techniques by conducting a pre-awareness survey [15, 16, 23, 24]. In the second phase, implement the proposed higher education awareness lifecycle to initiate passive learning on existing individuals in the ecosystem. In parallel implement the higher education training lifecycle to initiate active learning on new individuals entering the ecosystem. In the third phase, conduct a post-awareness survey [15, 16, 23, 24] to gather quantifiable data on the effectiveness of the proposed awareness and training lifecycle model.

References

[1] T. Thornburgh. Social Engineering: The "Dark Art", in Proceedings of the 1st Annual Conference on Information Security Curriculum Development, InfoSecCD Conference October 8, 2004, Kennesaw, GA, USA, 2005.

[2] F. Mouton, L. Leene, M. M. Malan and H. S. Venter. Towards an Ontological Model Defining the Social Engineering Domain, in: K.K. Kimppa et al. (Eds.): HCC11 2014, IFIP AICT 431, 2014, pp.266 – 279.

[3] F. Mouton, L. Leene, M.M. Malan and H.S. Venter. Social Engineering Attack Example, Templates and Scenarios, Computer & Security, Volume 59, 2016, pp.186-209. ISSN 0167-209. https://doi.org/10.1016/j.cose.2016.03.004.

[4] K. D. Mitnick, W. L. Simon. THE ART OF DECEPTION: Controlling the Human Element of Security, Wiley Publishing, Indianapolis, 2002.

[5] T. R. Peltier. Social Engineering: Concepts and Solutions, Information Systems Security; Nov 2006; 15, 5; ABI/INFORM Collection pg. 13.

[6] S. D. Applegate, Major. Social Engineering: Hacking the Wetware!, in Information Security Journal: A Global Perspective, 18:40-46, 2009, Taylor & Francis Group, LLC. ISSN: 1939-3555 print / 1939 – 3547 online. DOI: 10.1080/19393550802623214.

[7] R. Heartfield, G. Loukas and D. Gan. You Are Probably Not the Weakest Link: Towards Practical Prediction of Susceptibility to Semantic Social Engineering Attacks, in IEEE Access, vol. 4, pp. 6910 – 6928, 2016.

[8] M. Workman, Ph.D. Gaining Access with Social Engineering: An Empirical Study of the Threat, Information Systems Security, 16:6, 315 – 331, 2007. DOI: 10.1080/10658980701788165

[9] F. Mouton, M.M. Malan, K.K. Kimppa and H.S. Venter. Necessity for Ethics in Social Engineering Research, Computer & Security, Volume 55, 2015, pp.114 – 127. https://doi.org/10.1016/j.cose.2015.09.001

[10] J. Pierce, A. Jones, and M. Warren. Penetration Testing Professional Ethics: a conceptual model and taxonomy, in Australasian Journal of Information Systems, 13(2). 2006. https://doi.org/10.3127/ajis.v13i2.52

[11] D.B. Resnik and P.R. Finn. Ethics and Phishing Experiments, Science & Engineering Ethics, 2018, 24:1241 – 1252. https://doi.org?10.1007/s11948-017-9952-9

[12] G. Rotvold. How to Create a Security Culture in Your Organization: A recent study reveals the importance of assessment, incident response procedures, and social engineering testing in improving security awareness programs, Information Management Journal, vol. 42, no. 6, Nov-Dec, 2008, ABI/INFORM Collection, pp 32+.

[13] S. Mohammed and E. Apeh. A model for social engineering awareness program for schools, 2016 10th International Conference on Software, Knowledge, Information Management & Applications (SKIMA), Chengdu, 2016, pp. 392 – 397.

[14] K. Jansson & R. von Solms. Phishing for phishing awareness, Behavior & Information Technology, 32:6, 584-593, 2013. DOI: 10.1080/0144929X.2011.632650

[15] R.M. Groves, F.J. Fowler Jr, M.P. Couper, J.M. Lepkowski, E. Singer and R. Tourangeau. Survey Methodology. John Wiley & Sons, 2011, pp.149 – 253.

[16] T.L. Jones, M.A. Baxter, V. Khanduja. A Quick Guide to Survey Research. The Annals of The Royal College of Surgeons of England. 2013, pp.5 – 7.

[17] H. Aldawood and G. Skinner. An Advanced Taxonomy for Social Engineering Attacks. International Journal of Computer Applications. 177. 975-8887. 10.5120/ijca2020919744. Jan 2020.

[18] J. Jang-Jaccard and S. Nepal. A Survey of Emerging Threats in Cybersecurity. Journal of Computer and System Science, Volume 80, Issue 5, 2014, pp. 973 – 993, ISSN 0022-0000, https://doi.org/10.1016/j.jcss.2014.02.005

[19] E. Metalidou, C. Marinagi, P. Trivellas, N. Eberhagen, C. Skourlas and G. Giannakopoulos. The Human Factor of Information Security: Unintentional Damage Perspective. Procedia – Social and Behavioral Sciences, 147, 2014, pp. 424 – 428, DOI: 10.1016/j.sbspro.2014.07.133

[20] M. D. Richardson, P. A. Lemoine, W. E. Stephens, and R. E. Waller. Planning for Cyber Security in Schools: The Human Factor. Studies in Systems, Decision and Control, Educational Planning 2020, Vol. 27, No. 2, 2020, pp. 23 – 39, ISSN 2198-4190, https://doi.org/10.1007/978-3-030-43999-6

[21] W. Fan, K. Lwakatare and R. Rong. Social Engineering: I-E based Model of Human Weakness for Attack and Defense Investigations. I. J. Computer Network and Information Security, 2017, 1, pp. 1 – 11, DOI: 10.5815/ijcnis.2017.01.01

[22] I. Ghafir, V. Prenosil, A. Alhejailan and M. Hammoudeh. Social Engineering Attack Strategies and Defense Approaches. 2016 IEEE 4th International Conference on Future Internet of Things and Cloud, IEEE, 2016, pp. 145 – 149, DOI: 10.1109/FiCloud.2016.28

[23] H. Aldawood, T. Alashoor and G. Skinner. Does Awareness of Social Engineering Make Employees More Secure? International Journal of Computer Applications (0975 – 8887), Vol. 177, No. 38, Feb 2020.

[24] H. Aldawood and G. Skinner. Evaluating Contemporary Digital Awareness Programs for Future Application within the Cyber Security Social Engineering Domain. International Journal of Computer Applications (0975 – 8887), Vol. 177, No. 31, Jan 2020.

[25] H. Aldawood and G. Skinner. Analysis and Findings of Social Engineering Industry Experts Explorative Interviews: Perspectives on Measures, Tools and Solutions. IEEE Access, DOI: 10.1109/ACCESS.2020.2983280

[26] I. Corradini. Building a Cybersecurity Culture in Organizations, Chapter 3: Redefining the Approach to Cybersecurity. Studies in Systems, Decision, and Control 284, pp. 49 – 62, https://doi.org/10.1007/978-3-030-43999-6_3

[27] National Cyber Security Centre. The cyber threat to Universities. https://www.ncsc.gov.uk/report/the-cyber-threat-to-universities, Sep 2019, (Accessed 02/21/2020).

[28] PurpleSec LLC. The Ultimate List of Cyber Security Statistics For 2019. https://purplesec.us/resources/cyber-security-statistics/#Education, (Accessed 07/09/2020).

[29] BlackFog, Inc. The State of Ransomware in 2020. https://www.blackfog.com/the-state-of-ransomware-in-2020/, (Accessed 07/09/2020).

[30] B. Freed. Michigan State hit by ransomware threatening leak of student and financial data. https://edscoop.com/michigan-state-hit-by-ransomware-threatening-leak-of-student-and-financial-data/, EDSCOOP, May 2020, (Accessed 07/09/2020).

[31] C. Osborne. University of California SF pays ransomware hackers $1.14 million to salvage research: The malware infected crucial research stored in the UCSF medical school's network. https://www.zdnet.com/article/university-of-california-sf-pays-ransomware-hackers-1-14-million-to-salvage-research/#ftag=CAD-03-10abf5f, Jun 2020, (Accessed 07/09/2020).

[32] P. Waldie, C. Freeze. https://www.theglobeandmail.com/canada/article-four-canadian-military-schools-affected-by-cyberattack/, Jul 2020, (Accessed 07/09/2020)

[33] T. Nguyen. https://gitlab.com/chuck_x_chuck/social-engineering-attack-scenarios/, (Accessed 03/14/2020).

Applied Cyber Security for Applied Software Engineering Undergraduate Program

Yulia Cherdantseva, PhD
Cardiff University
UK
cherdantsevayv@cardiff.ac.uk

Phil Smart, PhD
Jisc
UK
philip.smart@jisc.ac.uk

Abstract—In the current landscape where a constantly growing number of cyber threats is accompanied by the increasing shortage of cyber security professionals, it is essential to provide a well thought-out hands-on cyber security education as a part of all Computer Science and Software Engineering degrees. This paper described the experience of designing and delivering a Cyber Security module to Level 5 students on a three-year BSc Applied Software Engineering program. The key goal of the module is to instil the importance of cyber security in software development, and to teach in practice modern security techniques. While being predominantly focused on web-application security, the module also covers foundational cyber security concepts, cryptography and network security, and discusses non-technical topics including security frameworks and security economics. The paper presents the outline of the module, the configuration of the virtual machine used, the structure and content of sessions, and student feedback.

Keywords—cyber security education, software engineering, web-application security

I. INTRODUCTION

"Knowledge isn't power until it is applied."

Dale Carnegie

Modern society at large and each of us individually need secure and trustworthy information systems. A workforce educated in cyber security is the key to building such systems. However, for the past several years reports on cyber security workforce have been showing a significant shortage of cyber security professionals as well as the lack of cyber security skills among IT professionals. At the end of 2016, 82% of employers globally admitted a shortage of cyber security skills; the global cyber security workforce shortfall is predicted to hit 1.8 million positions by 2022 [1].

A cyber security capability gap is recognized by academia, professional societies, and governments across the world, and there are various initiatives to address this gap. In 2017, professional societies including the Association for Computing Machinery (ACM) and the IEEE Computer Society (IEEE-CS) released university curriculum guidelines for cybersecurity degrees – CSEC 2017 [2]. In 2018, UK government published an Initial National Cyber Security Skills Strategy for public review and is currently considering the views collected before publishing the final strategy in the near future [3] .

In the US, the National Security Agency support and recognise Centers of Academic Excellence in Cyber Defense and Cyber Operations in order to advance cybersecurity skills [4]. In the UK, National Cyber Security Centre (NCSC) provides certification for cyber security degrees in Higher Education (HE), and has recently launched a new program for the Academic Centres of Excellence in Cyber Security Education encouraging broader commitment to cyber security teaching [5].

In the current landscape when a constantly growing number of cyber threats is accompanied by an increasing shortage of cyber security professionals, it is essential to provide a well thought-out hands-on cyber security education as a part of all Computer Science and Software Engineering degrees in HE. In this paper, we describe our experience of designing and delivering a Cyber Security module to Level 5 students on a three-year BSc Applied Software Engineering program at the National Software Academy, Cardiff University, UK (NSA-CU). The BSc program commenced in 2016 with the first cohort of students graduated in 2018.

The NSA-CU is a part of the School of Computer Science & Informatics at Cardiff University and is a center of excellence for software engineering education in Wales, UK. We adopted innovative industry-oriented teaching approach throughout curriculum. The NSA-CU works in partnership with the Welsh Government and industry leaders producing a supply of skilled, workplace-ready software engineering graduates.

The NSA-CU is driven by a *"learning by doing"* ethos strongly relying on project-based learning with continuous support from a wide range of industry partners from different domains. Every semester during this three-year program students participate in industry-led educational software development projects of progressing complexity. The projects are carefully chosen by academic staff to align with the learning objectives of modules in each semester. Industry partners set project requirements, run regular meetings with students in small groups to gauge progress and finally provide feedback for a final product which contributes to assessments. Industry experts regularly deliver guest sessions to our students. For example, for the cyber security module over the past three years guest sessions were delivered on the topics including, but not limited to GDPR, malware analysis, DDoS attacks, law and regulations, and penetration testing.

The rest of this paper is organized as follows. Section II provides an outline of the module. Section III describes the configuration of a virtual machine used in practical sessions. Section IV covers a set of hand-on exercises included in the module. Section V presents student feedback for the module, while Section VI contains concluding remarks and sketches the direction for future work.

II. MODULE OUTLINE

The module design was guided by Biggs' "Constructive Alignment" where all teaching components are integrated and tuned to support high-level learning [6]. The Intended Learning Outcomes (ILOs), which are listed below, are defined using active verbs and refer to action that could be verified empirically:

- ILO1: Appropriately use the key security concepts and terminology associated with the covered security topics in discussions and writing
- ILO2: Implement a range of countermeasures to secure a web-application
- ILO3: Implement appropriate database systems security countermeasures
- ILO4: Encrypt data in transit
- ILO5: Perform penetration testing of a web-application and produce a penetration testing report
- ILO6: Employ a range of techniques to secure network communications
- ILO7: Independently research a known security vulnerability and implement an appropriate solution for it
- ILO8: Be aware of cyber security standards and regulations, and understand the role of non-technical factors in cyber security

Teaching activities and assessments are closely aligned with the ILOs and designed to achieve them. ILOs are explained to the students. Each assessment has a set of ILOs associated with it. Related ILOs are explained to students at the beginning of each new topic/session helping students to gauge their progress better.

The Cyber Security module is delivered over the period of 11 weeks during 22 sessions, each being 2.5 hours long. In each session, a range of teaching methods takes place including traditional lectures; group and individual practical coding exercises, discussions, brainstorming, presentations; independent student research; planning; reflection; knowledge tests, and Q&A sessions. During each 2.5-hour session, we typically use a mix of activities switching approximately every 20 minutes. The "change up" approach [7] avoids interest loss that students typically experience as a lecture progresses, allows splitting material into manageable chunks, and gives them a chance to practice thinking about new concepts [8]. As an example, one of the activities is for students to research and present - while working in small groups - a recent cyber security incident (students are offered options to choose from). A discussion is then held about what could be learnt from each incident and how it could be prevented.

As the initial part of this module, students conduct a range of labs on the topics of database security, cryptography, and network security. The knowledge is then assessed by a class test. After that, students learn to pen-test and secure web-applications. The progress is assessed via a web-application security portfolio.

In this Cyber Security module, which is delivered during the Spring (second) semester, students work on securing web-applications they have developed for industry clients in the previous semester. The examples of projects include a token system for volunteers, an attendance monitoring system for sport clubs, a system to monitor behaviour of people with mild anxiety problems, a pilot training booking system, etc. Students work on projects in small groups of 3 or 4. Each software development project is a web-based system with a three-tier architecture: a MySQL database at the back end, a Java-based middle-tier developed using the Spring Boot framework which simplifies the creation of stand-alone enterprise-ready Spring-based applications and a presentation tier implemented with HTML/CSS/Java Script/JQuery. Students have solid programming skills in Java, which they developed during Year 1 and in the Autumn semester of Year 2. Students also undertake a Database Systems module focusing on relational databases in the Autumn semester preceding the Cyber Security module. Business logic may be implemented either in the database layer, or in the application layer based on a group's decision and the projects requirements. The front-end implementation varies from project to project as it is not dictated by assessment requirements, but is typically based on Thymeleaf, a server-side Java template engine for web environments. Students work on individual laptops which they receive for the duration of each academic year. All required software is preinstalled and configured in preparation for teaching. Students work in modern facilities with a start-up feel and look, providing flexibility and allowing students to work comfortably in small group.

The module is assessed via an automated class test in Week 5 and an individual web-application security portfolio due at the end of the module. A detailed discussion of the assessment methods is out of the scope of this paper.

The module is delivered by the authors of the paper, one of whom is an academic member of staff and a researcher in the field of Cyber Security, and another is a Trust and Identity Technical Expert at Jisc – a not-for-profit organisation providing digital services and solutions for higher, further education and skills sectors in the UK. The involvement of an industry expert in the development and delivery of the module further contributes to the practice-informed learning model [9] followed by the NSA-CU and provides multiple benefits to students that include, but not limited to developing a better understanding of cyber security practices, improving transferable skills and building professional relationships. The benefits of practice-informed learning for students, organisations and HE are extensively discussed in [9].

III. VIRTUAL LAB

Virtualization technologies are actively used for teaching Cyber Security. The most prominent example of a freely available pre-configured educational virtual cyber security lab environment accompanied by a set of practical exercises covering a wide range of cyber security topics is the SEED project that is active since 2002 [10].

In our approach to a virtual lab, we have been inspired by the SEED project. We adopted and extended SEED Ubuntu 16.04 VM with additional software in order to mimic the development environment that our students have on their laptops and to support practical exercises that we developed at Cardiff University. This approach allows our students to benefit from all exercises freely offered within the SEED project which are based on the SEED Ubuntu VM, in addition to the labs developed at Cardiff University that we offer to students. Students could develop, run and pen-test their web-applications within the VM as well as on their host machines.

The following additional software packages were installed on the VM: IntelliJ IDEA (Community Edition), Firefox with Live HTTP Headers and Cookies Manager extensions for examining and managing cookies, Burp suite for conducting brute force attacks, Fail2Ban used to ban IP addresses and limit login attempts for locally deployed web-applications, Ettercap to simulate a DDoS attack on a web-application on one of the local VMs, SQLmap to perform SQL injections attacks automatically, MySQL Workbench for a database user management exercise. All software installed is open-source and free. Oracle VM VirtualBox open-source hosted hypervisor is used for virtualization.

For most exercises on web-application security, a single VM is sufficient. For the exercises on network security and database replication multiple VMs are required. The VM(s) are deployed using a host-only network so that VMs can communicate between themselves, but are isolated from the campus network or the public Internet ensuring that no damage is accidentally caused. Students are instructed on the secure use of VMs and of all software provided, and their responsibility according to the Computer Misuse Act 1990.

IV. SESSIONS CONTENT AND HANDS-ON EXERCISES

Each session includes practical learning activities that turn declarative knowledge into functional knowledge and ensure that students acquire essential technical skills. We developed detailed step-by-step student lab manuals for most sessions, but the work is still ongoing to ensure their relevance in the current cyber security landscape. Each manual contains (a) background information required for an exercise, (b) explains ILOs addressed, (c) provides a step-by-step walkthrough for the exercise accompanied by screenshots and explanations, (d) outlines a set of revision questions, and (e) suggests alternative experiments.

The module begins with the introduction to cyber security, where the key concepts are covered and the foundational principles of the growing ISO/IEC 27000 family of standards. Students are encouraged to self-study ISO/IEC 27001 (ILO8).

To ensure continuity between modules within the program, we pick up from the Database Systems module taught in the previous semester and cover such aspects of database security as user management, secure storage of passwords, and database backup and replication. The practical exercises on encryption algorithms and hashing are demonstrated within a DBMS. During the Database Replication lab students configure a MySQL replica set with one master and one slave. The slave server is setup to replicate the master server's database by connecting to the IP address of the master. Once configured the slave server asynchronously checks the master server for updates to the database/s, as soon as there is a change the slave copies the change to its own database(s). This lab addresses ILO3 (Section II).

In the sessions on Network Security we cover the basics of network connectivity, core protocols and concepts from the TCP/IP stack, subnetting, and typical tools including ifconfig, nmcli, netstat, arp utility. In one of the exercises, students set up two VMs to communicate via ping messages, and then modify the Address Resolution Protocol (ARP) table on one VM to investigate the relationship between the IP and MAC addresses on a machine. Students also use Wireshark for network communication analysis examining all embedded layers of network frames, including IP packets, TCP segments and HTTP messages. It is invaluable to understand how network communication is achieved in order to learn how network traffic could be manipulated and protected. Firewall configuration is examined too. The above listed sessions address ILO6.

For the web-application security sessions (ILO2, ILO5) we developed an insecure vulnerable Java web-application for an imaginary company called BetterBuy who sells stationery and furniture online. The BetterBuy web-app is implemented using a three-tier architecture similar to the students' projects described in Section II. We have two versions of the application one implemented using JSP technologies and another as a Spring Boot application with JSF technologies. The latter BetterBuy application utilises Spring Boot for easy configuration of libraries, e.g. Tomcat and JSF mainly for the front-end representation and expression language it offers. In the development of sessions on web-app security we were guided by the Open Web Application Security Project (OWASP) Top Ten vulnerabilities [11].

The app is deployed locally within the VM and available using its own hostname www.betterbuy.com creating an illusion that students access it on the Internet. Our setting ensure that it is safe for students to pen-test the app and explore the inbuilt vulnerabilities. The code of the BeterBuy app is also available on the VMs and students can run the app on localhost and explore the runtime audit logs and error messages in IntellyJ IDEA, as well as observe the changes propagated to the MySQL database using MySQL Workbench. For example, among other vulnerabilities, we use the app for demonstrating SQL and JavaScript injections, direct-object reference vulnerabilities, insufficient user input validation, information leakage, and insufficient logging and monitoring.

During the session on securing data in transit, students employ pen-testing techniques using Wireshark to sniff unencrypted network traffic, including usernames and passwords, between their user-agent (browsers) and the web-server. In mitigation, students, then, learn how to configure an encrypted HTTPS connection for the application. Further, using Wireshark (or tshark/tcpdump), students examine traffic between the web-application server and a database server (each located on a different VMs) establishing that all commands sent to the database server are transmitted in plain text. Students then learn to set up an encrypted connection between the web-server and the database server as follows: enabling SSL Connection on MySQL Server with OpenSSL, creating a MySQL account that will require SSL, and configuring an SSL connection to MySQL in the Spring Boot Application.

In the summer 2018, we run an 8-week student project as one of the Cardiff University Student Education Innovation Projects (CUSEIP). Under supervision, a year 1 student was involved in setting up the VM adhering to the requirements of the NSA-CU and in the development of lab manuals for four sessions on web-application security including the following topics: user input validation, securing data in transit, authentication and authorization. The involvement of a student helped us to ensure that the material in the lab manual presented at the level accessible for the target audience. This project further contributed to student-led teaching when the student provided help and support to peers.

V. STUDENT SATISFACTION AND FEEDBACK

At the end of each semester, the NSA-CU runs module evaluation for each module. The Cyber Security module has received high scores of satisfactions from our students in 2017/18 and 2018/19 academic years. The feedback is provided by students using a Likert scale "Definitely Disagree" – "Mostly Disagree" – "Neither Agree nor Disagree" – "Mostly Agree" – "Definitely Agree" with the values 1 to 5 assigned to the answers respectively. Figure 1 shows consistently high average score of 4.41.

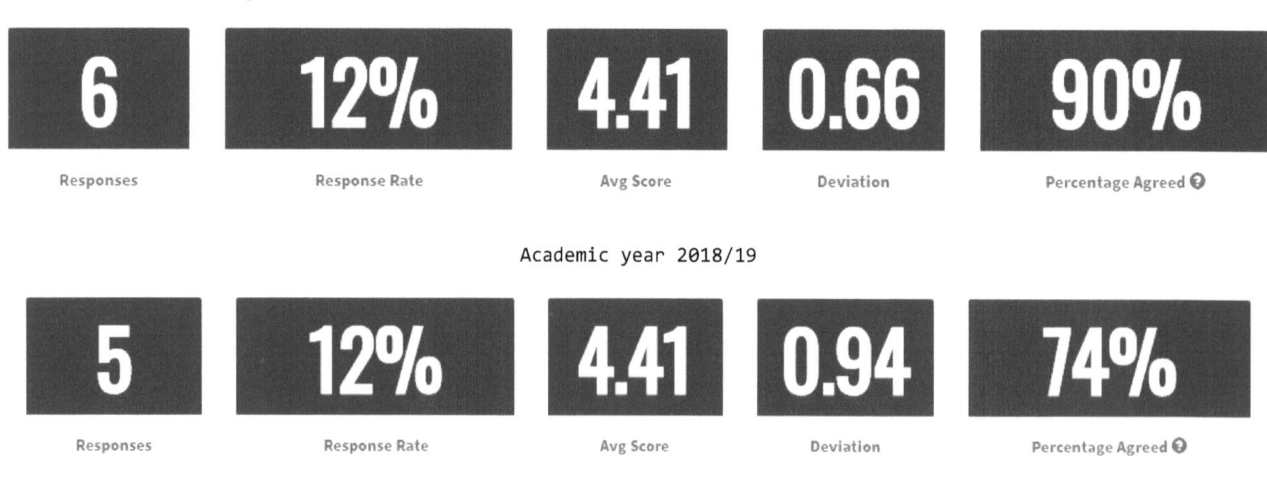

Fig. 1. Summary of Module Evaluation Data

In the module evaluation survey, students answer questions about Teaching and Learning, Assessment and Feedback, Organisation and Management, Learning Resources, Learning Community, Student Voice and rate their Overall Satisfaction. According to the student feedback in 2017/18 regarding Teaching and Academic Support 4 students choose "Mostly Agree" and 2 students - "Defiantly Agree" when rating their attitude towards the statement "*The module met my expectations in terms of the knowledge I have gained*". Figure 2 shows the answers in the section Teaching and Academic Support for 2017/18. Figure 3 shows the answers in the section Teaching and Learning provided in 2018/19.

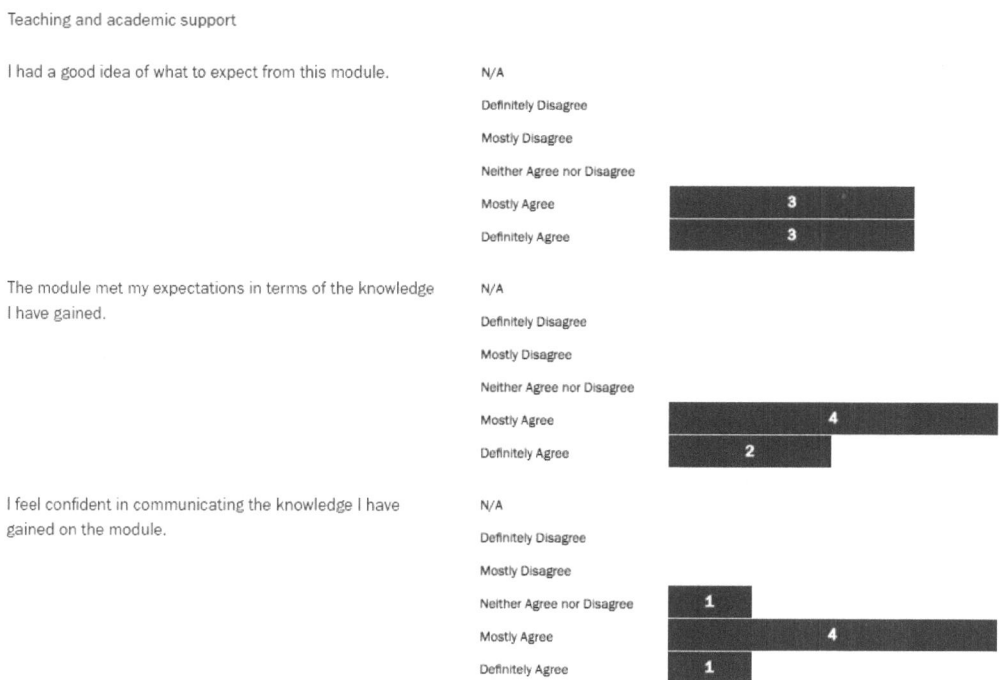

Fig. 2. Student Feedback on Teaching and Academic Support 2017/18

Fig. 3. Student Feedback on Teaching and Learning 2018/19

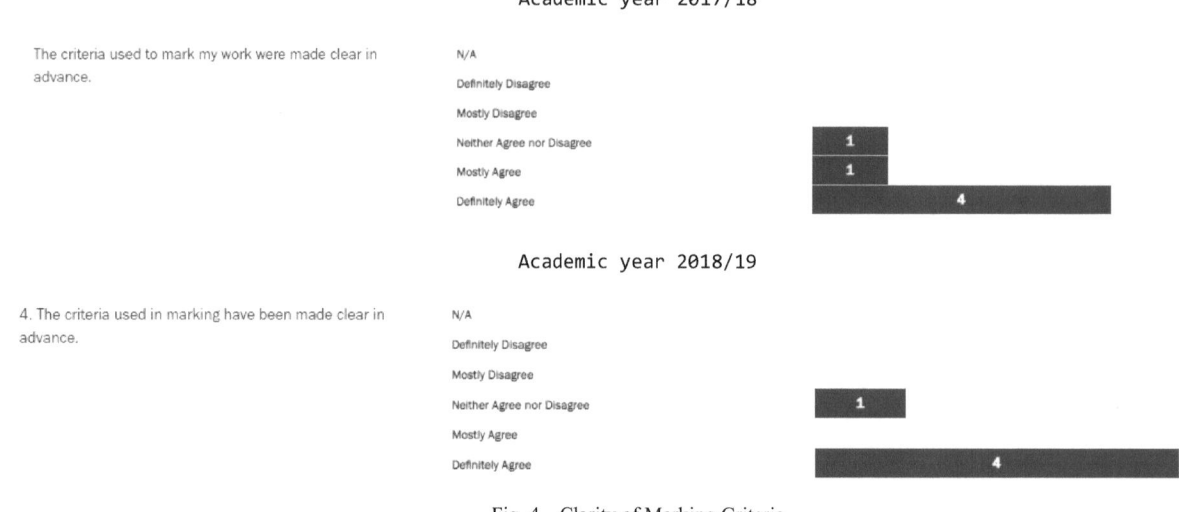

Fig. 4. Clarity of Marking Criteria

Figure 4 shows a consistent level of agreement with the statement "*The criteria used to mark my work were made clear in advance*" for 2017/18 and 2018/19.

In 2017/18 and 2018/19, in their feedback students indicated that they liked the following about the module:

- ✓ The teaching material was very clear and the guest speakers gave very good insight;
- ✓ Lots of practical exercises;
- ✓ Fun to learn about how to secure an application. The powerpoints were very detailed and great for referring back to and helped me a lot with my coursework;
- ✓ Made very interesting, hands-on and relevant. Well taught and lots of resources available;
- ✓ I liked the use of recordings to help students re-look over past lessons to relearn key things;
- ✓ Good range of guest speakers for related topics;
- ✓ Good feedback;
- ✓ The lectures were fun and taught me a lot. this was a mostly perfect module for me, the courseworks are perfect and well explained;
- ✓ The lecturer is engaging, which helps when covering particularly dry topics.

Among the things that the students would like to change about the modules the following suggestions have been listed:

- ✓ More help sessions;
- ✓ It would be nice to have more lab sessions using pen test tools like Metasploit;
- ✓ More time to cover the material;
- ✓ More time given for final project portfolio from lecture content delivery required to complete assessment;
- ✓ Other web application security examples for non-server-side templating applications.

All suggestions are considered during annual module review and reasonable adjustments are made.

Unfortunately, we do not have quantitative evaluation data in the same format for 2019-2020. However, one of our students have provided a video feedback for the module where the student said: "*This module was definitely one of my favorite in the second year of this course, I learnt so much about security which helped me to realize the effort that is going into securing a web-application, and above all, the benefits and the importance of implementing web-security. Having learnt some of the vulnerabilities in cyber security, it has made me more aware and now I believe I have sufficient knowledge and understanding and the skills into implementing and strengthening the security of a web-application.*" The video is available on request.

We hope that the feedback discussed above including the evaluation comments from our students will aid the reader in determining the value of reproduction and adoption of the module structure and material.

VI. CONCLUDING REMARKS AND WAY FORWARD

In this paper, we shared our experience with developing and delivering the Cyber Security module. In future, we plan to work further on the automated deployment of security VMs using system container technologies, such as the Docker platform and Vagrant. These technologies are already taught at the NSA-CU in the DevOps module, and using this valuable knowledge and skills within the Cyber Security module will be beneficial for students. This will also reduce time spent by students on performing VMs restoration and network configuration.

From the beginning, we aimed to develop detailed and complete lab manuals for every lab, however, we feel that lab manuals will benefit from going through multiple development cycles for improving clarity and accessibility of the material. We anticipate that the practical exercises we developed may be used in other security modules within Cardiff University and beyond. We hope that producing more hands-on cyber security teaching material will contribute to tackling the cyber security skills gap and the worldwide shortage of cybers security professionals.

ACKNOWLEDGEMENTS

We would like to thank our former student Ieuan Jones for help with the development of the lab manuals for web-application security sessions, and with setting up the VM, and our colleague Carl Jones for help with the development of the BetterBuy web-application.

REFERENCES

[1] W. Crumpler and J. A. Lewis, "The Cybersecurity Workforce Gap," CSIS, 2019.

[2] ACM, IEEE-CS, AIS SIGSEC, IFIP WG 11.8, "Curriculum Guidelines for Post-Secondary. Version 1.0 Report," 2017. [Online] Available: https://www.acm.org/binaries/content/assets/education/curricula-recommendations/csec2017.pdf

[3] H. Govenment, "INITIAL NATIONAL CYBER SECURITY SKILLS STRATEGY," A CALL FOR VIEWS. [Online]. Available: https://www.gov.uk/government/publications/cyber-security-skills-strategy. [Accessed 29 01 2020].

[4] NSA|CSS, "National Centers of Academic Excellence," [Online]. Available: https://www.nsa.gov/resources/students-educators/centers-academic-excellence/. [Accessed 29 01 2020].

[5] C. E., "Launch of the Academic Centres of Excellence in Cyber Security Education.," 23 January 2020. [Online]. Available: https://www.ncsc.gov.uk/blog-post/launch-of-the-academic-centres-of-excellence-in-cyber-security-education. [Accessed 24 01 2020].

[6] J. B. Biggs, Teaching for quality learning at university: What the student does., McGraw-Hill Education (UK)., 2011.

[7] Middendorf, J., & Kalish, A., "The "change-up" in lectures.," *In Natl. Teach. Learn. Forum*, vol. 5, no. 2, pp. 1-5, 1996.

[8] Verner, C., & Dickinson, "The lecture, an analysis and review of research.," *Adult Education*, , vol. 17, no. 2, pp. 90-91, 1967.

[9] GuildHE, "Practice-Informed Learning: The Rise of the Dual Professional," 2018. https://guildhe.ac.uk/wp-content/uploads/2018/11/Practice-Informed_Learning_Final_Nov_18.pdf [Accessed 29 01 2020].

[10] Wenliang Du, "SEED: Hands-On Lab Exercises for Computer Security Education," *IEEE Security & Privacy*, vol. 9, no. 5, pp. 70-73, 2011.

[11] OWASP, "OWASP Top Ten," [Online]. Available: https://owasp.org/www-project-top-ten/. [Accessed 29 01 2020].

Quantum Cryptography Exercise Schedules with Concept Dependencies

Abhishek Parakh
University of Nebraska, Omaha
Omaha, USA
aparakh@unomaha.edu

Vidya Bommanapally
University of Nebraska, Omaha
Omaha, USA
vbommanapally@unomaha.edu

Parvathi Chundi
University of Nebraska, Omaha
Omaha, USA
pchundi@unomaha.edu

Mahadevan Subramaniam
University of Nebraska, Omaha
Omaha, USA
msubramaniam@unomaha.edu

Abstract—The design of a gamified instructional paradigm requires careful identification of concepts, concept dependencies, and concept flow in order to achieve maximum student proficiency, in a subject matter, while maintaining engagement. This is especially true for difficult and counter-intuitive fields such as quantum cryptography. In this paper, we present an abstraction of concepts that are needed to learn quantum key distribution in a gamified environment. This is coupled with a powerful adaptive navigation algorithm that guides students from one exercise to the next in the game such that maximum proficiency is achieved in various concepts associated with each exercise. The student traverses through different lessons in the game achieving the lesson outcomes in an efficient manner. This represents the first of its kind abstraction of quantum cryptography concepts and a navigation algorithm for a gamified paradigm.

Keywords—serious games, engagement, exercise schedules, quantum cryptography

I. Introduction

In recent years gamification has become a trend covering a broad spectrum of multidisciplinary fields such as education, healthcare, defense, corporate training and advertising [1, 2]. Serious games have many definitions, the popular gist being games with a learning element along with an entertainment element [1, 2, 3]. [2] lists the advantages of serious games in various fields such as dance-pad for improving physical fitness through games, games for the purpose of rehabilitation, training games in corporate industry to minimize the teaching or the equipment costs and in education for improving logical thinking and so on. One of the challenging aspects of serious games is maintaining the player engagement, during the game, that might impact the learning outcomes [4][8-10, 21]. One of the factors that might affect the engagement is the cognitive load or application of knowledge. This is often related to design of exercises within the game and the distribution of relevant concepts, to be learnt, over these exercises [18, 19]. Failure to properly design the game may lead to lower engagement scores and lead to students spending long periods of time in navigational issues going from one exercise to the next. Navigational hints are a way of improving learning of player in the games also help in maintaining engagement [6] [7]. There are many ways to measure engagement of players in serious games depending on the game goals and various aspects inside the game [5].

Enhancing player learning abilities in serious games has become an area of research. In [11], authors try to enhance the learning ability of the players by implementing a pedagogical agent along with video tutorials in the game. These agents act as interactive assistants during the game play directing the player by providing necessary support through hints. [12] provides a design strategy for incorporating hints into the games where players leave the self-explanatory hints for the future players. [13] provides how serious games help in design and planning of a project to avoid accidents at workplace using a safedesign game.

An important feature of serious games is to adaptively improve the player performance [14]. The authors in [14] developed a virtual reality game to teach social engineering which assesses the player's performance by providing hints adaptively. Another way of adaptively improving the efficiency of the player is that prior game data is analyzed and hints are provided based on the current player performance [15] as well as update the assessments in the game dynamically. The authors used Bayesian network which is fed with the players game data, according to the data hints or feedback is provided in the help panel.

Quantum computing and cryptography is a growing field but remains inaccessible to a vast swath of student population because of the lack of courses at Universities and the lack of opportunities for hands-on training and experience. Given that this is a demanding field at the intersection of several disciplines such as computer science, Physics, mathematics and cybersecurity, it is difficult to maintain student interest, engagement and retention. One of the major challenges faced by educators, in this field, is the determination of appropriate breakdown of concepts and lessons and the flow between these concepts and lessons that must be followed for students, particularly, in a cybersecurity program. Multiple textbooks exist but most are written for students with strong Math, and Physics backgrounds. Furthermore, the flow that works in a textbook and traditional classroom setting does not necessarily translate to a gaming environment designed for teaching. This paper bridges this gap and presents a possible breakdown of concepts and lessons that may be used to develop a gaming environment for teaching quantum cryptography to cybersecurity students. Furthermore, we also present a navigation algorithm that can be used to direct a student between these concepts and lessons in order to gain proficiency in the subject. This flow was implemented and tested in an immersive gamified educational environment called QuaSim [11, 16, 17, 25, 26].

In a previous paper [7], the authors presented preliminary results on this concept flow graph. The previous results measured learning and engagement potential of the players in QuaSim using the knowledge concepts associated with the game and the player history. The paper attempted to improve the engagement and learning potential of the player by providing navigation hints thereby avoiding distractions to the player. [7] also introduced the concepts of hints in three different modes – manual, semi-automatic and automatic hints. In [7] QuaSim provided hints for the next exercise assuming the concepts that lead to learning goal in the game are independent of each other. In other words, we assumed that it is not required for the player to solve an exercise prior to solving another exercise. Each exercise has a value associated with it which determines the possibility of suggesting it as a next exercise to the player with reference to engagement potential. Exercises with new concepts (not yet encountered/solved by the player) in the current game session are given higher values and thus represent a higher engagement potential. Such exercises are suggested to the player iteratively. While, simultaneously learning potential is measured with respect to number of attempts the player takes before solving the exercise correctly. This paper, in part, presents further refinement of our previous results. In particular, we note that more often than not the concepts used and learned in one exercise depend on those in other exercises which may be deemed as pre-requisites by educators. In such cases, the next exercise maximizing the value metric must be chosen while taking these dependencies into account. This paper presents a novel algorithm that takes these dependencies into account while navigating through a landscape of concepts and lessons that are dependent on one another.

The paper structure is as follows: Section II discusses the guiding principles followed in identification of concepts and the abstract design of the game for quantum cryptography, Section III discusses our dynamic navigation procedure for traversing a concept graph for quantum cryptography, Section IV presents an overview of our game QuaSim and our updated navigation procedure with dependencies, Section V brings all the finer details together into a higher level view describing the various lesson dependencies in the game and Section VI concludes the paper.

II. A Systemic Approach to Teaching Quantum Cryptography

We distilled and identified the necessary concepts from quantum cryptography that a cybersecurity student needs to learn and internalize in order to understand the field. In doing so we employed a five-part model, called the Vowel Model, to develop the lesson plans [17]. This model helps to create learning efficiency and depth of content. The Vowel model consists of five instructional elements as described below:

A – Asking: In this first phase, the students can ask and get asked questions that are fundamental to completing a specific task, such as creating a quantum bit. This dialog phase allows for the creation of a testable hypotheses with a gaming environment for a cybersecurity student.

E – Exploring: The student is allowed to explore an immersive gaming environment and consult the oracle in the game to gain information about the challenge to be completed. This allows for the student to freely learn the content of a lesson before a formally structured instruction is delivered. This allows for the student to gain experience through trial and error and trying out different gaming elements.

I – Instruction: This allows for a formal instructional setting where the student in exposed to necessary concepts and ideas and completion of notational and symbolic exercises. This allows for the integration of important topics and demonstrate examples within the context of cybersecurity.

O – Organizing: This phase can be understood as a guided practice phase where the student actively engages with the game, completing gaming activities and exercises. The student often loops back to the Asking phase thereby addressing some of the early questions now based on formal instruction.

U – Understanding: This allows for the instructor to measure student progress in the game and proficiency in different concepts as the student attempts more and more exercises and proceeds through different lessons (levels) within the game.

A. Concepts, Exercises, and Schedules

Quantum cryptography involves an interplay of concepts from different inter-disciplinary domains including physics, mathematics, and computer security with subtle dependencies. A systematic approach including the organization of concepts, design of related exercises and a navigation approach enabling students to achieve proficiency in a stepwise fashion is crucial for effective instruction in this area. Such an approach can be adapted for several instruction modes including classroom lectures, educational games, and game-based teaching.

Informally we define a *quantum cryptography concept* (qcc) to be an indivisible unit of knowledge with a clearly stated learning objective(s) that are achievable by performing exercises and the learning progress (proficiency) can be assessed objectively. A qcc C is said to depend on qcc D if in order to achieve proficiency in C it is necessary to achieve proficiency in the concept D. A concept depends on a group of concepts if achieving proficiency in each member of the group is required to achieve proficiency on that concept. Quantum cryptography game unit consists of a set of $qccs$, $C = \{c_1, c_2, ..., c_k\}$ along with a set of exercises $E = \{e_1, e_2, ..., e_n\}$ that are designed to achieve proficiency over all the $qccs$ in C. Achieving proficiency in all the $qccs$ of C will result in meeting the learning objectives of the related unit. Each exercise in E is associated with one or more $qccs$ from C. Relevancy of concepts to exercises is given by a tuple $R(e_i)$ which gives all the concepts that are hosted by an exercise e_i. Also, $E(c_j)$ gives the set of exercises which host a concept c_j. Note that each exercise can involve multiple concepts and a concept can be associated with multiple exercises. However, for any two concepts c_j and c_k and exercise e_i, if the two concepts belong to $R(e_i)$ then c_j and c_k must be independent of each other. Similarly, the sets of exercises hosting two dependent concepts must be disjoint. To measure the *concept proficiency*, each concept c_j is assigned a numeric value of 1 if the player successfully solves an exercise where the concept c_j resides else it is assigned with 0. The learning goal is measured as game unit proficiency $P(C)$ which is the Boolean tuple of concept proficiencies in all the concepts in C initially assigned with a value 0 for each concept. Hence, the player is said to achieve the learning goal if all the values in the tuple are 1.

The dependency among concepts introduces a dependency among the related exercises (see next subsection) and the order in which these exercises can be scheduled for a learner in a gaming session. For instance, if any qcc hosted by exercise e_j depends on that hosted by e_i then exercise e_i must be scheduled before exercise e_j. Several schedules of exercises are possible for a quantum cryptography game unit involving multiple concepts and multiple exercises. In order to achieve learning objectives in a robust manner devising schedules that can be completed with reasonable effort is crucial. Given potential variability in the learning styles and the uneven learning rates of learners, a navigation algorithm is described below to dynamically adapt schedules for individual learners.

III. Adaptive Dynamic Navigation Procedure

The navigation algorithm helps the player to navigate through the exercise space while maintaining engagement, and frustration is minimized. The next exercise is proposed to the learner based on a numerical value calculated for each exercise in the game unit. This is an iterative algorithm where the value of each exercise is calculated at every iteration. The value is calculated using,

$$v_i = \langle \frac{1}{|E(c_j)|}, c_j \in R(e_i) \rangle \quad (1)$$

The value of each exercise is a tuple of values for each concept giving number of exercises the concept is relevant in. This value shows how essential is it to solve that exercise with respect to the concept and available exercises that cover the concept. The concept relevancy in all other exercises is updated with all the concepts that player has achieved proficiency in by setting the value to 0 as that concept is no more relevant to that exercise being achieved proficiency already. Also, the scenario proficiency is updated by assigning value 1 to the concepts where player achieved proficiency thereby tracking how far the player is from achieving the learning goal.

The above simple iterative procedure is sufficient to create customized dynamic schedule of exercises if there are no dependencies among the concepts in the schedule. When there exists dependency among the concepts, then an exercise involving a concept can be scheduled only after the learner has completed at least one exercise involving each of the concepts on which the original concept depends upon. A *concept graph* is a directed graph which represents relation between the concepts. There exists an edge from $c_1 \rightarrow c_2$ if concept c_2 is dependent on c_1. Using the concept graph and the set of tuples $R(e)$ relevant concepts for each exercise, an exercise graph is derived which is a directed graph. There exists an edge from $e_1 \rightarrow e_2$ if at least one concept in $R(e_2)$ depends on at least one concept in $R(e_1)$.

To select the next best exercise to the player taking into consideration the dependency among the concepts, edge weights are used. The value of each exercise (node value) is calculated using (1). The edge weight is calculated using the notion of *dependency overlap* and the *node value*. A *dependency overlap* from exercise e_i to e_j, $d(e_i, e_j)$ is

$$d(e_i, e_j) = N_{ji} - \delta * NR_{ji} \quad (2)$$

N_{ji} = number of concepts in e_j depending on a concept of e_i

NR_{ji} = number of concepts common between e_j and e_i

δ = redundancy factor.

The dependency overlap $d(e_i, e_j)$ allows us to pick the next exercise node e_j such that maximum number of required dependencies among the concepts in e_j are met while minimizing the repetitive learning of concepts across the exercises e_i and e_j. For example, suppose $R(e_i) = \{a, b, c, d\}, R(e_i) = \{e, f, c, d\}$, $R(e_k) = \{e, f, c, h\}$, $R(e_k) = \{e, f, c, h\}$, then exercise e_k is preferred over e_i as the next exercise after e_i since it reduces the number of repetitive concepts (from 2 to 1) while meeting the same number of dependencies as e_i. To schedule exercises in increasing order of complexity while providing opportunities to learn new concepts in each exercise (freshness), we further refine edge weight to from node e_i to e_j as follows.

$$W_{e_i} \rightarrow W_{e_j} = \left(\frac{d(e_i, e_j)}{|R_{e_j}|} * v_{e_j} \right) \quad (4)$$

Then, the next exercise is chosen based on maximal edge weight:

$$\text{Next exercise } (e_j) = \text{Max } \{W_{ei} \rightarrow W_{ej} \mid e_j\} \quad (5)$$
$$\text{is adjacent to } e_i\}$$

Note that the parameter δ proportionately reduces the redundancy among non-dependent concepts. For example, if there are 200 concepts and 199 concepts are redundant between nodes e_i, e_j then the dependency overlap if δ is $1 - (0.01 * 199) = -0.99$, which reduces the node value excessively that the significance of the node carrying 1 dependent concept is lost. Hence, δ should be chosen in a way that preserves the significance of the node while reduces the priority compared to other nodes with fewer redundant nodes. Given N concepts, the parameter can be set as follows:

$$\delta = 10^{-\text{ceil}(\log(N))} \qquad (6)$$

The main steps of the dynamic schedule generation procedure is as follows. Initially, the source nodes (exercise with no dependent concepts) are queued. Once an exercise is successfully completed, edge weights of the nodes adjacent to the current node are calculated and updated into a weight matrix and the node with maximum weight is queued to the player as the next best exercise. The progress vector is updated, and the values of the exercises are recalculated using (1) and the process is repeated until all components of the progress vector are 1 or there are no exercises left that cover the remaining concepts. We use two queues named visited queue (V) that queues the exercises for the player, processed queue (P) which queues the nodes successfully solved by the player in order to explore further for the next exercises. Below, a node represents an exercise in the exercise graph.

1. Enqueue the base nodes into V. Base nodes are nodes that do not have any dependencies.

2. Dequeue each node, provide to the player for solving. and enqueue this node into P.

3. Repeat the process until V is empty.

4. After all the base nodes are processed, calculate all the *node weights* (1) using nhints (navigation hints algorithm)

5. Dequeue node from P say D_p and calculate *edge weights* (4) for all the nodes adjacent to D_p using *edge weight*.

6. Pick the child node with *maximum* edge weight and enqueue to V.

7. Dequeue the node D_v and provide it to player for solving.

8. *If* the player successfully solves and exercise (node) *then* enqueue the node D_v in to P

    a. *Else* re-calculate the node weights of all the nodes and the edge weights of D_p.

    b. Pick the node with maximum value and enqueue to V.

9. Remove node D_p from the exercise graph.

10. Calculate the node weights, if weight = 0, remove the node from the exercise graph.

11. Repeat from step 5.

12. If no child nodes exist for the current node D_p and all concepts are not learnt, go to step 1.

13. Repeat steps 1 - 10 until there are no exercises left or all the concepts are learnt.

IV. QUASIM

In this section we introduce the QuaSim serious game, its navigation hint system and the novel extended concept dependency handling mechanism. QuaSim is a virtual gamified education paradigm that teaches basic concepts of quantum computing and cryptography. The goals of QuaSim are three fold. First, it allows the internalization of counterintuitive quantum concepts that sit at the intersection of Physics, mathematics, computer science and cybersecurity [22, 23, 24]. Second, it provides a immersive environment for hands-on learning in the absence of expensive quantum equipment and field-training opportunities. And third, QuaSim enhances student learning and proficiency in relevant concepts while maintaining engagement through a gamified interface.

Figure 1 shows screenshots of the game. There are four major lessons in the game namely polarization, basis and measurement, quantum communication, and BB84 quantum key exchange. There are several sub-lessons such as matrix and Dirac notations, linear combination, quantum communication, channel noise detection, eve detection, etc.

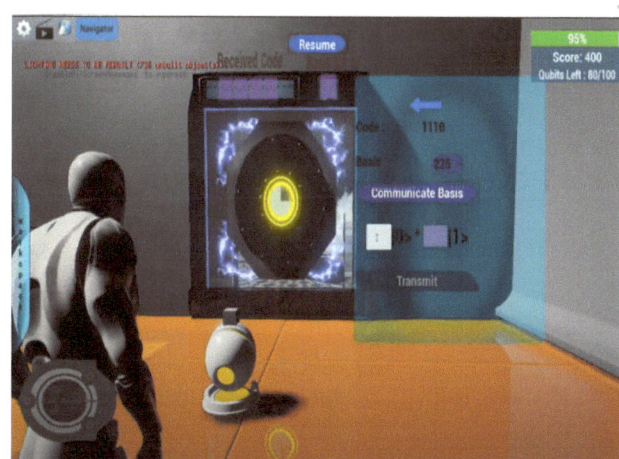

Fig. 1. Screen shots from QuaSim game showing lessons 2 measurement (top) and 3 quantum communication (bottom)

QuaSim has been developed in Unreal Engine 4. The game includes several features to support student gameplay such as a narrator (including a mission statement), an oracle (when students want to seek help or the system detects a student needs help), several hint mechanisms, embedded videos and quizzes throughout the game, a web browser, calculator, various controls to fine-tune the environment and finally and most-importantly support for multiplayer scenarios for up to three players. All events and actions performed by the player are recorded in the game including the solutions of the player and their attempts to solve each exercise. This is used to analyze student performance and need for intervention (through the oracle) on the fly. The game is played in three versions categorized based on the hint mode namely manual, semi-automatic, and the automatic mode. Manual mode enables players to access hints manually, in semi-automatic mode hints are provided to the player with an option for the player to reject or accept the hint whereas in the automatic hint mode hints are displayed to the user without an option to reject. Hints of two different types – solution hints and navigation hints called *shints* and *nhints*, respectively.

A. A Navigation Example with Dependencies

Considering the lesson 1 from the game, the navigation algorithm is executed using the concept dependency graph shown in Figure 2. The concepts from lesson 1 being same angle qubit polarization (S), orthogonal qubit polarization (O), opposite quadrant qubit polarization (Q), vector notation (V), linear combination (LC), Ket notation (K), and the notion of a basis (B). The distribution of these concepts among 12 exercises of lesson 1 are denoted as $P_1 – \{S,V\}$, $P_2 – \{O,V\}$, $P_3 – \{Q,V\}$, $P_4 – \{S,K\}$, $P_5 – \{O,K\}$, $P_6 – \{Q,K\}$, $P_7 – \{S,LC\}$, $P_8 – \{O,LC\}$, $P_9 – \{Q,LC\}$, $P_{10} – \{S,B\}$, $P_{11} – \{O,B\}$, $P_{12} – \{Q,B\}$. The dependency map for the exercises in the game is shown in Figure 3.

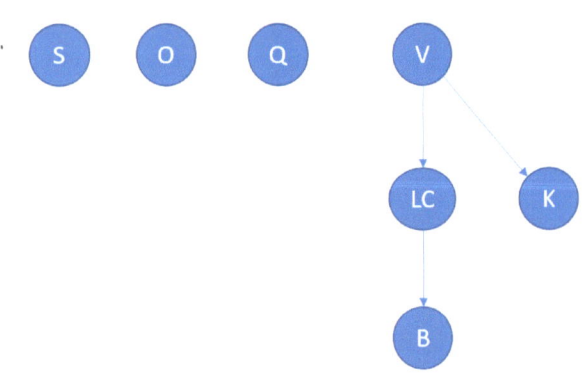

Fig. 2. Concept dependency graph of lesson 1.

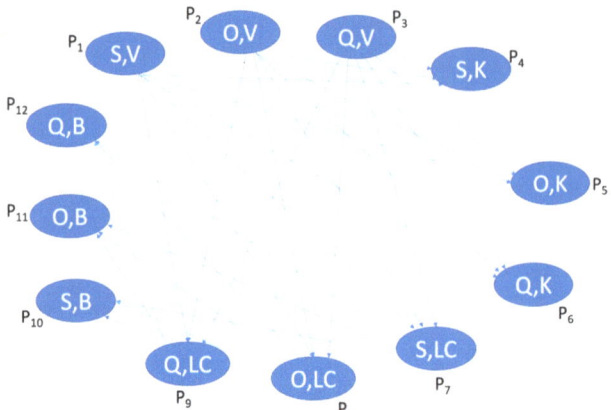

Fig. 3. Exercise dependency graph with 12 exercises of lesson 1.

Table I in Appendix shows a success scenario where the player successively solves the presented exercises in lesson 1. The edge weights are calculated using eq. 4 and next node is chosen using eq. 5. All ties are broken arbitrarily.

V. SUPER CONCEPTS AND INTER-LESSON DEPENDENCIES

While the concept and exercise graphs provide a fine grained view of a game unit, we can abstract these dependencies to a higher (lesson) level in order to determine the inter-lesson dependencies. This abstraction is represented using the notion of *super-concepts*; each super-concept is an encapsulation of all the concepts and the lesson's end goal. Each lesson in a game unit may be associated with one or more super-concepts and the super-concepts in turn may depend on one or more concepts or other super-concepts. To achieve the lesson's goal, therefore, the player should achieve proficiency in all the associated concepts of that super-concept. The concept dependency graphs along with the corresponding super concepts are shown in Figure 4. The dotted arrows do not represent a physical dependency rather abstract association of every concept with the super-concept. Unlike in Figure 3, the super-concept does not correspond to a physical exercise inside the game in Figure 4.

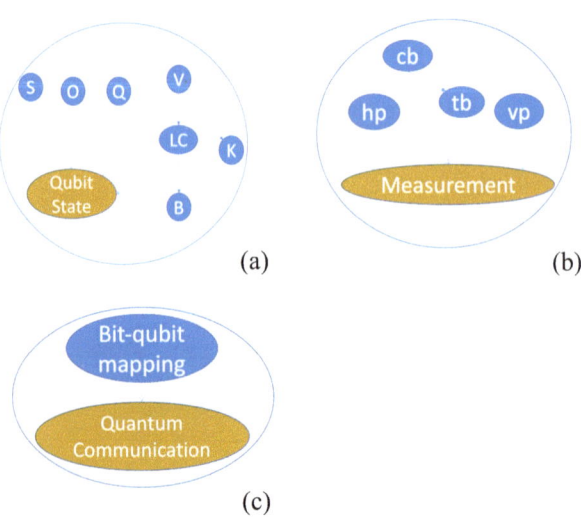

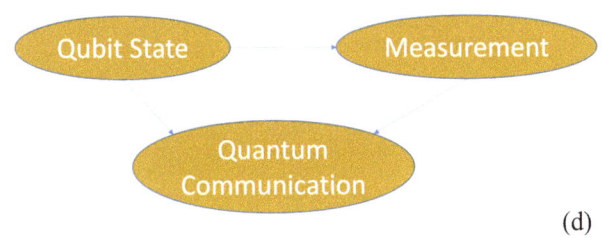

Fig. 4. Concept dependency graphs with *super-concepts* of lesson 1 (fig. a), lesson 2 (fig. b), lesson 3 (fig. c) and the lesson dependency graph (fig. d) of these *super-concepts*.

The concepts in lesson 2 Figure 4 (b) are computational basis (cb), basis transformation (bt), horizontal component (hc), and vertical component (vc) with the super-concept being measurement. The concept in lesson 3 shown in Figure 4 (c) include classical bits to quantum bit mapping with the super-concept of the lesson being quantum communication (qm). Similarly, Figure 4 (a) shows the super-concept for lesson 1 as qubit state (qs). As concepts dependency graphs are used to construct exercise dependency graphs, super concepts are used to construct lesson dependency graph shown in Figure 4 (d).

The lesson dependency graph provides the high-level overview of lesson navigation. In Figure 4, the measurement super-concept needs qubit state as a prerequisite. This dependency does not mean each and every concept of the super-concept are depending on each and every concept of the parent super-concept, rather the knowledge of the qubit state is necessary in-order to understand and solve measurement exercises on a higher level. For a game with multiple lessons, the lesson dependency graph is used to traverse through different levels in the game. Once a lesson node is being visited, the concept dependency graph of that super concept is used to form the exercise dependency graph to further traverse through that level in the game. The concepts in the graph could all be independent in which case navigation hints with independent concepts algorithm is executed instead.

Traversal through the lesson dependency graph can be done in two ways based on preserving engagement or freshness metric - a top-down approach guided by engagement or a bottom-up approach guided by modular concept structure. In top down approach, a schedule can be generated by moving to the next lesson in the graph even if the learning progress vector does not have a value 1 for all the concepts of the super-concept implying learning value of super-concept is not 1. This is to maintain the engagement by providing the player with new concepts for a change, and get back to the failed concepts later. Yet, the value of the current super-concept cannot be set to 1 even if all the concepts in the current concept are marked one, as the dependency is not yet satisfied. This will only be done once the player returns to the previous lesson node and successfully completed the remaining concepts. The second approach is a strict follow of the policy that parent node concept proficiency must be 1 before moving to the child node, else the player has to revert to the learning videos or tutorials to obtain the knowledge of the relevant concepts to continue further. There can also be a threshold proficiency of concepts, when met sets the super-concept proficiency as 1 to allow the player navigate through other lessons using the lesson dependency graph. These questions can be answered empirically by performing experiments, analyzing the engagement and learning potential of the players thereby reflecting on the efficiency of the approaches optimal way can be considered.

VI. CONCLUSIONS

The development of an educational gamified paradigm to teach counter-intuitive subjects such as quantum cryptography requires proper identification of concepts and concept dependencies. Equally important, in order to maintain student engagement, is an adaptive navigation mechanism to traverse the game such that the student achieves maximum proficiency in all the subject areas. This paper presented the first of its kind abstract model for designing a game for quantum cryptography. This model was implemented in our game QuaSim in order to dynamically schedule exercises in an adaptive and controlled manner. Future work will involve integrating the game in the classroom environment for easy adoption [20].

ACKNOWLEDGEMENTS

This project was partly supported by the National Science Foundation award #1623380.

REFERENCES

[1] Djaouti D., Alvarez J., Jessel JP., Rampnoux O. (2011) Origins of Serious Games. In: Ma M., Oikonomou A., Jain L. (eds) Serious Games and Edutainment Applications. Springer, London.

[2] Susi, T., Johannesson, M., & Backlund, P. (2007). Serious Games : An Overview (IKI Technical Reports). Institutionen för kommunikation och information.

[3] Ritterfeld, U., Cody, M., & Vorderer, P. (Eds.). (2009). Serious games: Mechanisms and effects. Routledge.

[4] Petko, D., Schmid, R., & Cantieni, A. (2020). Pacing in Serious Games: Exploring the Effects of Presentation Speed on Cognitive Load, Engagement and Learning Gains. Simulation & Gaming, 51(2), 258–279.

[5] Hookham, G., & Nesbitt, K. (2019, January). A systematic review of the definition and measurement of engagement in serious games. In Proceedings of the Australasian Computer Science Week Multiconference (pp. 1-10).

[6] Veinott E.S., Whitaker E. (2019) Leaving Hints: Using Player In-Game Hints to Measure and Improve Learning. In: Stephanidis C., Antona M. (eds) HCI International 2019 – Late Breaking Posters. HCII 2019. Communications in Computer and Information Science, vol 1088. Springer, Cham.

[7] Bommanapally, V., Subramaniam, M., Chundi, P., & Parakh, A. (2018). Navigation hints in serious games. *iLRN 2018 Montana*, 115.

[8] Harp, S. F., & Mayer, R. E. (1998). How Seductive Details Do Their Damage: A Theory of Cognitive Interest in Science Learning. Journal of Educational Psychology, 90(3), 414–434.

[9] Mayer, R. E., & Johnson, C. I. (2010). Adding Instructional Features That Promote Learning in a Game-Like Environment. Journal of Educational Computing Research, 42(3), 241–265.

[10] Rowe, J. P., McQuiggan, S. W., Robison, J. L., & Lester, J. C. (2009). Off-task behavior in narrative- centered learning

environments. In Frontiers in Artificial Intelligence and Applications (Vol. 200, pp. 99–106).

[11] Abeyrathna, D., Vadla, S., Bommanapally, V., Subramaniam, M., Chundi, P., & Parakh, A. (2018, December). Analyzing and predicting player performance in a quantum cryptography serious game. In *International Conference on Games and Learning Alliance* (pp. 267-276). Springer, Cham.

[12] Atorf D., Kannegieser E., Roller W. (2019) Study on Enhancing Learnability of a Serious Game by Implementing a Pedagogical Agent. In: Liapis A., Yannakakis G., Gentile M., Ninaus M. (eds) Games.

[13] Din, Z. U., & Gibson, G. E. (2019). Serious games for learning prevention through design concepts: An experimental study. Safety Science, 115, 176–187. doi: 10.1016/j.ssci.2019.02.005

[14] Drey, T., Jansen, P., Fischbach, F., Frommel, J., & Rukzio, E. (2020, April). Towards Progress Assessment for Adaptive Hints in Educational Virtual Reality Games. In Extended Abstracts of the 2020 CHI Conference on Human Factors in Computing Systems Extended Abstracts (pp. 1-9).

[15] Shute V., Ke F., Wang L. (2017) Assessment and Adaptation in Games. In: Wouters P., van Oostendorp H. (eds) Instructional Techniques to Facilitate Learning and Motivation of Serious Games. Advances in Game-Based Learning. Springer, Cham.

[16] Ostler, E., Parakh, A. and Subramaniam, M. (2018). QuaSim: The development of a virtual simulator for teaching topics in quantum cryptography, Society for Information Technology & Teacher Education International Conference, March 2018, Washington, D.C.

[17] A. Parakh, P. Chundi and M. Subramaniam, An Approach Towards Designing Problem Networks in Serious Games, 2019 IEEE Conference on Games (CoG), London, United Kingdom, 2019, pp. 1-8.

[18] Annetta, L. A. (2010). The "I's" Have It: A Framework for Serious Educational Game Design. Review of General Psychology, 14(2), 105–113. https://doi.org/10.1037/a0018985.

[19] Roungas, B. (2016). A Model-driven Framework for Educational Game Design. International Journal of Serious Games, 3(3). https://doi.org/10.17083/ijsg.v3i3.126.

[20] Bommanapally, A., Subramaniam, M., Parakh, A., Chundi, P. and Puppala, V. M. Learning Objects Based Adaptive Textbooks with Dynamic Traversal for Quantum Cryptography. Second Workshop on Intelligent Textbooks, In conjunction with 21st International Conference on Artificial Intelligence in Education, July 6th, 2020.

[21] Vadla, S., Parakh, A., Chundi, P. and Subramaniam, M. QUASIM: A Multi-dimensional Quantum Cryptography Game for Cyber Security, Journal of The Colloquium for Information Systems Security Education, Volume 6, Spring 2019.

[22] Parakh, A. and Subramaniam, M. Bootstrapped QKD: improving key rate and multi-photon resistance. SPIE Security + Defence, 10-13 September, Berlin, Germany, 2018.

[23] Parakh, A. Using fewer qubits to correct errors in the three-stage QKD protocol. SPIE Security + Defence, 10-13 September, Berlin, Germany, 2018.

[24] Parakh, A. Providing variable levels of security in quantum cryptography, SPIE Optical Engineering + Applications, 19 - 23 August 2018, San Diego, CA USA.

[25] McDermott, S., Vadla, S., Bommanapally, V., Parakh, A., Subramaniam, M. and Ostler, E. Teaching quantum cryptography using a virtual 3D educator: QuaSim, In Proceedings of 2017 National Cyber Summit (NCS'17), Huntsville, AL, June 6-8, 2017.

[26] A. Parakh, M. Subramaniam and E. Ostler, QuaSim: A virtual quantum cryptography educator, 2017 IEEE International Conference on Electro Information Technology (EIT), Lincoln, NE, 2017, pp. 600-605, doi: 10.1109/EIT.2017.8053434.

APPENDIX

TABLE I. EXECUTION OF DEPENDENCY ALGORITHM FOR LESSON 1.

Nodes in V	Nodes in P	Current node solved by the player	Node to explore children (E)	Edge Weights adjacent to node E	Node with Max value	Concepts learnt
P_1, P_2, P_3		P_1				$\langle S, V \rangle$
P_2, P_3	P_1	P_2				$\langle S, V, O \rangle$
P_3	P_1, P_2	P_3				$\langle S, V, O, Q \rangle$
	P_1, P_2, P_3		P_1	$P_1 \rightarrow (P_9, P_8, P_6, P_5) = \frac{1}{6}$, $P_1 \rightarrow (P_7, P_4) = \frac{0.99}{6}$	P_9	
P_9	P_2, P_3	P_9				$\langle S, V, O, Q, LC \rangle$
	P_2, P_3, P_9		P_2	$P_2 \rightarrow (P_4, P_6) = \frac{1}{6}$, $P_2 \rightarrow P_5 = \frac{0.99}{6}$	P_4	
P_4	P_3, P_9	P_4				$\langle S, V, O, Q, LC, K \rangle$
	P_3, P_9, P_4		P_3	$P_3 \rightarrow$ all nodes adjacent to P_3 have values 0		
	P_9, P_4		P_9	$P_9 \rightarrow (P_{10}, P_{12}) = \frac{1}{6}$, $P_9 \rightarrow P_{11} = \frac{0.99}{6}$	P_{10}	
P_{10}	P_4	P_{10}				$\langle S, V, O, Q, LC, K, B \rangle$
	P_4, P_{10}		P_4	<All concepts are learnt, end>		

Total of six exercises are solved in following sequence: $P_1, P_2, P_3, P_9, P_4, P_{10}$.

Evaluating the Effectiveness of Gamification on Students' Performance in a Cybersecurity Course

Fikirte Demmese
North Carolina A&T State University
Computer Science Dept.
Greensboro, NC, USA
fademmese@aggies.ncat.edu

Xiaohong Yuan
North Carolina A&T State University
Computer Science Dept.
Greensboro, NC, USA
xhyuan@ncat.edu

Darina Dicheva
Winston-Salem State University
Computer Science Dept.
Winston Salem, GA, USA
dichevad@wssu.edu

Abstract—The motivation of students to actively engage in course activities has significant impact on the outcome of academic courses. Prior studies have shown that innovative instructional interventions and course delivery methods have a vital role in boosting the motivation of students. Gamification tools aid course delivery by utilizing well established game design principles to enhance skill development, routine practice and self-testing. In this article, we present a study on how the use of a course gamification platform dubbed OneUp impacts the motivation of students in an online cyber security course. The study shows that more than 90% of the respondents agreed that OneUp has improved the effectiveness of the course delivery. In addition, 75% of the respondents want to use OneUp in their future courses. Furthermore, our analysis shows that OneUp has improved the median grade of students from B+ to A- compared to the same course delivered the previous year without using OneUp.

Keywords—cybersecurity education, gamification, self-learning, OneUp

I. INTRODUCTION

Students' engagement in course activities is an essential factor to attain the desired learning outcome of a course. Engagement depends on the quality of the course delivery system and the motivation enablers the instructor provides for the students to be proactive in the course activities [9]. Creating an inspiring learning environment is a proven measure an instructor could take to enhance students' motivation and engagement.

Gamification is a growing trend of leveraging game design principles and elements in non-gaming applications to enhance user engagement and motivation. It involves incorporating common game elements, such as points, badges, and leaderboard into the normal process of a non-gaming application. The early gamified applications were mostly for marketing [7]. Later on, gamification got increasingly popular in various fields, including business, health, wellbeing, military and education. Educational gamification tools aid course delivery by utilizing well established game design principles to enhance skill development, routine practice and self-testing. As a result, it helps students to improve their engagement in the course activities. Moreover, students' motivation and course engagement increase if satisfactory game-based elements were added while designing the course [8].

In this article we present a case study on the effectiveness of gamification to enhance the course delivery of a Software Security Testing course. The course was taught at North Carolina A&T State University (NC A&T) in Fall 2019. Following the recent tendency for Cybersecurity courses to be available in the form of distance learning [12], the course was offered as an online course. For the study we used the gamification platform OneUp as a supplementary study aid. OneUp is a gamification learning platform that is utilized to facilitate the process of gamifying academic courses [3]. A previous study has shown the effectiveness of using OneUp to gamify an on campus undergraduate Data Structures course to increase student motivation for out-of-class practice [4]. The study showed that the use of OneUp resulted in increased student engagement as well as reduced failing rate among students. The context of our study differs from the previous one in two aspects: first, the targeted course is a master level course, and second, the course is an online course. We were especially interested in the impact of using gamification in online courses, since the problem of engaging students in distant education is even bigger. We also wanted to explore how a generic gamification platform, such as OneUp, can be tailored to fit seamlessly into an online course delivery. Thus, the study was guided by the following questions:

Q1. Does gamification encourage online students to practice more?

Q2. Does gamification improve grades in online classes?

Q3. What is students' perception towards the platform and their engagement with it?

The remainder of the paper is organized as follows. Section II reviews briefly related work. The research methodology is described in Section III. Section IV discusses the principle findings of this study. Finally, Section V presents discussion of our findings and concludes the article.

II. RELATED WORK

Applying gamification in Computer Science courses is not a new idea. A number of studies have explored the application of gamification to support student learning and course delivery [2,8]. The game elements most frequently incorporated in gamified learning systems are points, badges and leaderboards. Huotari et al. [7] suggested that these gaming elements are particularly vital to the success of gamified platforms as they represent both the reward and competitive aspects of a learning system. Hakulinen et al. [6] demonstrated that awarding badges in Data Structures and Algorithms course can motivate students to study and to engage in desired learning activities. Their study did not enforce strict course policies, for instance, they had unlimited number of resubmissions for exercises to encourage students to keep trying until they solve the exercises correctly. Sprint and Fox implemented a flipped classroom with team-based gamification of student study choices [10]. They rewarded students for practicing "good" study habits, such as turning in assignments early and retaking quizzes for extra practice and found out that students did make better study choices, but these choices did not lead to higher final exam scores. Dicheva et al [4] described gamifying of a Data Structures course by using badges, leaderboard and virtual currency. The study showed that the gamifying of the course increased student engagement and reduced failing rates.

There have been only few attempts to gamify learning in Cybersecurity education. Tomcho and colleagues evaluated the effectiveness of gamification for an online military cyber education platform [11]. They applied unique game elements, Cyber Topic Map and Knowledge, Skill, and Ability (KSA) Trees in their experiment. Their study concludes that a careful gamification design and game elements will have a positive impact on motivation and engagement of learners with the platform. Another study applied Catch the Flag (CTF) tournament as a gamification process for cybersecurity courses [6,1]. The results showed that the tournament helped students to reinforce the learned skills and to apply them to specific challenges. Wood used Flipped Learning Adaptive Gamified Simulations (FLAGS) to improve correct first-time answers on hands-on laboratory tasks in cybersecurity distance learning [12]. In the experiment, existing simulation authoring software from the *Serious Factory* company was used. It enabled the employment of five gamification elements: player avatars, realistic environments, narrative context, feedback to answers, and time pressure. Although not statistically significant, the results showed higher scores within the experimental group.

Most of the studies on gamifying Computer Science courses have targeted undergraduate, face-to-face, predominantly programming courses. Differently, we targeted a graduate-level, online Cybersecurity course. Our study is different from the described above cybersecurity-related studies in both the context in which gamification was applied, as well as the used gamification elements. Moreover, published studies report mixed success in the application of gamification in various educational contexts, which requires more empirical evidence. This study contributes to filling this gap by assessing the effectiveness of OneUp-based gamification of an online Cybersecurity course.

III. METHODOLOGY

A. Course delivery strategies

In this study, we used the OneUp platform, to gamify the online course "COMP 725 - Software Security Testing". This graduate level course is offered only in the Fall semester and has comparatively low enrollment. In the study, we used Fall 2018 class (17 students) as a control group and Fall 2019 class (12 students) as an experimental group. The same instructor taught both classes using the same course materials including assignments and quizzes. All students in the experimental group signed an Informed Consent Form to participate in the study and students' usage of OneUp was voluntary.

The control group used only the course delivery platform Blackboard, which provided access to course modules along with quizzes created by the instructor. The quiz questions were included at the end of the reading material in each module. Our goal in gamifying the course was to encourage student self-study and practicing before taking the quizzes. OneUp supports gamified practicing, so we separated the quizzes from the reading materials, so that the students could first read them (in either Blackboard or OneUp), then practice and self-assess their knowledge in OneUp, and only then take the graded course quizzes in Blackboard. Thus, for the experimental group we introduced the OneUp platform not only for gamifying the course but also as a supplementary mechanism for delivering the course materials. Students were given 4-6 days to complete the reading and practicing. Blackboard quizzes were made visible after the due dates for solving the OneUp serious challenges.

B. OneUp platform and gamifying the course

The OneUp gamification platform [3] supports two kinds of quizzes, "warm-up" and "serious" challenges. Warm-up challenges are created for practicing and self-assessment and serious challenges are graded course assessments. OneUp offers various game elements, including avatars, badges, leaderboards, virtual currency, progress bar, etc. It is highly configurable, and the instructor can select the elements to be included in their gamified course.

To prepare the gamified version of the course, for each of the 15 course modules we created their own warm-up and serious challenges in OneUp: 31 warm-up challenges with a total of 170 problems and 15 serious challenges with a total of 134 problems. Further on, we configured the gamification elements for our course. We decided to use experience points (XP), avatars, leaderboard, badges, virtual currency (VC) and learning dashboard. We also created the gaming rules, according to which students would get their rewards (badges and VC). Below is some information describing our choices.

We allowed the students to select their own avatars from the available list of avatars. In the learning dashboard, each student could see aggregated information about their use of OneUp: their warm-up and serious challenges' scores, experience points, badges and VC collected so far. Badges were given to students in order to motivate them to practice more and we created 6 different kinds of badges. To earn a badge, a student had to satisfy one of the instructor's gaming rules. As soon as a badge was earned, it was displayed on the leaderboard. Most of the badges we created were associated with warm-up challenges. Table I shows sample badges used in the course.

TABLE I. SAMPLE BADGE CATEGORIES USED IN THE COURSE

Badge	Badge name	Earning rule
First Timer	First Warm-Up	Score > 75% for the first ever warm-up challenge
15 Practice Hero	Practice Hero Gold	Complete 15 distinct warm-up challenges
SUPER HERO	Super Hero Bronze	Complete 25 distinct warm-up challenges

The other feature we used was virtual currency (VC). We used VC as a reward for solving serious challenges and student's engagement in the course as a whole. Students earned VC for solving problems and could use it to buy a resubmission of assignments. We created earning and spending rules. For example, students must score 90% or above on a serious challenge to get one course buck. But if they scored 100%, they will get 2 course bucks. Students will also get one course buck for practicing 5 consecutive warm-up challenges with a score of 90% or above. When the collected VC reaches 15 course bucks, then students get the chance to spend it in the course shop.

IV. RESULTS

A. OneUp interaction

Students interaction with the inbuilt game elements such as points, avatars, leaderboards, badges, virtual currency, etc. is discussed below.

Avatars: Students were allowed to select their own personal avatars from an available list. Avatars help students to anonymize their identity and results. We were hoping to see that all students will have their own personal avatar, but surprisingly all students chose not to use a personal avatar.

Virtual Currency: During the course, 117 VC earning transactions were recorded. The course bucks were acquired by satisfying one of the earning rules specified by the instructor. Figure 1 shows the total VC earned for each module.

Badges: We set a total of 6 different kinds of badges for this course and all students participated in the experiment received at least one badge. 67% of the students received 4 and more badges. The most badges have been awarded for a first timer who completed 5 distinct challenges. We divided the badges based on the level of completion of warm-up challenges. 33% of the students completed more than 25 distinct challenges.

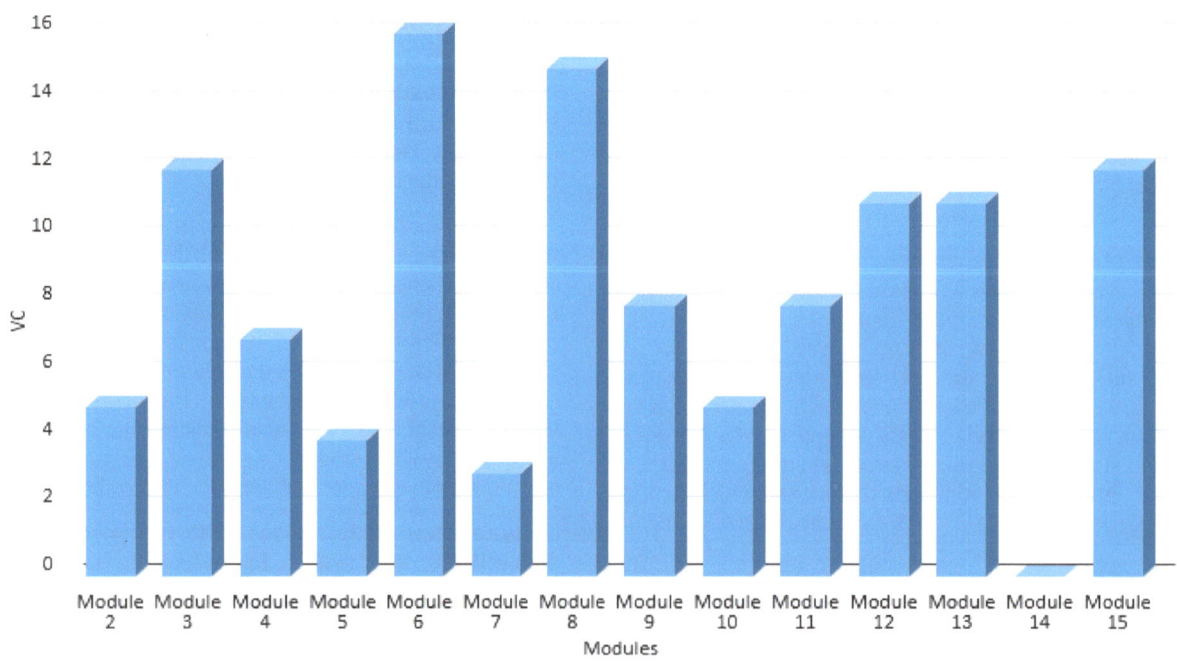

Fig. 1. Virtual Currency earned by Module

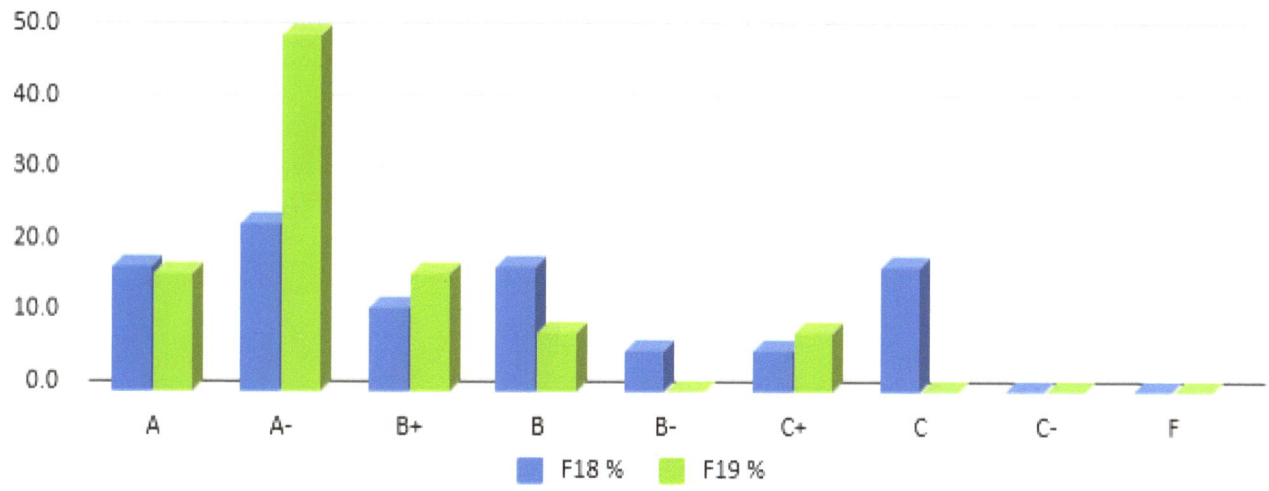

Fig. 2. Final Course Grade comparison

B. Student performance

Final coursework grades of both the control and experimental groups were evaluated to see the impact of gamifying the course. Figure 2 shows the distribution of final grades. As shown in the figure, the use of OneUp in the course has improved the median grade of students from B+ to A-.

C. Survey results

A survey questionnaire which contains 27 questions was given to the experimental group at the end of the semester. We used a numeric Likert scale from 1 (strongly disagree) to 5 (Strongly agree) with 3 as a neutral option. This survey helped us in understanding students' point of view towards gamifying a course and what specifically motivated them to engage in this course. Table II shows sample questions used in the survey grouped by the following categories: effectiveness of the tool, motivation, and level of engagement. The response for each sample question is shown in Figure 3.

TABLE II. SAMPLE SURVEY QUESTIONS BY CATEGORY

No.	Survey question
Q8	I felt more effective with regards to self-learning when using OneUp
Q9	Using OneUp made it easier for me to master course material & prepare for quizzes.
Q10	Using OneUp helped me to improve my grades.
Q16	A desire to boost my grades prompts me to practice in OneUp.
Q18	A desire to get new OneUp badges prompts me to practice in OneUp.
Q19	A desire to get new virtual currency prompts me to practice in OneUp.
Q21	When taking a warm-up challenge in OneUp I put in effort to complete it.
Q24	I do not take very seriously the warm-up challenges in OneUp (R).
Q25	When taking a warm-up challenge I do not pay much attention to my performance.
Q27	I intend to use OneUp if offered in future courses.

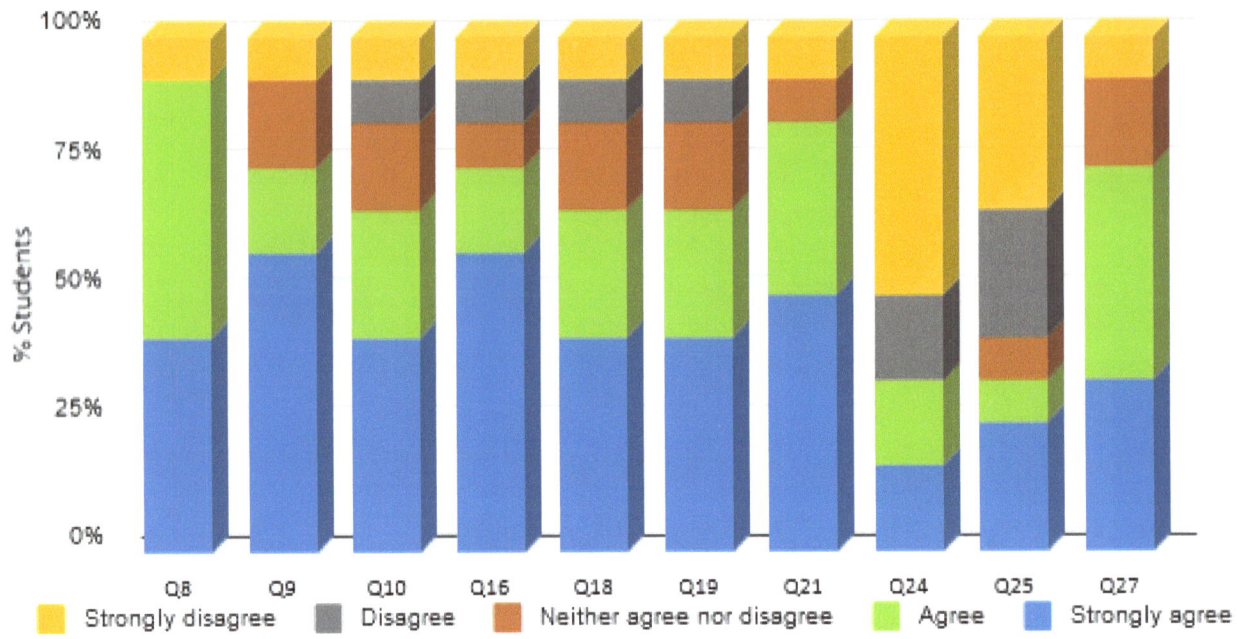

Fig. 3. Answers to the sample survey questions.

As shown in the figure, 90% of the students participated in this experiment agreed that OneUp has increased the effectiveness of self-learning and more than 65% of the students agreed that OneUp has helped them to improve their grades. Based on the results we got from the students' feedback, OneUp was considered a useful platform.

A desire to improve grades, earn badges and VC were the motivation for students to practice more. More than 75% of the students considered OneUp challenges seriously and would use the platform if offered in the future. This is one good result to the level of engagement we were expecting to achieve.

V. Discussion & Conclusion

In this study, we investigated the effect of gamifying a cybersecurity course on student's motivation and engagement. We used a graduate Software Security Testing course for this experimental study. We compared a gamified (experimental group) with a non-gamified (control group) where both groups took the online course. Our analysis shows that the OneUp gamification platform has increased the effectiveness of self-learning and motivation as well as helped to improve the median grade of students who participated in the study.

Since we were the first to offer a gamified course in the department, we were expecting a great enthusiasm in the students. We were also expecting that all students will practice in OneUp in order to get a chance to re-submit assignments. However, some students fail to login and practice for a couple of weeks. Then, we decided to add another benefit - serious challenge points count towards the final grades. This announcement motivated almost all students to login and practice more. We still noticed that some students would only concentrate on solving the serious challenges. These results show that students are motivated to practice if they think it will influence their final grade.

One of the limitations of this study is the small number of participants (12). Having a small number of participating students might make it easier to track their activities and achievements, however makes it difficult for us to understand whether the implemented gamification has improved student motivation to practice or not. For example, in our experiment, some students who didn't score much in OneUp got better final grades. As a future work, we are considering to study the impact of gamification on other computer science courses with a higher number of students.

Following our previous practice, where we used to post on Blackboard course modules, quizzes, and assignments every week, we did the same on the OneUp platform - uploaded the course materials on a weekly basis. But doing so constrained the students, since they had only a small number of problems to practice with. This, in turn, might have led to loss of motivation and eagerness for practicing. We believe that if we upload all course materials and resources at the beginning of the semester and have more warm-up challenges, students' motivation could be better than what we achieved now.

Acknowledgements

This work is partially supported by NSF under the grant DUE-1821189, DUE-1821960 and 1821965. Any opinions, findings, and conclusions or recommendations expressed in this material are those of the author(s) and do not necessarily reflect the views of the NSF.

REFERENCES

[1] Chothia, T., Novakovic, C., Radu, A. I., & Thomas, R. J. (2019). Choose Your Pwn Adventure: Adding Competition and Storytelling to an Introductory Cybersecurity Course. In Transactions on Edutainment XV(pp.141-172). Springer, Berlin, Heidelberg.

[2] Dicheva, D., Dichev C., Agre G., & Angelova G. (2015). Gamification in Education: A Systematic Mapping Study. Educational Technology & Society, 18(3), 75–88.

[3] Dicheva, D., Irwin, K., & Dichev, C. (2018). OneUp: Supporting Practical and Experimental Gamification of Learning. *International Journal of Serious Games*, 5(3), 5 - 21. https://doi.org/10.17083/ijsg.v5i3.236

[4] Dicheva, D., Irwin, K., & Dichev, C. (2019, February). OneUp: Engaging Students in a Gamified Data Structures Course. In *Proceedings of the 50th ACM Technical Symposium on Computer Science Education* (pp. 386-392).

[5] Gonzalez, H., Llamas, R., Montano, O. (2019) Using CTF Tournament for Reinforcing Learned Skills in Cybersecurity Course, Research in Computing Science 148(5), pp. 133–141.

[6] Hakulinen, L., Auvinen, T., & Korhonen, A. (2013, March). Empirical study on the effect of achievement badges in TRAKLA2 online learning environment. *In 2013 Learning and teaching in computing and engineering* (pp. 47-54). IEEE.

[7] Huotari, K.. & Hamari, J. Defining Gamification: A Service Marketing Perspective. The 16th International Academic MindTrek Conference, Tampere, Finland (2012).

[8] Moore-Russo, D., Wiss, A., & Grabowski, J. (2018). Integration of gamification into course design: A noble endeavor with potential pitfalls. *College Teaching*, 66(1),3-5.

[9] Putz, L. M., & Treiblmaier, H. (2019). Increasing Knowledge Retention through Gamified Workshops: Findings from a Longitudinal Study and Identification of Moderating Variables. In Proc. 52nd Hawaii Int. Conference on System Sciences.

[10] Sprint, G., Fox, E. (2020) Improving Student Study Choices in CS1 with Gamification and Flipped Classrooms. In 51st ACM Technical Symposium on Computer Science Education (SIGCSE '20), Portland, OR.

[11] Tomcho, L., Lin, A., Long, D., Coggins, M., & Reith, M. (2019). Applying Game Elements to Cyber eLearning: An Experimental Design. In International Conference on Cyber Warfare and Security (pp. 422-XV). Academic Conferences International Limited.

[12] Wood, S. W. (2019). Adapting Serious Gamification for Teaching Hands-on Skills in Cybersecurity Distance Learning (Doctoral dissertation, Capitol Technology University).

Enhancing Cyber Defense Preparation Through Interdisciplinary Collaboration, Training, and Incident Response

Tristen K. Amador
Regis University
Denver, CO, USA
tamador@regis.edu

Roberta A. Mancuso
Regis University
Denver, CO, USA
rmancuso@regis.edu

Erik L. Moore
Regis University
Denver, CO, USA
emoore@regis.edu

Steven P. Fulton
United States Air Force Academy
USAFA, CO, USA
steven.fulton@usafa.edu

Daniel M. Likarish
Regis University
Denver, CO, USA
dlikaris@regis.edu

Abstract—To enhance the capabilities of a cyber defense collaborative, a psychometric analysis team was embedded in a collaborative incident response team. Collaborative incident response community members included the State of Colorado, the Colorado National Guard, Regis University, private companies, and others. The collaborative training developed when National Guard leadership saw the Rocky Mountain Collegiate Cyber Defense Competition held at Regis, and planning began around the potential of collaborative training. The case presented shows the progressive efforts that allowed this to move from enhancing training exercises to being embedded during live cyber defense operations. Some outcomes of the psychometric evaluation are presented here as an embedded quantitative study within the framing case analysis. The case analysis is then used to formulate a generalized model designed to support opportunities for a range of interdisciplinary collaboration in support of technical endeavors with operations security requirements as exemplified by cyber defense. The resulting model provides a framework for expanding research to other disciplines.

Keywords—*Interdisciplinary Collaboration, Psychometrics, Psychometric Analysis, Sociotechnical, Cyber Defense, Cybersecurity, Collaborative, Incident Response, Colorado National Guard, Cybersecurity Training, Incident Response, Trust, Myers-Briggs Type Indicator, MBTI, Parker Team Player Survey, PTPS, Crew Cohesion Assessment Tool*

I. INTRODUCTION

To develop a roadmap for enhancing cyber incident response, an inter- organizational coalition of state governments, military defense teams, industry, and academic partners in the State of Colorado deployed psychometric analysis during a series of training exercises to address the sociotechnical dynamics in cyber defense activities. This paper details the pathway that enabled this interdisciplinary collaboration. It also presents a generalized model that may be used as a template for technical teams with operational security requirements that are attempting to extend beyond technical protections by leveraging relevant interdisciplinary expertise. A collaborative training and response community (CTRC) evolved from a group of like-minded academic, state, military, and industrial sector members. The authors' work with this group incrementally advances a trusted training environment where multiple interdisciplinary experts can be embedded with a defensive team to extend traditional incident response methods. Once trust and relationships were established in the training environment, the new capabilities could be used in live incident response.

The specific case presented in this paper incorporates psychometric analysis and feedback to enhance the adaptability of personality types and, ultimately, improve overall team performance. Initial observations took place during a Rocky Mountain Collegiate Cyber Defense Competition (RMCCDC) where the CTRC was also observing. It was during the competition, which involved the defense of a simulated financial institution, that the concepts regarding the teamwork analysis were formed and shared among the CTRC. Next, the psychometric analysts on the Regis faculty engaged the collaborative community in discussions regarding possible inclusion of psychometric analysis as another way of strengthening the cyber defense teams to be even more effective. In May of 2017, the analysts administered a series of tests to assess personality types and team player styles to better understand how successful teams work together.

II. CASE BACKGROUND

Since the RMCCDC is a large event held on a satellite campus of Regis, several faculty members from other disciplines at this satellite campus were aware of the cyber competition and suggested using a psychometric team analysis process to study the ongoing cyber team response. The close co- location of faculty members from different disciplines at this campus was critical in the early interdisciplinary brainstorming sessions and ongoing discussions.

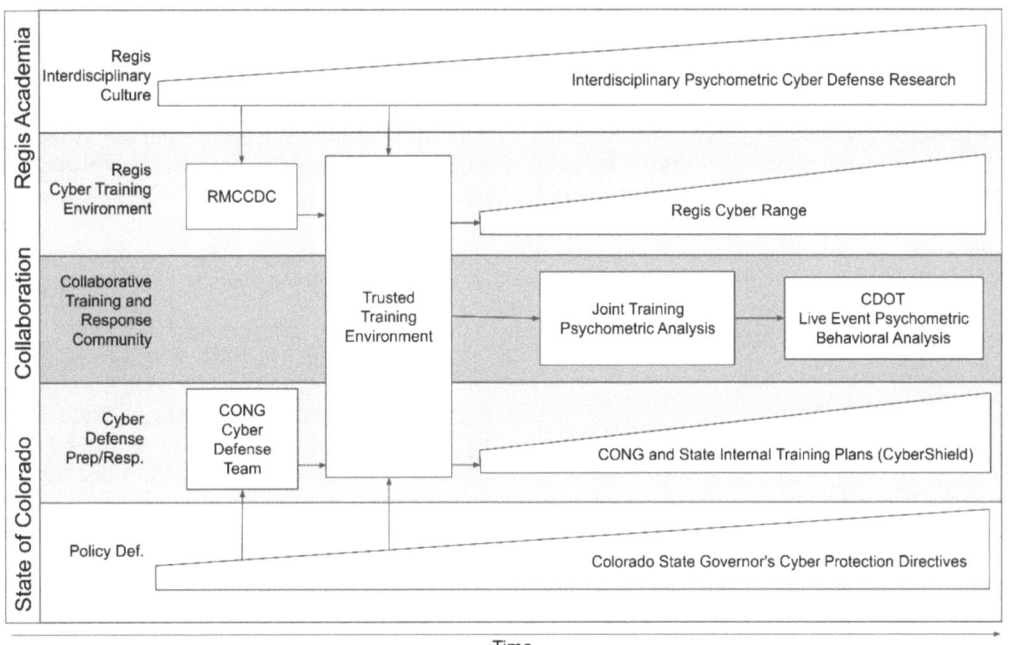

Fig. 1. Environment portraying the integration of psychometric analysis as part of an interdisciplinary effort. This analysis became a resource of the established trusted training environment.

This interdisciplinary organization of academics along with the CTRC, comprised of Colorado State employees, Colorado National Guard (CONG) military personnel and cyber industry experts began to jointly create a trusted training environment in which mistakes could be made without attribution and skills could be developed. This specific environment is outlined in Figure 1. The cross dimensional work identified as the Trusted Training Environment became the central pillar of the CTRC. It was here in this trusted environment where the differing organizations learned to trust each other. It was this environment that is the basis of our psychometric analysis training work. Details of this experience can be found in our earlier work [1]. As time went by, the level of trust following these events increased between each of the organizations. This allowed the research team to suggest new ways for the teams to work and new team environments in which to work.

There were two principle influences leading to the implementation of the Trusted Training Environment. The first was the progressive and incremental implementation of an early, competition-based challenge beginning with the CANVAS (Computer and Network Virtualization and Simulation) joint student technical and business training exercises supported by Regis University (RU) and the United States Air Force (USAF) [2]. The second was the decision to offer the RMCCDC [3] in Denver. The RMCCDC is a two-day collegiate cyber security team competition, established in 2005 [4]. RMCCDC offered physical cyber security exercises requiring the implementation of significant server and network infrastructure. This infrastructure allowed the RU cybersecurity faculty to offer collaborative training opportunities to local and state government agencies, the Colorado National Guard, private industry and critical infrastructure organizations, forming a CTRC. In the early days of our exercises, this community focused on advancing technical skills, providing RU the opportunity to build out a complex cyber range. When the community reached targeted levels of technical proficiency, the CTRC leaders observed that team performance could be further enhanced with non-technical training. This led to initial psychometric observations that were made during a recorded training exercise and was confirmed during the After Action Report (AAR) by the CTRC psychometric analysts. After these observations, the CTRC expanded activities to include the interdisciplinary psychometric analysts and formed the research team. Efforts to pilot the inclusion of psychometric analysis by RU in collaboration with the exercise partners resulted in incorporating team building that could enhance team performance. Based on those early interdisciplinary interactions, professors in health care management and psychology led to the addition of psychometric analysis to the capabilities employed to enhance cyber defense team performance. The case below came out of these initial interactions.

III. CASE METHODOLOGY

An embedded case study methodology is an appropriate research instrument for analyzing the insertion of psychometric research into a collaborative environment requiring high levels of trust. Creswell and Creswell's embedded case study methodology [5] is based on a post-positivist perspective and is designed to address sociotechnical dynamics. The authors used as the example a cross-sectional study, where the application of the Myers-Briggs Type Indicator (MBTI) and the Parker Team Player Survey (PTPS) instruments provided analytic tools in an effort to enhance performance within cybersecurity training environments that require operations security. The case includes brief qualitative analysis to provide a reference for a generalizable model of integrating experts from diverse disciplines within cyber defense training, and provides a reference case for facilitating this type of work. Embedding a quantitative research methodology into a case study has been explored previously as Scholz and Tietje described in 2002 [6] and guided us in creating a model for injecting a range of disciplines into technical training environments requiring high levels of trust because of factors like operational security requirements.

The questions this work answers are the following: Is there a viable path to incorporate interdisciplinary expertise and tools into a cyber defense training program and incident response operation? Also, is there a generalizable model that can be abstracted from the case that might be transferable to other cyber defense situations and other interdisciplinary work? Prior to the research questions described here, the leadership of the CTRC started by asking how we could work together to "make a good team even better." This initial question drove the authors to formulate the research questions as we looked outside the cyber defense discipline for methods of enhancing operational capabilities. Working with psychometric analytical techniques and embedding this in a larger framework is the method we chose to provide a formal method of reflection on the efficacy of this work. The insights in the conclusion are formulated into a generalizable model designed to guide future work.

IV. CASE RESEARCH CONTEXT

High functioning teams in cyber security incident response are critical given the prevalence, substantial cost, and rising complexity of cybercrime. In regard to medical and other types of incidents, Uitdewilligen *et al.* describe "multidisciplinary crisis management teams consist of highly experienced professionals who combine their discipline-specific expertise in order to respond to critical situations characterized by high levels of uncertainty, complexity, and dynamism" [7]. Cybersecurity teams are characteristic of these highly experienced professionals working within uncertainty, complexity, and dynamism that Uitdewilligen *et al.* discuss. Our research suggests that convening and responding as a collaborative and cohesive team are vital to a team's success, yet we have much to learn about how we intentionally create these high-functioning, collaborative teams.

Willems *et al.* [8], in discussing disaster response in the medical field, describe some of the interprofessional, non-technical skills needed which include skills such as "physical self-care including survival skills, psychological self-care, flexibility, adaptability, innovation, and improvisation" which they call the "skills for austere environments." Additional skills identified by Willems *et al.* include cognitive strategies such as "big picture thinking, situational awareness, critical thinking, problem solving, and creativity". Interprofessional attributes include characteristics such as "communication, team-player, sense of humor, cultural competency and conflict resolution skills". Other studies support the importance of non-technical skills in incident response teams. For example, Tokakis *et al.* [9] found that leaders with strong decision-making abilities, communication skills, and emotional intelligence were instrumental in the integration of crisis management teams in the public sector.

Another study investigating non-technical skills included software engineers and concluded that specific attributes such as managing expectations, creating a "safe haven," asking for help, creating shared success, and perseverance are key attributes among the most expert of engineers [10]. Li *et al.* state, "this reinforces the perspective that software engineering is a sociotechnical undertaking, and not just a technical one." Additionally, much of the work of Li *et al.* also focused on the importance of effective decision making among software engineers, especially as they are "tasked with making decisions in increasingly more complex and ambiguous situations, often with significant ramifications."

Numerous studies suggest that additional skills, beyond technical skills, impact team effectiveness in incident response. What remains unclear is how to develop and ultimately advance team-work skills in more insular technical cultures, specifically in a cybersecurity team. Our research suggests that one way to further develop the human side of cyber skills is to more fully understand personality trait preferences and role diversity of cyber team members. Utilization of instruments such as the MBTI may be important for team development because past studies [11] have indicated that the MBTI can successfully predict group performance in crisis management; it also successfully predicts the style in which individuals communicate, make decisions, and manage change and conflict.

Further, because certain personality types tend to be over-represented in certain careers [12], it may be advantageous to develop strategies that capitalize on or compensate for the ways that particular personality types prefer to contribute in their social and work environments. As cited in Hammer [13], people who prefer Introversion on the MBTI are more likely to choose careers that do not necessitate frequent social interaction, such as Information Technology (IT). In addition, people who prefer the Sensing and Thinking (ST) facets of the MBTI tend to be drawn to facts and objective analysis [14]. They often choose careers that are technical and practical in nature, consistent with positions in IT as well as law enforcement and the military [15]. In studies of organizational team performance, ST individuals also tend to show the most risk avoidance and are more inclined to take risks only in an environment consistent with their type [16]. In addition, the researchers measured Crew Cohesion, a global assessment of team performance.

Both role and type diversity within teams are variables that predict team performance. Research on team-work suggests that diverse groups often perform better, working more quickly and more consistently than similar groups [17]. The Parker Team Player Survey (PTPS) is an assessment tool that identifies role diversity, specifically whether team members perform primarily as the communicator, collaborator, challenger, or contributor [18]. Teams that encompass all of these roles are theorized to be most effective. Utilizing established assessment tools is critical as we begin to understand how cyber defense teams can work together to ensure rapid, efficient, and effective response to the ever-changing landscape of cyber threats.

V. Background of the Psychometric Analysis

Our exploratory research included a pilot study that focused on personality trait preferences and role diversity within the CONG. The CONG team is comprised of cyber defense experts. The members of this team had been working together in CTRC exercises for several years and use a leadership structure based initially on individual military rank and civilian government leadership, adjusting this with individual skill set. Inclusion of an active cyber defense team is a unique feature of our research.

The cyber defense physical exercise analyzed in this pilot study used the scenario of defending a financial institution. As described earlier, this was developed originally as a challenge for the RMCCDC to allow the visiting college teams to identify and recognize vulnerabilities in a networked environment. The exercise was repurposed for the CONG exercise for two reasons: to allow the cyber defense teams to practice their expert technical skills and team collaboration, and to allow the researchers to observe type and role diversity within the CONG during a challenging training exercise.

VI. Psychometric Methodology and Results

In the pilot, the authors hypothesized that team members would show greater preference for Introversion versus Extroversion, Sensing versus Intuition, and Thinking versus Feeling on the MBTI, in contrast to preferences reported by the general population. An additional hypothesis was that teams with greater role diversity (exhibited by the PTPS) would exhibit better performance. The Crew Cohesion Index will be used to track the team's effectiveness over time.

Thirteen members of the CONG (11 men, 2 women) participated in a cybersecurity exercise at Regis University. Of the participants, eleven were Caucasian, one was African American, and one was Asian. The median age of participants was 35, with ages ranging from 28 to 47 years. Approximately 46% had college degrees. Of the 13 participants, 54% had worked together as a team. Approximately 42% considered themselves to be novices in cybersecurity, while 58% had at least some level of experience.

Myers-Briggs Type Indicator. The MBTI personality inventory was used to identify the variability of personality type in each team. It is a highly valid and reliable research-based assessment tool that has been in use for over 60 years. According to the Myers Briggs Company, over 88% of Fortune 500 companies use the MBTI as a hiring tool and hundreds of universities use it as an assessment tool. Approximately 1.5 million individuals complete the MBTI online each year [19]. MBTI certified practitioners engage in a minimum of 30 hours of training in order to administer the MBTI and interpret the assessment results. Moreover, there are several thousand peer reviewed research studies that have utilized the MBTI. Researchers and practitioners who are experts in survey methodology and personality assessment confirm that it is one of the most scientifically sound measures of personality type in the field of psychology.

The MBTI identifies differences in personality type using four central dichotomies, two that capture differences in attitudes (Extraversion – Introversion and Judging – Perceiving) and two that capture mental functions (Sensing – Intuition and Thinking – Feeling) [14].

The Parker Team Player Survey [18] is a reliable and valid assessment tool that identifies the level of role diversity within a team environment. In team activities, each member brings with them a specific set of strengths based on a combination of personality, communication and leadership skills, and past experience. The PTPS assesses the current strengths of each individual and suggests ways to increase each person's effectiveness as a team player. In the current study, participants were asked to indicate the role they typically perform (communicator, contributor, collaborator, or challenger) in team settings.

The Crew Cohesion Assessment Tool [20] assessed team performance during the cybersecurity exercise, including the quality and quantity of collaboration, communication, team rapport, and team cohesiveness.

Of the seven participants who completed MBTI assessments, three reported Extraversion as their type preference while four reported Introversion. Six of our participants preferred Sensing while one participant showed a greater preference for Intuition. Finally, all seven participants showed a greater preference for Thinking rather than Feeling. All 13 participants completed the PTPS to assess their role diversity. Results indicated that four were Contributors, three were Collaborators, two were Communicators, and none were Challengers, with the remaining participants exhibiting dual roles that did not include the Challenger.

Trends in the data gathered from the Crew Cohesion Assessment showed slight decreases in Communication, Trust, Effectiveness, Leadership, Teamwork, and Conflict as the exercise progressed.

Preliminary findings of the pilot support our hypothesis that there would be a greater preference for Introversion rather than Extraversion. Also consistent with the hypotheses, we found a greater preference for Sensing versus Intuition, with only one participant preferring Intuition. This is in contrast to the general population, where 70% prefer Sensing and 30% show a preference for Intuition [14].

Also supporting the hypotheses, there was an oversampling of Thinking versus Feeling. This is consistent with qualities predominant in the fields of IT, law enforcement, and the military, and is in contrast to the general population, where 60% indicate a preference for Thinking versus 40% for Feeling [14]. PTPS data showed moderate role diversity, with three of the four roles represented.

These findings suggest for those intentionally constructing and developing cyber teams that strategies leveraging type and role diversity may improve performance. For example, cybersecurity response teams could benefit from the ability to attend to both details and the bigger picture. Thus, diverse team members with Sensing and Intuition, could approach their task with greater flexibility and creativity when generating solutions to cyber threats. A team that incorporates both logic and emotions (i.e. both Thinking and Feeling) could exhibit greater cohesion, exhibited by increased trust, enhanced teamwork, and more effective conflict management [8]. Moreover, increasing diversity along both the Sensing-Intuition and Thinking-Feeling dimensions could encourage less risk avoidance, a critical piece of crisis management [16]. Drawing from research on the PTPS, it could also benefit response teams to include a team member who can adopt the role of Challenger to present difficult questions and question accepted paradigms [18].

Similar to preliminary results in the pilot, research from Willems *et al.* [8] on the non-technical skills of disaster response teams in the medical field also suggests that diversifying team type enhances performance. For example, Willems *et al.* stress the importance of flexibility, adaptability, improvisation, big picture thinking, and creativity as critical non-technical skills for team members.

Willems *et al.* suggest that inter-professional attributes such as communication, team-player, and conflict resolution skills could significantly diversify the knowledge, skills, and effectiveness of team members. Willems *et al.* also suggests that "effective teamwork, clear leadership, role adjustment, and conflict resolution" are skills that disaster response teams should focus their development efforts.

Tokakis *et al.* [9] recommend that leaders of crisis management teams specifically improve their emotional intelligence competencies in order to enhance overall team integration and performance as well as goal attainment. Noting that the Crew Cohesion scores were decreasing as the pilot exercise progressed, observation also suggests that further training emphasis on leadership core competencies and emotional intelligence could address this.

While the pilot study had the inherent limitation of small sample size, the observations in the pilot and the work of Tokakis *et al.* [9] suggest that further work developing and testing psychometric instruments could support the goal of identifying qualities that embody more effective cyber response team members. Such work in the future should incorporate larger numbers of participants since small sample size was a limitation in this study.

VII. GENERALIZING THE PSYCHOMETRIC CASE

In order to assist those with similar goals of increasing collaboration with teams requiring operational security, the authors generalize the interdisciplinary environment in Figure 2, modelling the embedded psychometric analysis of cyber defense training into embedded interdisciplinary support for a trusted training environment.

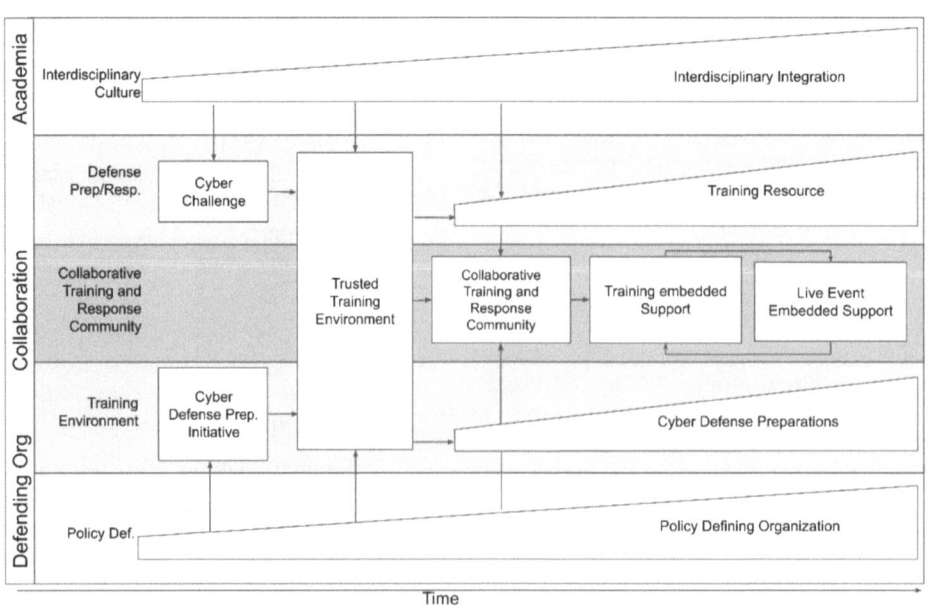

Fig. 2. Generalized model portraying the integration of embedded support as part of an interdisciplinary effort. This new embedded support becomes a resource of the established trusted training environment.

The model identifies a roadmap connecting academia and a defending organization resulting in a CTRC. This is achieved by identifying bridge points connecting their internal development paths to achieve a common trusted training environment. These bridge points, represented by arrows in Figure 1, include interdisciplinary observations, training pilots, and policy adjustments that demonstrate incremental value. Applying this model to the analysis of additional cases could result in enhancing training and live incident response for a variety of incident response teams that may not yet have the advantage of interdisciplinary support. The model from top to bottom is formulated to reflect the bridging of complex academic organizational cultures and their interaction with quite disparate groups like military units, civilian government agencies, other academic institutions, and private security companies.

The authors intend to apply the generalized model across a broader range of cyber incident responders, digital business continuity teams, and disaster recovery policy development. In addition, the team is identifying places to use interdisciplinary contributions to technical degree programs. This harkens back to the original discussion between the cyber defense community and the psychologists, suggesting that they were looking for ways to "make strong teams even stronger."

REFERENCES

[1] Moore, E., Fulton, S., Mancuso, R., Amador, T., Likarish, D., (2019, June), A Short-cycle Framework Approach to Integrating Psychometric Feedback and Data Analytics to Rapid Cyber Defense. Information Security Education, Education in Proactive Information Security, IFP AICT 557, proceedings of the 12th IFIP WG 11.8 World Conference, WISE 12

[2] Collins, M., Schweitzer, D., & Massey, D. (2008, June). Canvas: a regional assessment exercise for teaching security concepts. In Proceedings from the 12th Colloquium for Information Systems Security Education.

[3] Regis University Site for the Rocky Mountain Collegiate Cyber Defense Competition, https://rmccdc.regis.edu/rmccdc/

[4] White, G. B., & Williams, D. (2005, October). The collegiate cyber defense competition. In Proceedings of the 9th Colloquium for Information Systems Security Education.

[5] Creswell, J. W., & Creswell, J. D. (2017). Research design: Qualitative, quantitative, and mixed methods approaches. Sage publications.

[6] Scholz, R. W. & Tietje, O. (2002). Embedded Case Study Methods: Integrating Quantitative and Qualitative Knowledge. London: Sage Publications Inc. ISBN 0-7619-1946-5

[7] Uitdewilligen, S., and Waller, M. J. 2018. "Information Sharing and Decision- Making in Multidisciplinary Crisis Management Teams," Wiley Journal of Organizational Behavior (39), pp. 731-748.

[8] Willems, A., Waxman, B., Bacon, A. K., Smith, J., Peller, J., and Kitto, S. 2013. "Interprofessional Non-Technical Skills for Surgeons in Disaster Response: A Qualitative Study of the Australian Perspective," Journal of Interprofessional Care (27), pp. 177-183.

[9] Tokakis, V., Polychorniou, P., and Boustras, G. 2018. "Managing Conflict in the Public Sector During Crises: The Impact on Crisis Management Team Effectiveness," International Journal of Emergency Management (14:2), pp. 152- 166.

[10] Li, P.L., Ko, A.J., and Zhu, J. 2015. "What Makes a Great Software Engineer?," in Proceedings of the 2015 IEEE/ACM 37th IEEE International Conference on Software Engineering, Florence, IT, pp. 700-710.

[11] Sample, J. A., and Hoffman, J. L. 1986. "The MBTI as a Management and Organizational Development Tool," Journal of Psychological Type (11), pp. 47- 50.

[12] Schaubhut, N. A., and Thompson, R. C. 2008. MBTI Type Tables for Occupations, Mountain View, CA: CPP, Inc.

[13] Hammer, A. L. 1993. Introduction to Type and Careers, Mountain View, CA: CPP, Inc.

[14] Myers, I. B., McCaulley, M. H., Quenck, N. L., and Hammer, A. L. 2009. MBTI Manual: A Guide to the Development and Use of the Myers-Briggs Type Indicator Instrument, Mountain View, CA: CPP, Inc.

[15] Beyler, J., and Schmeck, R. R. 1992. "Assessment of Individual Differences in Preferences for Holistic-Analytic Strategies: Evaluation of Some Commonly Available Instruments," Educational and Psychological Measurement (52:3), pp. 709-719.

[16] Walck, C. L. 1996. "Management and Leadership," in MBTI Applications: A Decade of Research on the Myers-Briggs Type Indicator, A. L. Hammer (ed.), Mountain View, CA: CPP, Inc., pp. 55-80.

[17] Blaylock, B. K. 1983. "Teamwork in a Simulated Production Environment," Research in Psychological Type (6), pp. 58-67.

[18] Parker, G.M. 2008. Team Players and Teamwork (2nd ed.), San Francisco, CA: Jossey-Bass.

[19] The Myers-Briggs Company. 2017. The Myers-Briggs Type Indicator (MBTI). Retrieved June 30, 2020 from https://www.themyersbriggs.com/en-US/Products- and-Services/Myers-Briggs.

[20] WFLDP Toolbox. 2018. Crew Cohesion Assessment Tool, April 16. (www.fireleadership.gov, accessed October 20, 2018)

Tempting High School Students into Cybersecurity with a Slice of Raspberry Pi

Sandra Gorka
Pennsylvania College of Technology
Williamsport, PA, USA
sgorka@pct.edu;
cyber.pct@gmail.com

Alicia McNett
Pennsylvania College of Technology
Williamsport, PA, USA
amcnett@pct.edu

Jacob R. Miller
Pennsylvania College of Technology
Williamsport, PA, USA
jmiller3@pct.edu

Bradley M. Webb
Pennsylvania College of Technology
Williamsport, PA, USA
bwebb@pct.edu

Abstract—Improving the Pipeline is an NSF grant project [1] to extend the Information Assurance and Cybersecurity pipeline into the high school environment by offering an after-school for college credit course to students. This paper discusses the use of an isolated and portable Raspberry Pi network within the course.

Keywords—computing education, cybersecurity education, K-12 education

I. Introduction

The Raspberry Pi computer has been used within computing to facilitate education in topics such as introductory computer science (CS0), parallel computing, computer security and cluster computing [2-6]. The Raspberry Pi has also been used to teach computing in secondary education [1]. One of the main attractions of the Pi is its low cost. While somewhat limited in speed compared to a more traditional desktop computer, it is generally still sufficient to illustrate the functionality and capabilities necessary to conduct an experiment or teach a particular concept. Where additional processing speed is necessary, the low cost of the Pi platform allows for integrating multiple units to perform a given task. This makes the Pi, or a Pi network, an attractive teaching and proof-of-concept platform. In this paper, we discuss the use of a collection of Raspberry Pis networked together in a "briefcase" providing for a portable and isolated network-in-a-box (NIB). Our NIB was used to create an isolated cybersecurity-lab-in-a-box (CLIB).

II. The Network in a Box

The original NIB, a former student's senior project, had the Pis mounted directly to the case of the box. This gave the entire system a very low profile. However, we envisioned instances where it may be necessary for students to remove and manipulate individual boards and then replace them into the case. As a result, our CLIB mounts the Raspberry Pi units on a rail system installed in the case. See Figure 1.

The Pis are held in place using 3D-printed clips that allow them to be readily removed and reinstalled while holding them securely when mounted. See Figure 2. The Pis are powered by a central USB power hub and networked together via an 8-port switch. With the Pis mounted on the elevated rails, the power supply and switch are mounted under the rails in the bottom of the case. This allows for up to six Pis to be mounted comfortably in the box. Although the operating systems on the Pis can vary, our implementation uses three Linux distributions: Kali Linux [7], Raspian [8] and RaspOwn [9] (a vulnerable Linux distribution for the Pi).

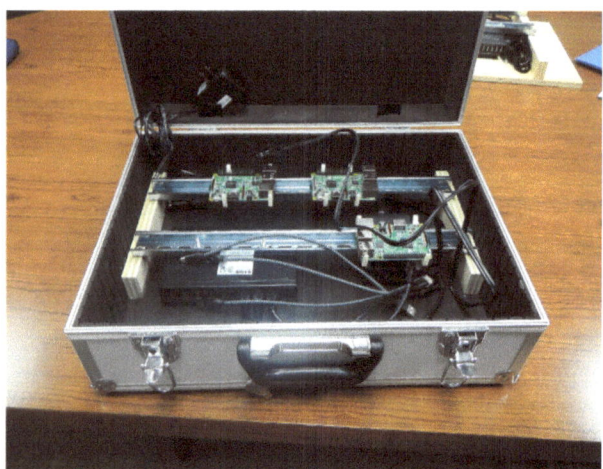

Fig. 1. Photo showing the completed CLIB. The case is an inexpensive aluminum "briefcase" with a foam lining adhered to the inside. Rails are mounted to plywood blocks glued to the inside of the case. Pis are mounted in clips to the tops of the rails. The switch and USB power supply are mounted to the bottom of the rails using screws and zip-ties. This leaves a small amount of space beneath the switch and power supply for network cables, power cords, the switch power supply and the power cord for the USB hub. There is also space for a portable monitor and keyboard (not shown) if desired.

In order to use the lab, it is necessary to connect a monitor and keyboard to at least one of the Pis. Our original vision incorporated an HDMI portable monitor and a small Bluetooth keyboard. This would allow everything to be packed in the box for portability. While these worked, they were not as comfortable to use as simply plugging in a more traditional monitor and keyboard. In addition, our Information Technology Services group has a store of unused monitors and keyboards. It made sense to use the "free" monitors and keyboards rather than purchase additional equipment.

Fig. 2. Photo showing the prototype as well as the clips used to mount the Pis to the rails. The rails are commonly used to mount electrical devices such as controllers and relays to a backer board. A search on the Internet yields several sources for clips and holders that will mount Raspberry Pis to these and similar rails. The clips we chose were selected due to their minimal materials cost and ability to remain clear of all the Pi's ports and connectors. They also lent readily to unmounting and remounting the Pis.

III. Activities using the CLIB

This section provides an overview of several of Raspberry Pi activities completed by the students. Readers interested in the full details of the activities can request them from the authors.

A. Connecting the CLIB

The first activity using the CLIB was targeted more at creating a network. Student were grouped in teams of 2 – 3 students and given a CLIB box, keyboard, mouse and monitor. The CLIB box contained all of the components of the CLIB and the necessary cables, but none of the cables were connected. Students were required to connect the Pis to both the USB power hub and the switch. Students were also required to connect the monitor, keyboard and mouse to a Raspberry Pi designated as the primary Pi. Students could then power the CLIB to determine if the primary Pi was properly connected to the keyboard, mouse and monitor. Students then tested the network functionality of the CLIB using the next activity.

B. Network Addressing

The starting point of this activity typically follows the previous activity. However, this activity can be completed after giving the students a CLIB with all of the cables properly connected.

This activity was completed after a class discussion on MAC and IP addresses, subnet masks and default gateways. Students experimented with several Linux commands as follows:

- `ifconfig` to determine the MAC and IP addresses of the primary Pi.
- `route` to determine the default gateway.
- `ping` to determine whether or not an IP addresses was in use.
- `arp` to see the IP address to MAC address mapping in the ARP lookup table.

C. Networks and Programming

In this activity students used the CLIB to code two Python scripts. Students were previously introduced to Python programming and this provided an opportunity to combine networking and programming concepts in a pair of activities.

The first script was a Python script that performed a ping sweep of IP addresses. The script pinged a total of ten IP addresses, some of which were not connected to a Pi and some of which were connected to a Pi. Students were given the code to implement and were asked questions about what the script accomplished. They were also asked questions about what the output tells them about the network and the computers on the network.

The second script was also a Python script that determined the MD5Sum of a file. Students were previously exposed to the concept of hashing and how it could be used to verify the integrity of a file. The student executed the program with a file to determine its MD5Sum. The file was then modified and the program executed again. To determine its new MD5Sum. Students were asked to address how such a program can be used to identify when a file has been modified. It should be noted that at this activity does not make use of the networked aspect of the CLIB as the activity was restricted to a single Pi.

D. Future Activity – Using nmap

This activity is currently accomplished using virtual machines (VMs). We had planned on using the CLIB, however extenuating circumstances such as inclement weather and COVID-19 prevented the use of the CLIB for this activity.

In the VM version of this activity, students use a Kali Linux VM to execute a nmap scan another Linux VM. In the CLIB version, students will use the Raspberry Pi with Kali installation to execute a nmap scan on the Pi with the RaspOwn installation. After the scan is complete, the students would review the output to determine the name of the computer scanned, its IP address, its operating system, which ports are open and what services are associated with the ports.

IV. Benefits

One of the primary benefits of the CLIB is its isolated environment. This is important as students just beginning study in cybersecurity can be both intimidated and careless. Students may be reluctant to experiment for fear of breaking things. Other students are often anxious to "just get started" and don't always follow the complete instructions when setting up an experiment. Of course, on an open network, this can be disastrous. With the CLIB being a self-contained environment, students can experiment without worrying about anything getting "loose" and wreaking havoc. For the most part, if anything does cause a catastrophic failure (e.g. launching a DoS attack or fork bomb) you simply reboot the affected systems and all is as it was.

The CLIB can be quickly reconfigured to use different OSs simply by replacing the SD card in each Pi. This can prove beneficial if a student unintentionally damages an installation - a fresh SD card can be inserted into the Pi and have it back to "normal" in minutes. We made several copies of each SD card for this reason. During teaching/lab sessions when something went wrong, it was simple to start over with a fresh card and diagnose the problem later. Additionally, OSs can be configured to create a particular scenario and then easily replaced for a subsequent activity. While not a focus in this course, scenarios for diagnosing configuration and network problems can be easily built and swapped out for lab or testing purposes.

In addition to using the CLIB for cybersecurity coursework, it can be used for projects/lessons within many other areas of IT. One of the labs we conducted had the students build the network and demonstrate its functionality. This was a precursor to demonstrating networking scanning and reconnaissance techniques. We divided the class into groups of two or three students. We supplied each group with the CLIB components and instructions on how to configure the various OS installations. They assembled the hardware, configured the network and then demonstrated the functionality by writing a small application to exchange data among the various computers in the network. After verifying the networks operated correctly, we began looking at tools for scanning and reconnaissance.

The other main benefit of the CLIB is the cost. The college supports an isolated security lab for our cybersecurity classes. This lab is significantly more sophisticated than a box full of Raspberry Pis, but the cost is also significantly higher. The security lab is capable of supporting several hundred simultaneous VMs and virtual networks; however, the price tag ran in the tens of thousands of dollars for that functionality. By contrast, the CLIB, sans monitor, keyboard and mouse, can be built for about $230 (2017 prices). It will not support hundreds of VMs, but that functionality is not necessary. In addition, the students responded very positively to the "visceral" knowledge they acquired by being able to see and touch the machines they were working with. It was much more engaging than an icon of a VM on a screen.

Another benefit of the low cost is that high schools could fund one of these CLIBs to use in teaching a similar security class. In addition, they can get extra mileage out of the expenditure through using it to support networking and programming classes as well. It would be helpful in any instance where having access and control over the server and/or network along with the client is desirable. Moreover, the cost is such that even individual students could afford to construct a NIB/CLIB for about the price of a cheap laptop.

Another significant benefit of the CLIB stems from its portability and low cost. One difficulty of our on-campus security lab is access control. In order for the students to do assignments in the lab, they would have to be physically on campus. While we did use the lab for on-campus events [10], most students would not have been able to access the lab in general. One intended mission of the CLIB was to accompany the students back to the high school where they could use it during the school week when not on the college campus. While there were concerns that the CLIBs could be damaged or compromised, again the overall feeling was that financially, there was very little at risk. Additionally, this would be less risky and preferable to trying to manage off-campus access to our isolated security lab.

While taking the CLIB to the high school was an intended part of the project, feedback from the students raised two issues. None of them felt there would be time enough in their regular school days for them to use the CLIB at the high school. Most, if not all, of the students who participated were very active in extra-curricular activities, so things like study halls were simply not available in their schedules. Additionally, the students felt they would get more mileage out of the CLIBs in the classroom and by coming to campus. Several students arranged their after-school schedules in order to come to campus early to do work with the CLIBs. As a result, the CLIBs were never deployed to the high schools but were utilized to support in-class lab activities.

V. RESULTS

Prior to the exercise outlined above, several students in the class had never built a physically connected network before. Many had never installed and configured servers before. Most had attached wireless devices on home networks, but had never really taken the time to understand the subtleties of network addressing, subnetting and the like. Moreover, other than creating access passwords, they had never considered the exposure of their data while in transit over the network. Assembling the network, configuring the services, scanning the servers and later monitoring the traffic gave them all an appreciation (wakeup call!) of what happens to their data and the sometimes difficult task of protecting it.

In spring 2019, sixteen students completed the activity and 14 of them indicated that the activities were interesting. Several commented during the exercise that they had never done anything like this before and found it very enlightening. Some of the more experienced students, having helped assemble physical networks before, found the build part of the exercise only "kind of" interesting. Generally, all the students felt the exercise was worthwhile and were very engaged with the subsequent cybersecurity parts of the labs.

Visual observation indicated that several students were initially timid about physically interacting with the hardware. We encouraged more experienced students to work with inexperienced students. While the instructors were encouraging with everyone, getting encouragement from their peers vastly helped some students overcome their fears. Once engaged, the students enjoyed the activity and appeared to be confident about dealing with the hardware.

While these results may seem limited and relatively unsurprising, the value of the confidence gained by some of the students was immeasurable. Students who just an hour earlier were leery of even opening the briefcase, were now willing to assemble a network, jump into configuring and troubleshooting network services, and monitoring the network and servers for illicit behavior. While all of these activities had been discussed in class over the prior few weeks, nothing brought the concepts home like these little networks.

In addition, many students expressed that they had a much better feel for what was going on with their data. Security concerns over things like cloud storage, smart home appliances, online banking, and having their entire life on their phone suddenly seemed to snap into a sharper focus now that they had experienced managing a network first-hand. Based on their comments, it seems unlikely they would have received the same experience from virtual networks in our security lab.

VI. STUDENT FEEDBACK

At the end of the experiment, we asked the students to provide feedback on the Raspberry Pi activities. In particular, we asked them what they learned and for any general comments they had on the exercises.

Feedback was generally positive in nature. Students indicated that they enjoyed the activity and that it was a fun way to learn about the Raspberry Pi. Informally, when we asked if we should continue with the Pi labs, the response was a resounding yes. Several students offered advice that we should try to incorporate them more.

VII. POSTMORTEM

For every up there is a down. When we first planned the incorporation of the CLIBs into our class, they seemed very necessary. Several of the activities we had planned could not be carried out safely on an open network; some still cannot. However, during the two years between the time we wrote the proposal and began the work, virtualization got better, new resources became available and a lot of material was published to do many of the planned activities on-line in a safe manner. While we cannot do everything on-line, many of our planned activities became a lot easier to do via various websites targeting cybersecurity training. Other activities became much more doable via VMs than they had before. This was mostly a function of better performance in the VM software making VMs a lot less cumbersome and a lot more responsive.

We believe the CLIB still represents a valuable asset. No amount of VM magic will replace the learning that happens when students can see, touch and manipulate the physical objects. The thrill a student gets when he or she powers up a complex collection of devices and sees it function is immeasurable. But do you need a CLIB? We think it depends. If you can securely configure a virtual network so that nothing hostile being played with by a novice can ever escape, then there are some consultants that would like to hire you. There is no way to make every activity that you might want to do in cybersecurity training and research absolutely safe. The CLIB gives you adequate protection at a very low price.

But whether or not you need a CLIB for safety is somewhat peripheral to the point of the activity. If you want to engage, inspire and retain students, then we think the CLIB performs in a way that VMs just cannot do. For the cost, we can think of no better way to give students the sense of learning and accomplishment that these boxes accomplished.

It seems that Raspberry Pi is excellent bait.

ACKNOWLEDGMENTS

This material is based on work supported by the National Science Foundation under Grant No. 1623525. Any opinions, findings, and conclusions or recommendations expressed in this material are those of the author(s) and do not necessarily reflect the views of the National Science Foundation.

The authors would also like to acknowledge and thank Sebastian Peipher for the inspiration of his network in a box project and his advice as we began creating ours.

REFERENCES

[1] Improving the Pipeline: After-School Program for Preparing Information Assurance and Cyber Defense Professionals. In *Proceedings of the 18th Annual Conference on Information Technology Education (SIGITE '17)*. ACM, New York, NY, USA, 167–167. https://doi.org/10.1145/3125659.3125665

[2] Francesco Cuomo, Eric Mibuari, Komminist Weldemariam, and Osamuyimen Stewart. 2013. Leveraging Raspberry Pi for Interactive Education. In *Proceedings of the 4th Annual Symposium on Computing for Development (ACM DEV-4 '13)*. ACM, New York, NY, USA, Article 16, 2 pages. https://doi.org/10.1145/2537052.2537068

[3] Kevin Doucet and Jian Zhang. 2019. The Creation of a Low-cost Raspberry Pi Cluster for Teaching. In *Proceedings of the Western Canadian Conference on Computing Education (WCCCE '19)*. ACM, New York, NY, USA, Article 7, 5 pages. https://doi.org/10.1145/3314994.3325088

[4] Brian Krupp and Andrew Watkins. 2019. CS0: Introducing Computing with Raspberry Pis. In *Proceedings of the 50th ACM Technical Symposium on Computer Science Education (SIGCSE '19)*. ACM, New York, NY, USA, 832–838. https://doi.org/10.1145/3287324.3287488

[5] Suzanne J. Matthews, Joel C. Adams, Richard A. Brown, and Elizabeth Shoop. 2018. Portable Parallel Computing with the Raspberry Pi. In *Proceedings of the 49th ACM Technical Symposium on Computer Science Education (SIGCSE '18)*. ACM, New York, NY, USA, 92–97. https://doi.org/10.1145/3159450.3159558

[6] Adam H. Villa. 2016. Hands-on Computer Security with a Raspberry Pi. *J. Comput. Sci. Coll.* 31, 6 (June 2016), 4–10. http://dl.acm.org/citation.cfm?id=2904446.2904447

[7] Kali 2019. Kali Linux - Raspberry Pi. Retrieved June 12, 2019 from https://docs.kali.org/kali-on-arm/install-kali-linux-arm-raspberry-pi

[8] RASP [n. d.]. Raspberry Pi Downloads. Retrieved June 12, 2019 from https://www.raspberrypi.org/downloads/

[9] RasPwn 2016. RasPwn OS. Retrieved June 12, 2019 from http://raspwn.org/

[10] Allison Chapman and Margot Rinehart. 2019. Capture the Flag as a Testing Platform. Online. Retrieved June 16, 2019 from http://ccscne.org/wp-content/uploads/2018/09/StudentPostersDocument-2019-Final.pdf CCSCNE 2019, Student Poster Abstracts, April 12 - 13, 2019, West Haven, Connecticut, 37.

Integration of Blockchain Concepts into Computer Science Curriculum

Eric Sakk
Department of Computer Science
Center for the Study of Blockchain and Financial Technology
Morgan State University
Baltimore, MD, USA
eric.sakk@morgan.edu

Shuangbao Paul Wang
Department of Computer Science
Morgan State University
Baltimore, MD, USA
shuangbao.wang@morgan.edu

Abstract—In this work, we consider the nexus between blockchain technology and computer science curriculum. While it is possible to introduce the blockchain paradigm using a single course, the depth of a single topic can often be sacrificed at the expense of covering a breadth of information. As blockchain is an emerging technology, it is important to embed various concepts throughout the undergraduate curriculum with the depth necessary to reinforce each facet. Using a just in time approach, we define exactly where and how blockchain topics relevant to computer science should be introduced. As a means for active learning pedagogy, we introduce a lab framework for students to gain hands-on experience. Finally, we describe collaborations with industry to provide mentorship and internship opportunities.

Keywords—blockchain, hash function, proof of work, computer science Introduction

I. INTRODUCTION

Blockchain is an emerging technology that is transforming the way business and financial institutions process transactions. Given this current state of affairs, it is critical that computer science training involve technical aspects of such processes. In addition to tutorials and instruction available from industry [8, 9], many academic institutions have begun to offer curricula containing specific courses dealing with blockchain technology [4, 10]. While the offering of full courses through academia or industry is sensible, the applications are so vast that it can become difficult to achieve the necessary technical depth. Within the computer science major, our approach is to weave aspects of blockchain technology throughout the existing undergraduate curriculum. This allows for concept immersion and reinforcement through the revisiting of ideas at various stages with increasing depth.

With regard to computer science training, key topics most relevant to blockchain technologies are found within courses dealing with:

- Introductory and Advanced Programming Techniques
- Data Structures
- Computer Networks
- Network Security
- Cloud Computing
- Cryptography
- Machine Learning and Artificial Intelligence

The main goal of this work is to demonstrate how blockchain concepts can be integrated into these key topics. For the purposes of illustration, examples are presented using the Python programming language.

II. INTRODUCTORY PROGRAMMING TECHNIQUES

At the heart of any programming curriculum are basic constructs necessary for algorithm implementation. Beginning at the introductory level, key concepts to be covered generally include:

- Variable types
- Arithmetic and logical operations
- Loops
- Functions
- Lists
- Nested lists and nested iterations
- Methods and basic object oriented programming

Instead of introducing lists in Python, other programming languages might include rudimentary data structures exhibiting similar behaviors such as arrays, structures or cell arrays.

To emphasize the practice of the above concepts, we propose the implementation of a blockchain cryptocurrency example that grows in complexity as new programming constructs are introduced and developed. Key components of an introductory level example include:

- Variable types for the blockchain participants requiring both sender information and receiver information
- Transaction information

- Account balance computations
- Verifying transactions before adding them to a set of open transactions
- Adding a new block to the blockchain with a validated set of open transactions
- Methods for hash function implementation
- Nested list data structure for storing the complete blockchain

These initial components are enough to demonstrate simple cryptocurrency transactions from which students can glean understanding of how a blockchain works. Furthermore, existing libraries for Python make for fast implementation of operations involving a fair amount of complexity such as SHA-256. For instance, the Python library '*hashlib*' [2] can be used to implement hashes and message digests with straightforward method calls that can easily be applied at the freshman level. When used in tandem with the 'json' library [3], it becomes possible to encode any data structure available in Python that one might choose to represent the blockchain. For example, assume '*encodedBCBlock*' represents a variable encoded from the most current block within the simulated blockchain. Then a command as simple as

```
hashlib.sha256(encodedBCBlock).hexdigest()
```

can be used to generate the associated block hash formatted with hexadecimal characters. This is the beauty of using Python as an introductory language. Many computationally intensive operations that would be unraveled in greater depth within upper level courses can be easily programmed using existing Python libraries. A novice programmer can then experience immediate results that do not get bogged down with the finer details of an intense computation.

Figure 1 shows an abbreviated version of a menu shell in the form of a while loop for achieving blockchain functionality. This snippet of code encompasses many of the key programming concepts outlined above. After introducing variable types, lists, boolean operations, loops, and functions, the blockchain example can be initiated. The code for each menu item can then be successively added as the details of each new operation is introduced. As a concrete example from Figure 1, choice number five allows a new block to be added to the blockchain. As part of this process, Proof of Work must be established.

Figure 2 shows some sample Python code that performs a simple iterative search for a hash containing an instance of the correct nonce. This type of code is highly instructive at the freshman level as it involves simple data structures, loops, boolean operations, and function calls applied in the context of blockchain implementation.

```
1   def input_selection():
2       usr_inputvalue = input('Make your selection: ')
3       return usr_inputvalue
4   
5   exit_the_menu_loop = False
6   while(not exit_the_menu_loop):
7       print()
8       print('Select a blockchain operation')
9       print('1: Output the complete current blockchain')
10      print('2: Output a list of current users along with their balances')
11      print('3: Verify balances for the current transaction')
12      print('4: Add a new transaction to the set of open transactions')
13      print('5: Add a new block to the blockchain')
14      print('6: Hack the blockchain')
15      print('q: Quit')
16      print()
17  
18      user_vals = ['1', '2', '3', '4', '5', '6', 'q']
19      user_selection=input_selection()
20      if user_selection not in user_vals:
21          print('Invalid input, please try again')
22      elif user_selection == 'q':
23          exit_the_menu_loop = True
24  
```

Fig. 1. Example 'while' loop.

```
80  def test_nonce(candidates, prev_hash, pwcounter):
81    teststr=(str(candidates)+str(prev_hash)+str(pwcounter)).encode()
82    teststr_hash=hashlib.sha256(teststr).hexdigest()
83    return teststr_hash[0:4]!='0000'
84
85  def proof_of_work(prev_block):
86    prev_hash=blockhash(prev_block)
87    pwcounter=0
88    while test_nonce(candidates, prev_hash, pwcounter):
89      pwcounter+=1
90    return pwcounter
```

Fig. 2. Proof of Work example.

III. Sophomore Level Concepts

A. Data Structures

The example from the freshman level can be expanded when discussing concepts from a typical data structures course in a number of ways. For instance, the nested list data structure could be implemented in the form a linked list where each node would correspond to a given block. In addition, algorithmic complexity examples involving various loops and methods would be a natural consequence of revisiting techniques previously introduced in earlier courses.

B. Advanced Programming Techniques

An advanced programming course should involve deeper aspects of object oriented programming (OOP) and the construction of dedicated classes. In addition to rephrasing the introductory blockchain example with more sophisticated OOP concepts, projects for this level involve the programming of smart contracts for digital property transactions. Software engineering projects naturally include the design of user interfaces for smart contract transactions similar to those available for Ethereum using, for example, Solidity [7].

IV. Upper Level Concepts

A. Computer Networks

Basic understanding of computer networks involves introducing concepts such as network protocols, network architecture, fault tolerance, and software defined networks. Hence, deeper immersion into blockchain and cryptocurrency concepts such as proof-of-work, proof-of-stake and 51% attacks naturally arise in this setting. The example introduced at the freshman and sophomore levels can now be phrased in a context where multiple network nodes have stored copies of the current blockchain. Course projects involving the mining of new blocks and analyzing various tradeoffs for achieving scalability, throughput maximization and latency minimization would be appropriate at this level.

B. Network Security, Cryptography, and Cloud Computing

Assuming computer networks as co- or prerequisite material, detailed understanding of hash functions and nonces for block mining, public key cryptography for wallets, as well as authentication and key distribution are necessary to provide the necessary depth of understanding for blockchain implementation. After mining, each block will be submitted as a new transaction. In the cloud computing course, techniques to setup AWS EC2, VPC and create interfaces are introduced where the blockchains are hosted in a cloud environment. With this material as a foundation, undergraduate research projects can be offered in order to simulate and analyze various facets of mining and blockchain security. Advanced topics such as IoT security and quantum cryptography are also introduced at this level [11, 14].

C. Deep Learning and Artificial Intelligence

This is an extremely fertile area of research [1, 5, 6], the basics of which can be discussed after basic deep learning concepts have been introduced. For instance, deep learning applications where the training data cannot be exposed (e.g. health informatics) require privacy - preserving methodologies. Blockchain architectures have recently been proposed addressing such classes of problems involving trusted data. At this level, it would be expected that students have a command of blockchain technology and would engage in simulation, projects and research involving deep learning applications of blockchain.

V. Experiential Learning via the AI and Cloud Computing Lab

Learning is an integration of interaction. The interaction might exist between learners and instructors/computers or between learners and the real world [15]. While traditional approaches tend to focus more on lectures, emerging fields in Computer Science require students to be equipped, not only with knowledge, but also skills [12, 13].

For this study, we have setup an AI, IoT, and Cloud Computing Lab for upper level students in order to teach AI,

Cloud Computing, and Cybersecurity through hands-on, experiential learning. Currently we have acquired a number of AWS DeepLens, DeepRacer, and IoT Buttons, as well as different types of Echos. Figure 3 shows the architecture of the AI lab in the AWS Cloud. It demonstrates how to process blocks submitted to the cloud with the help of AI.

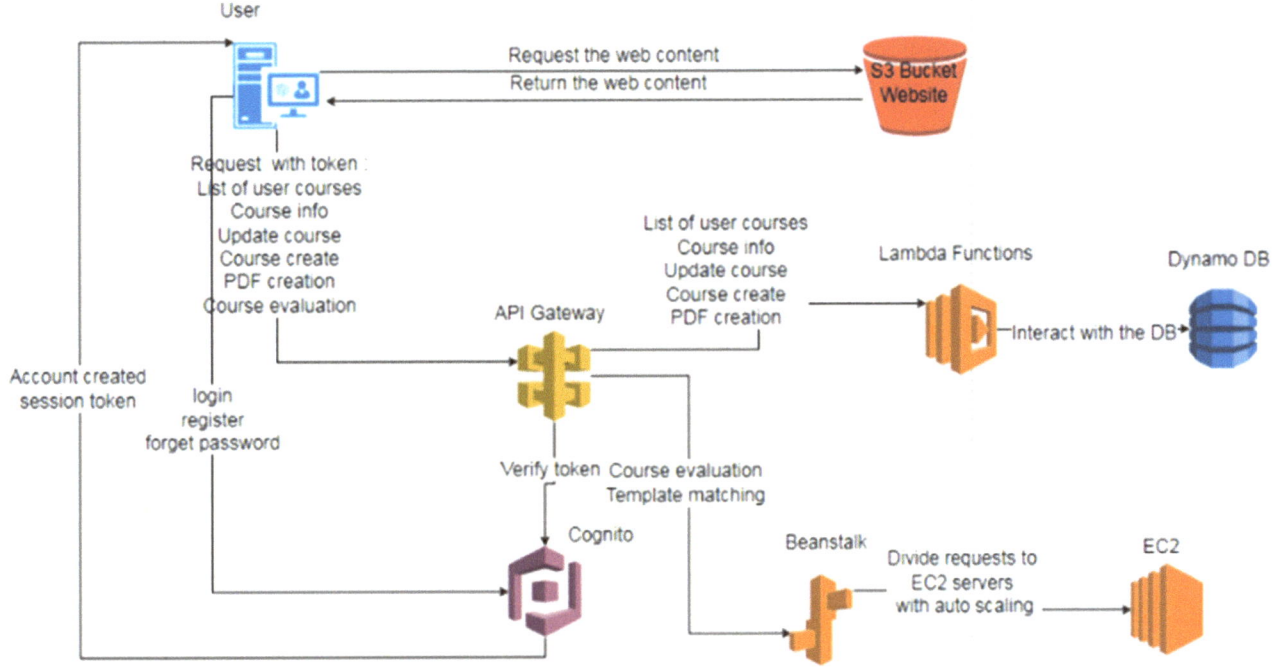

Fig. 3. Diagram of an AI-assisted Block Processing Lab in the AWS Cloud.

We are currently collaborating with Google, Facebook, and JP Morgan Chase where engineers from these companies are invited to participate in the teaching of classes, to aid in the development and mentoring of projects, and to provide summer camp and internship opportunities. A pipeline has therefore been established to study blockchain and other emerging areas in Computer Science allowing for internships and full-time employment within various high-profile tech companies.

VI. EXPERIMENTS AND FURTHER DISCUSSION

The methodology presented in this work is new to our department and a phased-in blockchain integration plan is currently under evaluation. Some courses will begin phase-in during the 2020-2021 academic year with the goal of generating academic performance data to measure student learning as a function of introducing blockchain concepts. The goal for Fall 2020 will be to compare the performance of two cohorts: one with blockchain concepts introduced and one without.

At present, we have generated data from a sample of ten students in a junior-level course entitled Introduction to Cryptography. Specifically, a course unit dealing with hash functions has been taught with blockchain as the foundational example. Furthermore, this unit allows students to numerically experiment with Python code involving proof of work. The intent is to compare student performance in this cohort against a Fall 2020 cohort. This group will not apply blockchain as the primary vehicle for introducing and applying hash functions. Anecdotal data from previous iterations of this course without blockchain suggests that the current cohort has been much more engaged when presented with the blockchain application.

With regard to best practices, various approaches have been cited involving curricular a la carte itineraries as well as global subjects adapted to each person [16]. In addition, while blockchain has been introduced into curricula involving business applications, for example [17], the distributed approach presented here of introducing blockchain into computer science curricula, to the best of our knowledge, has not been tested. We are effectively on new ground and it will take some time to infuse our courses with this new material.

VII. CONCLUSIONS

In this work, we have outlined a framework for integrating blockchain technology into all levels of a computer science curriculum. This approach addresses the 'breadth-vs-depth' dilemma that might be encountered within a single course addressing blockchain applications. In this way, the necessary depth can be achieved over time by introducing blockchain concepts in courses where they are most appropriate. Furthermore, an AI, IoT, and Cloud Computing Lab has been established so that students can learn by doing. The main benefit achieved is a deeper understanding through practical implementation and simulation.

ACKNOWLEDGEMENTS

Funding for this work was provided in part by the Center for the Study of Blockchain and Financial Technology at Morgan State University.

REFERENCES

[1] X. Chen, C. Ji, J. Luo, W. Liao, and P. Pan Li. 2018. When Machine Learning Meets Blockchain: A Decentralized, Privacy-preserving and Secure Design. *IEEE International Conference on Big Data* (2018), 1178–1187.

[2] Python Documentation. 2020. *hashlib — Secure hashes and message digests.* https://docs.python.org/3/library/hashlib.html [Accessed Feb. 29, 2020]

[3] Python Documentation. 2020. json — *JSON encoder and decoder.* https://docs.python.org/3/library/json.html [Accessed Feb. 29, 2020]

[4] MIT. 2020. *blockchain.mit.edu.* blockchain.mit.edu/ [Accessed Feb. 29, 2020]

[5] P. Mohassel and Y. Zhan. 2017. Secureml: A system for scalable privacy-preserving machine learning. *IEEE Symposium on Security and Privacy* (2017), 19–38.

[6] R. Shokri and V. Shmatikov. 2015. Privacy-preserving deep learning. *Proceedings of the 22nd ACM SIGSAC Conference on Computer and Communications Security* (2015), 1310–1321.

[7] Solidity. 2020. *Solidity 0.6.1 documentation.* https://solidity.readthedocs.io/en/v0.6.1/ [Accessed Feb. 29, 2020]

[8] Global Software Support. 2020. Blockchain Explained Step by Step. https://www.globalsoftwaresupport.com/blockchain-explained-step-by-step/ [Accessed Feb. 29, 2020]

[9] Global Software Support. 2020. *Cryptocurrency (Bitcoin) Explained Step by Step.* https://www.globalsoftwaresupport.com/cryptocurrency-bitcoinexplained -step-by-step/ [Accessed Feb. 29, 2020]

[10] Stanford University. 2020. *The Stanford Center for Blockchain Research.* https://cbr.stanford.edu/ [Accessed Feb. 29, 2020]

[11] Paul Wang, A. Ali, U. Guin, and A. Skjellum. 2018. IoTCP: A Novel Trusted Computing Protocol for IoT. *The Colloquium of Information Systems Security Education (CISSE)* (2018), 165–180. Issue 1.

[12] Shuangbao Wang. 2016. Dual-Data Defense in Depth Improves SCADA Security. Signal (2016), 42–44. Issue 10.

[13] Shuangbao Wang and William Kelly. 2017. Smart Cities Architecture and Security in Cybersecurity Education. *The Colloquium of Information Systems Security Education (CISSE)* (2017). Issue 2.

[14] Shuangbao Wang, M. Rhhde, and A. Ali. 2020. Quantum Cryptography and Simulation: Tools and Techniques. *ACM Proc. of International Conference of Cryptography, Security and Privacy (ICCSP)*, pp 36-41.

[15] Shuangbao Paul Wang and William Kelly. 2017. Video-based Big Data Analytics in Cyberlearning. *Journal of Learning Analytics* 4, 2 (2017), 36–463.

[16] A.R. Bartolomé. 2020. Blockchain in Educational Methodologies. In: Burgos D. (eds) Radical Solutions and eLearning. Lecture Notes in Educational Technology. Springer, Singapore

[17] W. Dettling. 2018. How to Teach Blockchain in a Business School. In: Dornberger R. (eds) Business Information Systems and Technology 4.0. Studies in Systems, Decision and Control, vol 141. Springer, Cham

Author Index

Amador, Tristen K.	86
Bhatia, Sajal	57
Bommanapally, Vidya	72
Chaput, Robert L.	1
Cherdantseva, Yulia	65
Chundi, Parvathi	72
Demmese, Fikirte	80
Dicheva, Darina	80
Enright, Esther A.	30
Fulton, Steven P.	86
Girard, John	9
Gorka, Sandra	92
Hoppa, Mary Ann	19
Hu, Yen-Hung (Frank)	19
Justice, Connie	30
Likarish, Daniel M.	86
Loo, Sin Ming	30
Mancuso, Roberta A.	86
McNett, Alicia	92
Miller, Jacob R.	92
Moore, Erik L.	86
Nguyen, Thai H.	57
Parakh, Abhishek	72
Pham, Binh An	44
Pittman, Jason M.	38
Robinson, Nikki	38
Sakk, Eric	96
Sample, Char	30
Shelton, D. Cragin	30
Smart, Phil	65
St.Clair, Nelbert	9
Subburaj, Vinitha Hannah	44
Subramaniam, Mahadevan	72
Taylor, Eleanor	30
Wang, Shuangbao Paul	96
Webb, Bradley M.	92
West, Tobi A.	49
Whitman, Michael E.	1
Williams, Dominicia	19
Yuan, Xiaohong	80

www.ingramcontent.com/pod-product-compliance
Lightning Source LLC
Chambersburg PA
CBHW051153220526
45473CB00003B/760